"Packed with a wealth of case studies, historical facts, and actionable recommendations, *A Clinician's Guide to Gender-Affirming Care* is a powerful actualization of the authors' commitments to creating trans justice. Chang, Singh, and dickey go beyond simply compiling information to create a compelling, deeply empathetic, and effective resource that bridges the gap between helping professionals and the trans communities they serve. A must-read for all aspiring trans allies and coconspirators!"

—**Lily Zheng**, diversity consultant, and coauthor of
*Gender Ambiguity in the Workplace*

"Chang, Singh, and dickey have created the essential guide for clinicians who want to dive deeper into developing and expanding their skills for affirmative gender-related care. It is practical, comprehensive, and reminds providers that competent gender-related work begins with the clinician's personal examination of their gender socialization. Experiential activities guide clinicians to dive deeper into their own socialization as they develop their clinical knowledge of gender-related and transition care. *A Clinician's Guide to Gender-Affirming Care* is a necessary reference for all mental health providers."

—**julie graham, MFT**, nationally recognized specialist in gender
health care; consultant on gender-related healthcare and trauma
issues for gender and sexual minorities; director of Gender Health SF

"As healers, we are taking on a major responsibility when we devote ourselves to helping others. It can be such an enormous gift, but it's profoundly important that we fill our souls with the best tools to meet our clients' needs. It's time for a paradigm shift, and this book provides a path to freedom from the shackles of transphobia that will revolutionize your healing practice."

—**Danielle Castro, MA, MFT**, research director at the
Center of Excellence for Transgender Health, and the Division of
Prevention Science at University of California, San Francisco

"One of the biggest challenges to offering competent care and support to trans and other gender-diverse people is society's tendency to assume that a singular gender narrative exists. Academic research, professional association guidelines, media stories, and standards of care have too often been crafted from the individual experiences of too few. How deeply refreshing it is to find a resource that gently, persistently encourages the clinician to consider an individual's gender pathway within an ever-widening context of individuality, family, culture, and systems. *A Clinician's Guide to Gender-Affirming Care* supports the clinician in not only considering the intersecting identities of their patient—their age, sexuality, race, faith, and more—but factoring themselves into the equation. This guide provides many illustrative examples of complex people in an easy-to-read format that will surely make this text a dog-eared must-have in any clinician's practice."

> —**Aidan Key**, K-12 gender education specialist, author,
> national speaker, and director of the parent support organization
> Gender Diversity

"This unprecedented resource for clinicians and service providers seeking to deepen their analysis of gender and capacity to provide care to trans people is accessible, reflective, complex, thorough, and practical. *A Clinician's Guide to Gender-Affirming Care* situates trans mental health care in a sociopolitical context requiring practitioners to contend with the medical and mental health systems' ability to perniciously perpetuate structural violence. Finally, a comprehensive resource that gives clinicians a road map to be in deep solidarity with trans, nonbinary, and gender nonconforming people who deserve access to care rooted in dignity and justice."

> —**Erica Woodland, MSW, LCSW**, healing justice practitioner,
> psychotherapist, consultant, and founding director of the
> National Queer and Trans Therapists of Color Network

# A CLINICIAN'S GUIDE *to* GENDER-AFFIRMING CARE

## WORKING *with* TRANSGENDER & GENDER NONCONFORMING CLIENTS

Sand C. Chang, PhD
Anneliese Singh, PhD, LPC
lore m. dickey, PhD

CONTEXT PRESS
An Imprint of New Harbinger Publications, Inc.

## Publisher's Note

Distributed in Canada by Raincoast Books

Copyright © 2018 by Sand C. Chang, Anneliese A. Singh, and lore m. dickey
New Harbinger Publications, Inc.
5674 Shattuck Avenue
Oakland, CA 94609
www.newharbinger.com

Cover design by Amy Shoup

Acquired by Elizabeth Hollis Hansen

Edited by Rona Bernstein

Indexed by James Minkin

---

Library of Congress Cataloging-in-Publication Data on file

20    19    18

10    9    8    7    6    5    4    3    2    1          First Printing

Sand dedicates this book to all those who work toward collective liberation, those who are not afraid to ask the hard questions, and the many people and furry creatures who have inspired their creative, emotional, spiritual, and professional growth. A special thank you to Theo Chang for reminding me to breathe, and to Zelda Sesame for reminding me to play.

Anneliese dedicates this book to her beloved partner, Lauren Lukkarila, and to the trans, nonbinary, and cisgender freedom fighters and angelic troublemakers who have demanded—and continue to demand—justice in mental health care. The journey has been longer than our lives, and may we remember the ancient roots of trans liberation.

lore dedicates this book to his trans ancestors and those whose shoulders help him to stand tall as an out, queer, trans person. His mentors have held his feet to the fire and he is a better person as a result. Whether traveling by himself or with others on the path of life, he never walks alone. We need to see and hold one another. I see and hold you.

# Contents

## Part 5: Special Topics and Concerns

## Appendices

# Foreword

I am excited to write this foreword for *A Clinician's Guide to Gender-Affirming Care: Working with Transgender and Gender Nonconforming Clients*! As an Indian American, as a woman, as a trans person, and as a psychologist who advocates for trans-affirming mental health practice, I find this book especially meaningful. Like a growing number of the most "fortunate" trans people, I live with a level of freedom, respect, and celebration for my whole self that I had never dreamed possible. For example, I reviewed this manuscript while flying to Jacksonville, FL, to take my fiancé, Teri, a trans man, to see my parents, who have been wonderfully affirming of my trans identity, my womanhood, and our engagement. I am reminded of the song "What a Wonderful World."

However, not everyone in my community has the opportunity to live their lives so freely or fully. We have experienced decades of mistreatment, including at the hands of mental health professionals and other health care providers. Rates of suicidality, depression, anxiety, housing insecurity, and other challenges in our community are still at very high levels, while trans visibility is still nascent in our society, and all too often, trans people are still caricatured. Despite all these challenges, as trans people, we are reemerging from hiding, silence, and invisibility, and taking our rightful place in society. As we do so, disentangling ourselves from oppression, we redefine our personal narratives and our collective story. We do so speaking on the authority of our own individual, lived experience, reaching consensus where possible, and creating space for plurality where consensus is neither possible nor desirable.

What role do you have in this? We need mental health clinicians who have the awareness, knowledge, and skills to work with our community in affirming ways. But even more importantly, we need mental health clinicians who are well-versed in the community's advocacy needs to develop a more trans-affirming society and world. Whether you are trans or cisgender, this book provides you with the opportunity to engage in introspective work to deepen your understanding of not only the needs of your trans clients, but also of yourself as a clinician working with and advocating alongside them. We are living at a time in trans mental health when we can move beyond "basic skills" of affirming practice to more advanced and nuanced topics. These topics are, of course, not "advanced" to the trans people who live with them. Rather, what is being advanced is *your* understanding, and in turn your ability to deepen your affirmative clinical work. This will allow you to support redimensionalizing and recontextualizing trans identities within complex, holistic human identities, which I believe is crucial to trans happiness. If the topics covered here are "advanced," the goal is basic. Being fully embraced and living fulfilling lives must not be luxuries of fortunate trans people, but basic human rights for trans people, and for *everyone*.

The authors themselves deserve much credit for the underlying work, raising our basic awareness and bringing us to a point of readiness for this discussion. I have known Drs. Chang, Singh, and dickey through their longstanding advocacy for trans and gender nonconforming mental health in professional associations, such as the American Psychological Association and the World Professional Association for Transgender Health. I have been continuously impressed by their educational efforts to ensure that trans-affirming practice is foundational practice that all mental health professionals should be able to provide. As I read this book, I believe Drs. Chang, Singh, and dickey break new ground in trans mental health, as they provide a comprehensive approach for mental health professionals that will benefit not only clinicians who are brand new to working with trans clients but also longtime providers who want to ensure their current skills are in line with the most current and affirming practice, offering both insight and practical solutions to providers of any experience level. Now, the authors guide you, the reader, toward fully understanding trans people as people and, in turn, beginning to have real discussions with them. Having had marginal experiences as a therapy client myself, I think to myself, *Now* that *would be a wonderful world*.

—Mira Krishnan, PhD, ABPP

# Preface

To our ancestors and transcestors who have paved our paths

To our beautiful and fierce community

To those who have survived

To those who are no longer with us

To those whose names we will never know

To those who have had to make difficult choices

To those who continue to fight against injustice and toward autonomy and resilience

To all the badasses who continually breathe life and renewal into our struggle

To those who lift up their communities

To those who strive to center trans voices

To those who have allowed us to hear their truths, witness their processes, and aid in their healing

The purpose of this book is to provide a deeper knowledge base and practical skills for clinicians providing affirming mental health care to trans clients. Over our years of working with trans clients, as well as navigating our own personal challenges as queer, trans, and nonbinary clinicians, we have recognized a need for greater awareness and cultural responsivity to trans people within professional communities. Our aim is to provide you, the reader, with a guide to serving trans clients across many aspects of care that goes beyond an introductory level. We know that many trans clients feel the need to educate their providers in order to receive competent care. We hope to provide a means for you to educate yourself so that your clients do not carry this unnecessary burden.

Although the term *clinician* is used most often in this book, we also use several other terms, sometimes interchangeably, to refer to mental health providers who interact with trans clients, including counselors, therapists, psychotherapists, psychiatrists, somatic practitioners, and healers. This book may also assist other health care providers in working with trans clients.

As clinicians, we have a great responsibility. We have the capacity to perpetuate harm when operating from a place of ignorance, unchecked privilege, or bias. We also have the capacity to witness and help our clients in powerful ways, to assist in healing not only at the individual level but also in ways that intervene with systems that deny autonomy and resilience. We see every interaction with clients as an opportunity to contribute to their greater physical, mental, emotional, and spiritual well-being—these are opportunities that we do not want to miss.

We have aimed to provide you with basic competencies as well as more advanced skills in dealing with the nuances that many oversimplified depictions of trans identities fail to offer. The field of trans health is rapidly evolving, and continual learning is a necessity. We recognize that advanced training, such as in-person didactic training or participation in consultation groups, may not be accessible to you.

This book is based on our many years of collective experience working in the field of trans health, expert consensus, knowledge gained from our respected colleagues, and our own personal experiences. We have made an effort to incorporate evidence-based research with the acknowledgment that this body of research is still small yet growing. Because the research and practice related to trans health is continually evolving, we encourage you to develop a network of colleagues on whom you can rely to keep your knowledge and practice current and to challenge your approaches to clinical work with trans clients. Whether you are working to build a practice that includes work with trans people or you have been working with the community for many years, we hope that the information in this book allows you to grow as a provider and ally to the trans community.

In our writing, we felt it was important for us to be transparent about our background, positionality, and relationship to this work. Sand is a nonbinary, genderfluid Chinese American (they/them/their). lore is a White, queer, trans man (he/him/his). Anneliese is a mixed-race, queer, nonbinary Sikh (she/her/hers and they/them/their). We do not speak for all trans clients, as there is no universal truth that represents clients of all gender identities and backgrounds. Although our experiences differ based on our background and work settings, we share a vision for the type of world in which we want our trans clients, loved ones, and communities to live. We envision a world in which trans people can access affirming care from all health care providers, a world in which therapeutic and assessment work with trans clients is demystified and thereby liberating, a world in which gates have been replaced by bridges, and the very real factors of anti-trans bias and oppression are, at the very least, understood and ultimately eradicated. We invite you to join us in working toward this vision.

# Introduction

Throughout this book, we draw from several theoretical frameworks with the perspective that there is no one-size-fits-all approach for working affirmatively with trans clients. A useful, overarching question when considering counseling interventions is, "What is gender affirming and culturally affirming for *this trans client* at *this particular time* and *in this particular sociopolitical context?*"

This question can remind us that clients not only have different needs based on who they are in the world (e.g., cultural intersections such as race, class, religion), but they also need interventions to be tailored to developmental stages and situational factors. What is affirming for one client today may not be the best counseling intervention for the same client at a different time; similarly, that same counseling intervention may not be appropriate for another client even if that other client seems to be presenting the same clinical concern. In the following section we discuss the frameworks that have informed our clinical perspectives.

## Theoretical Foundations of Trans-Affirming Mental Health Care

Theoretical frameworks incorporated throughout this book include:

- Client centered

- Inclusive, nonbinary view of gender

- Global, multicultural

- Sex-positivity

- Relational, psychodynamic, and attachment theory

- Family systems

- Social justice

- Feminism

- Intersectionality

- Trauma-informed and resilience-based

- Cognitive behavioral therapy

- Dialectical behavior therapy

- Acceptance and commitment therapy

- Developmental

First and foremost, trans-affirming counseling interventions are *client centered*. This means that self-determination and autonomy are seen as key in providing affirming care. In simple terms, this means that clients have the right to say who they are. Providers working with trans clients can demonstrate respect for clients' self-determination in many ways. The first requirement, however, is that counselors interrogate the persistent messages they have been socialized with regarding sex and gender. This includes unlearning ways of relating to others that may be automatic or unconscious; for example, you may have to consciously replace commonly used expressions (e.g., "both men and women") with more affirming, inclusive alternatives (e.g., "people of all genders"). Of course, it is important to take into account the ways that a trans client's self-determination may be limited or thwarted by the influences of systems of oppression—from trans prejudice to racism to other oppressions.

Another underlying aspect of trans-affirming counseling is an *inclusive, nonbinary view of gender* that challenges the gender binary categories of male/man/masculine and female/woman/feminine. You will learn the importance of recognizing that although some clients identify with binary genders (i.e., identify as men or women), others do not. Some clients may identify as both, neither, or somewhere in the middle. These identities include but are not limited to *genderqueer, gender nonconforming, gender neutral, ambigender, gender variant, neutrois,* and *nonbinary*.

A truly inclusive trans-affirming approach to counseling acknowledges and integrates a *global and multicultural* framework for understanding gender diversity, as gender may be experienced, labeled, and expressed in different ways based on culture and geographic context. Because the dominant narratives of trans health and identity are limited in terms of representation, we aim to center the vastly underrepresented and undervalued needs, experiences, and narratives of trans people of color. The journey of global and multicultural competence includes the self-attitudes we examine, the knowledge we can acquire, and the resulting skills we can develop to affirm the multiple intersections of cultural identities trans clients have.

When we work with trans people in counseling, striving to be inclusive of sexuality is as important as being affirming of the broad range of gender identities and expressions with which clients identify. We emphasize a *sex-positive* approach that does not pathologize variations from compulsory heteronormativity (Williams, Prior, & Wegner, 2013). A sex-positive approach is one that not only allows for diversity in sexual orientation (e.g., gay, bisexual, pansexual, lesbian, straight, queer), but also affirms other dimensions of sexuality, including relational diversity (e.g., monogamy, consensual nonmonogamy, polyamory), kink/BDSM practices, and a broad spectrum of asexuality.

*Relational, psychodynamic,* and *attachment theory* perspectives inform some of the interventions you might use with trans clients. One of the key influences of these perspectives is the acknowledgment that the relationship dynamics between you, as clinicians, and the clients with whom you work can greatly affect the course and outcomes of your clinical practice. The feelings trans clients may have about you (traditionally termed *transference*), your feelings and reactions toward them (traditionally termed *countertransference*), and the extent to which these dynamics are acknowledged, explored, or managed can be powerful factors that contribute to the success or failure of treatment. The client-provider relationship allows an opportunity to heal previous relational wounds and increase the potential for greater relational fulfillment in the future. For example, many trans clients report having had their identities invalidated by mental health providers; working from an affirming stance provides an opportunity for clients to have a corrective experience in being accurately mirrored and understood. We also apply a *family systems* approach and acknowledge the role of social support and influence in shaping clients' experiences. With this approach, we consider interventions that include and target family members, partners, coworkers, friends, and other significant communities (e.g., church, school).

The theoretical foundations of our approach to trans-affirming counseling include *social justice* (Toporek, Gerstein, Fouad, Roysircar, & Israel, 2006), *feminism* (Brown, 2010), and *intersectionality* (Crenshaw, 1991). Therefore, we recognize that all social identities are complex; we resist thinking of trans clients as one-dimensional based on their gender identities. In other words, being trans is one aspect of identity among many others. Depending on each person and the particular time in their lives, trans identity and experience may feel more or less salient. Because the intersectional and interactive natures of cultural identities are important influences on our clients' experiences in the world, knowing that gender both influences and is influenced by other significant markers of power and privilege (e.g., race/ethnicity, sexual orientation, social class, religion/spirituality, ability status, immigration status) is critical to our work. Trans clients' multiple and intersecting social identities greatly impact their access to resources, vulnerability to discrimination, and experiences with others, including their health care providers. Therefore, trans-affirming counseling explores how medical and mental health industrial complexes and related power dynamics may create barriers to accessing appropriate trans-affirming health care. Medical and mental health care systems are not exempt from the influences of oppression, capitalism, and consumerism that do not always center the needs of trans clients, and may at times be exploitative. Challenging these systems and advocating for our clients is important when providing trans-affirming counseling.

We believe that work with trans clients must be *trauma-informed* and *resilience-based*. A trauma-informed approach to working with trans clients requires not only attunement and understanding of the signs, symptoms, and effects of trauma, but also responsiveness to the ways that trauma can be treated or healed—or worsened—in the course of therapeutic work (Richmond, Burnes, Singh, & Ferrara, 2017). As clinicians, we seek to understand the ways that trans clients face and cope with trauma they encounter, whether it be overt, specific incidents or the cumulative effects of repeated microaggressions. In turn, the ways that we address trauma (and coping) must include attentiveness toward recognizing and building resilience, including clients' individual and community strengths and resources (Singh, Hays, & Watson, 2011). Because many trans clients experience trauma while seeking medical and mental health care, our work can be an opportunity to restore positive associations with health care providers.

We suggest utilizing structured, mindfulness-based approaches such as *cognitive behavioral therapy* (CBT), *dialectical behavior therapy* (DBT), and *acceptance and commitment therapy* (ACT) where useful. There are strong links between thoughts, feelings, and behaviors, and to address any one of these aspects of experience in isolation may not be effective for our clients (Austin & Craig, 2015). For example, unhelpful or self-defeating beliefs may need to be challenged and replaced in order to help clients move away from behaviors that are harmful to them. Mindfulness-based approaches are ideal for this. For clients with self-injurious behaviors, for instance, DBT (Linehan, 2014) can be an excellent approach. In addition to validating feelings, it provides skills-based alternatives to reduce behaviors that are not in the clients' long-term best interest while reducing the experiences of emotional distress through the development of strengths-based coping mechanisms.

A client's stage of identity development should be a consideration in treatment planning and interventions; therefore, a *developmental* framework is useful in working with trans clients. Age, generation, and cohort are important to consider with regard to developmental stages. For example, a client who is just coming into an awareness of having a trans identity will have different needs from a client who started their transition twenty years ago.

As trans-affirming providers, we endorse the perspective that our clients may benefit from a wide range of approaches, some that call for greater insight and understanding and others that emphasize more active coping strategies and skills. We can encourage greater awareness of self, others, and the world while not losing sight of the need for active, behavioral interventions and solutions for the challenges our clients face. Concerns related to gender identity or expression and decisions related to different aspects of transition may require a great deal of exploration. However, approaches that encourage insight alone (e.g., classical psychoanalysis) are often not the most useful for trans clients, as the reality of anti-trans bias, as well as the need to take actions to cope or seek medical care, require more solution-focused strategies for dealing with client concerns.

## The Structure of the Book

We begin each chapter with an overview of content followed by essential trans-affirming knowledge and case examples that can help you to understand how to apply trans-affirming concepts, skills, and techniques in your clinical practice. You will notice that some of the case examples occur within the context of the clinician-client interactions, while others speak to common experiences trans clients may have in society. As you read through the case examples of counseling interactions, you may imagine yourself in the role of the clinician and ask yourself what you might do similarly or differently. For the case examples that focus on trans client experiences in the world, imagine how you might address these concerns as if you were counseling this client. These foundational concepts and examples are not meant to be exhaustive, but they will help to inform your affirming practice with trans clients. At the end of each chapter, you will find two lists (except in chapter 1, which has one list) of reflection questions that are designed to allow you and your clients to explore the material in the chapter in greater depth. The questions for clinicians can be used as a training tool, in a consultation group, or for personal reflection. The questions for clients can be used in session; they are meant to help the client gain insight and for the counselor to further understand and conceptualize the client's concerns. We hope you will find this guide to be practical in terms of building knowledge and skills as well as inspiring personal and professional growth.

This book is divided into five parts. Part 1 addresses trans communities and health in context. Chapter 1 explores the ways that our gender training (formal and informal) may permeate the language and actions we engage in when communicating with others. It is important for us to explore the biases, beliefs, and values we hold that may impact our ability to build a trusting and productive relationship with our clients. Chapter 2 addresses the importance of demonstrating humility and prioritizing client self-determination. By exploring our own knowledge and the gaps that exist, we are able to join with our clients in a way that ensures they have a clear understanding of the approach we take in our work with them. Too often trans clients have been subjected to the expectations of their cisgender (non-transgender) counselors. As a result, trans clients have been forced to tell stories about their identity that are not consistent with their lived experience for the purpose of gaining access to care. In prioritizing the self-determination of our clients, we allow the client to set the direction and pace of the work and goals they have set for themselves. In chapters 3 and 4, we explore the context relative to the cultural landscape in the United States and the historical reality of trans health care. Understanding the context around which our clients have lived will help us to frame the work we engage in, including trauma-informed and resilience-based work. Chapter 5 focuses on raising awareness and building skills that are necessary for people of all genders and sexualities.

Part 2 explores the foundational skills that allow for trans-affirming care. In chapter 6, we focus on the many roles of the mental health provider. Chapter 7 addresses the importance of applying affirming assessment and diagnostic skills, which then informs treatment interventions and recommendations. In chapter 8, you will learn about the individual, community-based, and institutional barriers that uphold cisgenderist and heterocentric norms and stigmatize any deviations from them. In chapter 9, we examine resilience, both individual and community-based, that allows trans people to cope with or overcome adversity. As clinicians, we may aid clients in developing resilience and applying resilience experiences in other parts of their lives to their current concerns.

Chapter 10 examines the mental health challenges that trans clients experience that may be distinct from or overlapping with gender concerns. We discuss the ways these clinical concerns can be addressed in a sensitive and affirming way.

Part 3 is devoted to deepening an understanding of transition-related care. Chapter 11 lays out different aspects of transition that clinicians should be familiar with, including social, medical, and legal dimensions of transition. Chapter 12 is the most extensive chapter, as it contains details of medical transition (e.g., hormones, surgery), a sample referral letter, and trans-affirming questions you can explore with clients related to each of these medical interventions. This is followed in chapter 13 by information about interdisciplinary, collaborative care with providers and trans communities. Development of collaborative resources will help to ensure that we are addressing clients' needs in the context of their social environments.

Part 4 goes into greater depth on applications of counseling and psychotherapy and the use of different therapeutic modalities. Chapter 14 examines the ways that we can build an affirmative practice for trans clients in individual counseling. Chapter 15 emphasizes the importance of relationship and family counseling, as our clients' well-being is greatly influenced by their relationships and social systems. Chapter 16 addresses the ways that clients may benefit from group counseling or support, especially during earlier stages of gender exploration and transition. The final two chapters in this section, chapters 17 and 18, explore developmental and lifespan concerns with a consideration of the needs of youth and older adults.

Part 5 covers special topics in our work with trans clients. Chapter 19 addresses the importance of creating trans-affirming environments, and chapter 20 discusses how we, as clinicians, can engage in advocacy. Chapter 21 is centered on the experiences of trans clinicians, which is a topic that has received little attention in the field. This chapter may be informative for cisgender clinicians in ally development.

We've also included two appendices: appendix A is a glossary of trans-affirming terms, and appendix B contains a number of resources that can support your ongoing learning in working with trans clients, including publications on guidelines, competencies, and standards; trans-affirming organizations; and books and articles for further reading. We hope you will find these useful for your practice. These and other resources can be found on the website devoted to this book, http://www.newharbinger.com/40538. (See the very back of this book for more details.)

This book was written by and for mental health providers who work with trans clients. We cover topics in ways that center trans clients' needs in our practice. The information covered in each chapter, combined with case examples and reflection questions, will be useful regardless of the amount of experience you have in working with trans communities. It is our sincere hope that the practices we suggest will help to shift the experiences of trans clients and forge connections that allow trans clients to feel understood, respected, and supported.

# PART 1

# TRANS COMMUNITIES AND HEALTH IN CONTEXT

# CHAPTER 1

# Challenge Your Gender Training

As you learn to provide trans-affirming care, you will gain not only important knowledge about trans people and communities, but also a greater capacity to self-reflect. In doing so, you will explore your own history with gender and privilege so as to provide trans clients the services they need and deserve. This exploration often involves interrogating your biases and assumptions, unlearning habitual ways of relating, and acquiring new skills. In addition, developing accountability is a foundation for solidarity, which is crucial in any movement toward liberation and justice. For cisgender clinicians working with trans clients, it is important to develop skills as an ally, which involves action rather than simply claiming an identity. Demonstrating true allyship means being a consistent, trusted, and accountable presence in trans clients' lives, educating colleagues, and interrupting transphobia. Recent social justice movements have seen a trend of replacing the term *ally* with *co-conspirator*, a term that denotes greater action and demonstrated solidarity (Miller, 2018).

Clinicians working with clients who are different from them are not immune to mistakes, but rather can admit to, learn from, and correct mistakes when they inevitably occur. Even providers who are highly skilled and knowledgeable in working with some trans clients may fall short when working with trans clients and communities that are culturally different from them. And even if clients' cultural identities are similar to those of the clinician, there can be large within-group differences in cultural practices. Some providers may be experienced and competent in working with White trans feminine clients with class privilege but less skilled at working with trans masculine clients, trans people of color, or those who are poor or lack access to financial or basic life resources (e.g., safe housing, secure employment).

We encourage you to reflect on your reasons for choosing this work, as well as how your social location informs how you approach the work. When providers do not acknowledge or take steps to manage the impacts of their privilege, they may interact with clients in ways that consciously or unconsciously reinforce harmful and oppressive power dynamics that exist in society. The result of this type of practice can be seen in the historical representation of counselors engaging in exploitative gatekeeping practices that interfere with the health and lives of many trans people.

The self-reflection required to be a true ally to trans clients can be an emotional but rewarding process that you will find benefits you and your clients, as well as your clients' family, friends, larger communities, and other providers. Although it may not be realistic or even desirable to completely erase our gender socialization, humility—the capacity to approach others graciously and be accountable for what we say or do—can serve as a source of strength that enables us to recognize and challenge these biases and make conscious choices about our behavior. There is no "there" to arrive at that will indicate that this work is done; the more you can embrace this as a lifelong journey, the more you will grow along with your clients and with societal changes. Let's start by looking at the ways we are all subject to gender training.

# Gender Training

"Are you a boy or a girl?"

"Act like a lady."

"Boys don't cry."

"What a good girl you are."

"You throw like a girl."

These all-too-common messages are part of gender training in many cultures, but they are particularly salient in Western and colonized cultures. We define *gender training* as the rigid, pervasive messages that we receive from a young age about what it means to be a boy/man or girl/woman, including rules about appearance, behavior, emotional expression, preferences and dislikes, and ways of relating to others. Many of us have internalized the gender binary system so deeply that the ways it informs our attitudes, speech, and behaviors are largely unconscious and automatic. In order to change what we are doing (or thinking), we need to know and understand what we are doing (or thinking).

The statements at the beginning of this section are examples of specific, overt messages about gender roles and rules. However, there are many more subtle cues that we may internalize, even if they are not explicitly said to us:

*Women should shave their legs and underarms.*

*It's not okay for boys to cry; if they do, they will be seen as weak or gay.*

*Girls are bad at math and science.*

*Men are not supposed to show affection toward each other.*

*Women should take care of others.*

You might be thinking, *What harm is there in categorizing people based on gender, especially people who are not trans?* Or, *What if the intentions behind these assumptions are good?* As far back as we can remember, we are inundated with messages about rules pertaining to gender, and we are taught that if we break these rules we will be regarded as bad, deviant, or even mentally ill. Here are some examples:

- When John sees his son Tyler playing with his sister's dolls, he gets very angry. He scolds Tyler and threatens to ground him if it happens again.

- Math is Gina's favorite subject, and she usually gets A's on her math assignments. Once, when she does poorly on a quiz, her teacher says, "It's okay, I know you girls aren't good at math."

- Erin is a tomboy, and everyone accepts her as she is—until puberty. At that point, other girls start to gossip about her being gay. Her mom, who is worried about how this could negatively affect Erin, forces Erin to grow out her hair, pierce her ears, and wear feminine clothing and makeup.

In each of these examples, the end result is the same—the message of conformity often gets internalized, making it hard for anyone to feel free to authentically express their gender. Such gender dynamics do not just affect trans people; they affect people of all genders. However, the consequences of this internalization differ across populations. The gender binary negatively impacts everyone, but the real consequences for cisgender and trans people are not the same. For example, some female-assigned people have negative reactions to being asked (or forced) to wear dresses. This can be harmful to both cisgender and trans people who do not feel comfortable wearing this type of clothing, but for trans people this may create a disconnect that is deeply troubling and related to gender identity (not just gender expression). In all cases, we encourage increased awareness about the ways that we enact the rules of the gender binary. Again, the goal is not to eliminate or flatten the construct of gender, but to allow for self-determination and a diversity of experiences.

## Reflecting on Your Own Gender Socialization

If you think back to your earliest memories, you may be able to locate one in which a parent or caregiver communicated how successful you were at being a boy or a girl. Conversely, think of a memory in which a parent or caregiver criticized you for not fulfilling their expectations for your gender. Consider your parents, how they expressed their genders, and where they received their gender training. How much was that training embedded in race, national origin, or religion? What do you imagine were the consequences for them of breaking the rules? How invested were they in how you expressed your gender? Consider, too, the gender training you might have received from teachers and classmates or in sex education and health classes.

Consider what you have read about relationships. For instance, a popular book in the 1990s was *Men Are from Mars, Women Are from Venus: A Practical Guide for Improving Communication and Getting What You Want in Your Relationships* (Gray, 1992). Not only did this framing rely on the binary, it also suggested that problems between men and women in relationships stemmed from gender differences. Books like this were highly stereotyping of men and women and did not allow any room for people who did not fit these stereotypes.

In professional training, we encounter gender bias and the reinforcement of gender-role stereotypes. For example, the Minnesota Multiphasic Personality Inventory–2 (MMPI-2; Butcher, Graham, Ben-Porath, Tellegen, & Dahlstrom, 2003) contains a scale that purportedly measures masculinity and femininity. Examples of items on this scale are "I like mechanics magazines" and "I think I would like the work of a librarian." These scales suggest that masculinity and femininity are immutable, intrinsic, and one-dimensional rather than dynamic, complex, and socially constructed. What are the ways in which your clinical training has reinforced binary gender essentialism?

To become more aware of your gender biases and socialization, try this mental exercise, which you can also download in worksheet format at http://www.newharbinger .com/40538.

## *Exercise:* Uncovering Unconscious Bias

Imagine in your mind a man and a woman. Don't think too much about it. Just go with the first images available to you. Hold those pictures in your mind. Notice what physical or personality characteristics these imaginary figures have. Notice the racial or ethnic background of these figures. Notice their body shapes and sizes. Then ask yourself why these images or representations for men and women are most available to you. Notice how you feel about these representations, including how it feels to compare yourself to them. Imagine what it would be like for your trans clients to compare themselves to these images.

Now bring up a picture of a trans man and a trans woman. Don't think too much about it. Just go with the first images available to you. Notice what physical or personality characteristics these imaginary figures have. Notice the racial or ethnic background of these figures. Notice their body shapes and sizes. Ask yourself why these images or representations for trans men and women are most available to you. Imagine what it would be like for your trans clients to compare themselves to these images.

Ask yourself:

• *What biases about gender or transgender people did I notice I have in this exercise?*

- *What can I do when I become aware of biases affecting my clinical judgment and practice?*

- *If I am neglecting to think about the wide range of trans people in the world, what effect does this have on each client who comes to work with me?*

This exercise may help uncover unconscious bias related to your gender socialization by bringing awareness to assumptions about what it means to be a man, a woman, or even a trans person. You might have gained insight into ways in which the ideals you hold for "men" and "women" are based on White, attractive, heteronormative, cisgender norms—and possibly assumptions about other identities (e.g., ability, socioeconomic status).

As clinicians, we are encouraged to invest in our own emotional growth in order to guide others through growth or healing work. Many of us have been in counseling, sometimes as an academic requirement in our training programs. Reflecting on your choice of therapist in the past, or how you might approach finding a therapist in the future, may also reveal some biases. You can ask yourself whether, at different points in your own emotional development, you would have been or would be open to working with a trans therapist. We encourage cisgender therapists who would not feel comfortable seeing a trans therapist to reflect on this discomfort and to question their readiness for working with trans clients if this is the case. This reflection may help you understand the emotional risk involved for trans clients meeting with clinicians who may not have firsthand experience with navigating the world as a trans person, as the following case example illustrates.

## CASE EXAMPLE. Clinician Microaggressions: *Working with Andrea*

*Andrea (she/her/hers) is a mixed-race (Latinx/White) thirty-three-year-old who identifies as a "transsexual woman." Andrea hopes that her counselor is trans-affirming and can help her with some issues in her marriage. Within the first few minutes of the intake session, the counselor says, "Wow—you look like a 'real' woman!" Andrea stays for the entire session but feels confused and frustrated because even though she named her marriage concerns as the reason she is seeking counseling, her counselor focuses on her gender instead. Andrea ends up talking about her social and medical transition to educate her counselor. Andrea never comes back to counseling, relying on her friends for support with her marriage concerns instead.*

In this example, we see that the counselor not only sensationalizes Andrea's appearance, but also fails to address Andrea's presenting concerns. The counselor makes the common mistake of assuming that all trans clients seek counseling to discuss gender.

# Acknowledging Privilege and Intersectionality

Acknowledging one's privilege in the context of multiple domains of identity is key in providing trans-inclusive, culturally sensitive care. Peggy McIntosh (1991) discusses the idea of an "invisible knapsack"—one that White people wear, filled with privileges enjoyed by those who have dominance in society: the ability to reliably be in the company of people of one's own race, the ability to speak without being taken as a representative of one's own race, the ability to feel welcomed rather than ostracized in society and public life, and so on. She acknowledges the many ways that she experiences privilege by never even having to notice the ways that others are not afforded the same privileges; White people often wear this knapsack without even knowing it (McIntosh, 1991).

Kimberlé Crenshaw (1991) coined the term *intersectionality* as a framework that considers the additive and interconnected nature of cultural identities, systems of oppression, and the power, privilege, and marginalization that may result. Using intersectionality as a framework for understanding, we cannot focus on one aspect of identity or oppression (e.g., race/racism) to the exclusion of another (e.g., class/classism). It is overly simplistic, in most cases, to say that a person is either privileged or marginalized. A person may have privileges based on some identities while also experiencing marginalization based on other identities. A woman can have cisgender privilege yet still experience racism. A man can have male privilege yet experience anti-trans bias. When working with trans clients, it is important to take into account the multiple contexts of their lives (de Vries, 2012). Without this consideration, our work will be one-dimensional and unlikely to be effective in affirming the client as a whole person, as is demonstrated in the following example.

## CASE EXAMPLE. Considering Cultural Intersections: *Working with Danté*

*Danté (they/them/their) is a seventeen-year-old Black first-year college student who identifies as gender neutral. Danté seeks counseling for the first time at their university counseling center. During the phone intake, they request a counselor who is skilled at navigating both racial and gender identity concerns as well as coping with the stress of being a first-generation college student. They would like to discuss how being a first-generation college student brings up guilt for them and creates a sense of divide between them and their family.*

*Since Danté identifies as gender neutral, the intake counselor decides to assign them to Hannah, a White queer woman who has experience working with trans and nonbinary students. When Danté shows up for their first session, they share some of the challenges they have been facing. They are taken aback when Hannah states, "Let's just focus on gender first. It seems like that is your biggest concern. Then we can discuss what you're experiencing as an African American and as a first-generation college student." Danté feels shut down in the conversation. They also feel uncomfortable because they identify as Black and do not identify as African American. They do not understand how they can discuss their gender in isolation, as it feels so intertwined with their racial identity.*

Danté is self-aware; they know that their identity concerns must be addressed simultaneously and that it is not possible for them to only focus on one concern or another. They are also frustrated that Hannah used a term to describe them that does not feel resonant or authentic for them. Overall, Hannah did not center Danté's presenting concerns or reflect back the language they use for themself.

Some cisgender people can become defensive when thinking about intersecting identities. We encourage our readers to sidestep what feminist scholars have called the "Oppression Olympics" (Davis & Martinez, 1994). Instead, people can strive to be mindful of what they experience at their own unique intersections of culture and identity, as well as how these intersections confer particular privilege and marginalization in different contexts. For example, a White cisgender woman may deny having gender privilege because she does not have male privilege; being narrowly focused on her experience of being a woman in relation to men (i.e., in the context of the gender binary) may obscure the ways that she benefits from being cisgender and having White skin privilege. This limited view may cause her to fail to recognize the ways that misogyny affects trans women and how femininity, for them, may be policed differently.

What follows is a brief list of cisgender privileges. Whether you are cisgender or trans, we encourage you to come up with your own examples of how cisgender privileges are enacted in your social environments.

## Cisgender Privileges

- Being able to use public restrooms, locker rooms, or other sex-segregated spaces without fear or even having to think about it

- Not having to think about which gender box to check on an application or form

- Never having to worry about other people getting your pronouns wrong

- Never having to worry about educating your doctors about how to provide you with appropriate health care

- Having identification documents that have the correct name and gender marker

- Not having to constantly defend your medical decisions or have them be seen as a political statement

- Not having to worry about representing all people of the same or similar gender (e.g., representing all trans women)

- Not having to worry about what the police officer will say or do if you get pulled over while driving and have to show your driver's license

- Not being expected to answer deeply personal questions about your body or genitalia

- Being able to participate on athletic teams without scrutiny about whether your gender identity is acceptable for the team and league

What did you notice as you read through the above list? Whether you are a trans or cisgender clinician, you may have actual or perceived cisgender privilege that affords you differential access to resources. A lack of cisgender privileges does not simply bring up negative emotions—there can be serious physical, emotional, and financial consequences. For example, not having documentation that reflects one's identity can be a barrier to employment. Lack of employment, in turn, may make it difficult to access insurance coverage or afford co-pays for medical services. In some states, documentation of gender-affirming surgeries is required in order to change one's gender marker on identification documents. Lack of employment can result in barriers to safe and affordable housing. As you can see, this is a self-perpetuating cycle of barriers to well-being that trans people often experience. Another example is not having safe, accessible restrooms to use, the consequences of which range from health problems (e.g., urinary infections) to violence or even death. It is vital for clinicians to understand how being subject to enactments of cisgender privilege and the ways it manifests, including within the clinical encounter, can negatively impact trans people.

## Gender as a Reality

Although gender norms are socially constructed, they are still meaningful. When facilitating gender-related trainings, we are often asked questions such as "What if there were no gender? What if we, as a society, got past the construct of gender? Would there still be trans people? Isn't the answer to get rid of gender so there would be no need for transition?" The fact is that we do not live in a gender-free or culture-free world, and the pressures of gender-role expectations significantly affect people's lives. We want to caution our readers against thinking that all people should be gender-free or gender nonconforming or that there is something inherently wrong with having a binary gender presentation. This is where skills of embracing complexity and holding multiple truths is essential. We have clients who identify with the binary gender system, and we do not aim to convince these clients to change their gender identities or expressions. However, when we see that binary ideals are causing harm, we invite an exploration that allows for more flexibility. For example, a trans masculine client who identifies strongly with a more traditional, binary, masculine gender role and disparages others who do not adhere to this role may benefit from having rigid ideas about gender challenged. This is different from a client who has a binary identity, feels secure in this role, and does not impose the gender binary on others.

# Who Is Responsible for Trans Education?

Much of this chapter has addressed the necessary self-reflection for mental health providers who work with trans clients. Another facet of this work is challenging yourself to consider whose responsibility it is to ensure that trans people's needs are understood.

Providers new to working with trans people may rely on their clients to educate them about trans identities and communities. Although we encourage providers to be open to learning from each client, as individual clients' needs may vary greatly, we also caution against expecting this from your clients. There are complex ways in which trans people may be asked to advocate for their communities' needs. It is important to recognize trans people as experts and leaders; however, it should never be an expectation that just because a person is trans, they have the desire or capacity to be in a teaching role. A client who presents with depression or anxiety is never asked to explain these clinical conditions. As a provider, you should take primary responsibility for educating yourself by reading and exposing yourself to trans communities. Furthermore, if you are a provider in an institutional setting, you may want to arrange training for your staff in order to ensure basic competency and skills in interacting with trans clients.

Cisgender providers who offer trans education to colleagues or trainees are encouraged to reflect on their privileged identities and how unconscious bias may inform their approaches to speaking about trans people. We encourage humility and refraining from assuming "expert status" on a group to which you do not belong. In later chapters, you will learn more about what it means to be a "gender specialist" or gender therapist and how to respectfully engage as a provider who works with trans clients.

# Conclusion

Being a gender-affirming clinician requires a commitment to ongoing self-reflection and concrete actions. Being a gender therapist or being in solidarity with trans people means understanding systems of power and privilege, not just those related to gender but also those related to race and class. This is a necessity; it is not optional. It is impossible to consider oneself in allyship with trans people without being in allyship with poor people and people of color. In the next chapter, we take the idea of gender training one step further by emphasizing the importance of humility and respecting self-determination.

# Going Deeper: Questions for Clinicians

*Questions for Clinician Self-Reflection*

1. What early memories can I recall of being expected to behave a certain way because of my gender?

2. How have the following people influenced my beliefs about gender?

    A. Parents

    B. Other family members

    C. Classmates or teachers

    D. Romantic interests or partners

3. How has my gender influenced or been influenced by other identity markers: race, ethnicity, class, ability, sexual orientation, religion, and other identities?

4. How have I benefited from conforming to gender expectations?

5. What were the consequences of not following gender expectations?

6. How have I participated in reinforcing binary gender socialization (e.g., engaging in jokes regarding gender norms, expecting a person to conform to preconceived gender rules, imposing traditional gender norms on my children)?

7. How have I communicated to others (e.g., friends, children, coworkers, clients) how successful or unsuccessful they have been at following the rules of the gender binary system?

8. How might I be able to change these messages or behaviors to be more inclusive of trans people's experiences?

9. Why have I chosen to work with trans clients? If cisgender: How do I approach my work with humility and an awareness of my cisgender privilege? If trans: How do I approach my work with humility and an awareness of how my trans experiences inform my approach to working with trans clients who are different from me?

10. Would I consider going to a trans clinician for my own counseling or therapy? Why would or wouldn't I choose to do this, and what does this tell me about beliefs or biases that may be embedded in this decision?

# CHAPTER 2

# Respect Client Self-Determination

We believe the basis of all trans-affirming care is this: to respect client self-determination. This foundation may be an aspiration with all clients, but it is even more essential when working with trans clients, who often have negative experiences when seeking health care due to the fact that most clinicians never receive formal training on working with trans people.

There are many facets of respecting our trans clients' self-determination, and we can demonstrate humility as we do so. This humility includes understanding that even if we have some, many, or even extensive trans-affirming skills, we must continuously learn about the areas in which we still need to grow our awareness, knowledge, and skills. Some may be more concrete, such as specific affirming language that we use *with* and *about* our clients, while others are subtler and reflected in our approach to care. In this chapter, you will learn skills for communicating with and about trans clients, including "quick tips" for skillful and respectful interactions, which can all be downloaded from http://www.newharbinger.com/40538. We provide examples of non-affirming or outdated language along with more trans-affirming alternatives.

## Using Gender-Affirming Language

Language matters. As trans people are frequently subject to harmful or inaccurate speech in their everyday lives, it is important for us to take extra care to choose our words thoughtfully (Smith & Shin, 2012). In doing so, we can avoid or minimize the trauma that trans people face in dealing with microaggressions (Nadal, Skolnik, & Wong, 2012) and discrimination (James et al., 2016). Affirming language is not about political correctness, right or wrong, or threatening the right to freedom of speech. It is about encouraging the use of culturally inclusive language that does not harm or alienate people whose experiences or mere existence are already denied, marginalized, or criminalized. When working with trans clients, our words have the power to affirm or deny their truths about who they are. Thoughtfulness in choosing our words, even small changes, can make a significant difference in helping someone else to feel safe, welcome, and affirmed.

We acknowledge that terminology related to gender identity has changed significantly over the past few decades, and it continues to evolve. Furthermore, what is affirming for some may not be for others, and these variations are often related to cultural background and context. Therefore, we cannot emphasize enough the importance of *following the client's lead* and using the terminology that feels appropriate for each individual. When we inevitably make mistakes when referring to trans people, we can exhibit our humility by correcting ourselves and apologizing to the trans person (or others who witnessed the mistake) for having misspoken.

## Respecting a Trans Person's Correct Name

A trans person's given or birth name is not always affirming of their gender identity. A trans person may choose a different name that better fits their gender identity or is gender neutral. Regardless of whether the person has legally changed their name, it is important to address them by their correct name, which is the one they designate or choose for themselves. You may hear some clients use the term *dead name* to refer to their given name; we have not chosen to adopt this term because many trans people do not find this term affirming or true of how they conceptualize their relationship to their former names or ways of identifying in the world.

### Quick Tips for Respecting Trans People's Names

- Ask what name a person wants you to use.

- Never use someone's given name without their permission.

- Never ask what someone's given name is *unless absolutely necessary* (e.g., for insurance billing if policy is under the name given at birth). It is generally respectful to ask someone to write down or spell out their name rather than have them say it out loud.

- Refrain from putting the person's chosen name in quotation marks.

- When discussing a client in the past or pre-transition (e.g., during childhood), use the person's current or chosen name *unless the client makes this distinction.*

**Examples of non-affirming usage:**

- "What is your preferred name?"

- "What is your real name?"

- "I knew Jay when he was Jenny."

**Examples of affirming usage:**

- "What name do you go by?"

- "I've known Jay since he was a teen."

## CASE EXAMPLE. Using Respectful Language: *Working with Jamal*

*Jamal (he/him/his) is a nineteen-year-old African American trans man who has not changed his legal name. During the first session at a community mental health clinic, Dr. Knowles asks Jamal what his "real name" is. When Jamal asks why this information is important, Dr. Knowles says, "I was just curious." Jamal feels uncomfortable with Dr. Knowles's curiosity, as it is motivating her to ask inappropriate questions. Jamal takes a risk and decides to advocate for himself by letting Dr. Knowles know that he feels uncomfortable. Dr. Knowles immediately gets defensive, stating that she is a trans ally, has a trans partner, and has never had a problem with any other trans clients. This early in treatment, the relationship between Jamal and Dr. Knowles is tenuous, and it is not likely that it will get better from here. Jamal decides that the counseling center is not a safe space for him to get support.*

In this example, Dr. Knowles fails to respect Jamal's chosen name and places unnecessary value on knowing his given name. In addition, Dr. Knowles did not follow Jamal's lead or show humility when given feedback. Instead, she imparted a message of shame and that Jamal was being difficult (unlike her other trans clients).

## Using Correct Pronouns

Pronouns are units of speech we use to refer to someone or something. In English, we typically use the gendered pronouns *he/him/his* and *she/her/hers* to refer to someone in the third person. Some trans people use *he/him/his* or *she/her/hers* pronouns, while others use gender-neutral pronouns such as *they/them/theirs, ze/hir/hirs, ey/em/eir*, or others.

Failing to use the correct pronouns to refer to someone, whether intentional or accidental, is a microaggression. We recommend against using the term *preferred pronoun* or *preferred gender pronoun* (PGP) for the same reasons we avoid referring to someone's name as a preference. For trans people, being referred to with the correct pronouns (or name, for that matter) is not simply a preference but rather a part of who they are that should be recognized. Instead of saying "preferred pronouns," we can simply refer to them as "your pronouns." If you do not know someone's pronouns, you can ask, "What are your pronouns?" or "What pronouns do you use?"

Clients who use singular they/them/their pronouns may be met with the most resistance from others. Therefore, it can take extra intention and practice for others to use these pronouns correctly and in an affirming way. In addition, we suggest refraining from referring to pronouns as "male" or "female," as gender identity does not always correspond with the associated pronouns.

## CASE EXAMPLE. The Impact of Using Incorrect Pronouns: *Working with Dee*

*Dee (they/them/their) is a thirty-one-year-old Latinx genderqueer client who is seeking help through a binge-eating support group at a community mental health clinic. During their intake with Dr. Kim, they indicate being genderqueer and using they/them/their pronouns. Dr. Kim appears to be receptive. She lets Dee know that the clinic is a "safe space" for trans clients and that the group check-ins usually start with name and pronoun introductions.*

*However, during the first group, even though Dee indicates their pronouns, they feel disappointed when other members repeatedly use she/her/hers pronouns to refer to Dee. Dr. Kim does not seem to notice and even uses the wrong pronouns herself to refer to Dee. Dee wonders if this group will allow them to get the help they need if their pronouns (and gender identity) are not respected.*

In this case, Dee is in a common predicament about how to advocate for their needs, and they feel the stress of having to choose between getting treatment for their eating disorder and having their gender identity respected. Ideally, Dr. Kim would have noticed her error, apologized, and corrected the behavior for herself and other group members moving forward, thereby modeling self-correction for the group. This example illustrates that simply labeling spaces as "safe" falls short of taking necessary action to create an affirming space.

## Quick Tips for Respecting Pronouns

- When you've made a mistake with pronouns, immediately correct yourself and avoid going into shame, justification, defensiveness, lengthy apologies, or explanations. Simply correct yourself and move on.

- Include a fill-in field on intake forms that allows all clients to designate their pronouns.

- In group settings, consider having people introduce themselves with their name and pronouns. This is a simple intervention that can raise awareness.

- If someone else uses an incorrect pronoun and you notice this, take initiative and gently correct that person so that the person being referred to does not have to carry this responsibility on their own.

**Examples of non-affirming usage:**

- "What are your preferred pronouns?"
- "Do you use male or female pronouns?"

**Examples of affirming usage:**

- "What pronouns do you use?"
- "My pronouns are he/him/his. What are your pronouns?"

## Describing Gender Identity or Designation

There are many words to describe gender identity, and this is part of the creativity and resilience of trans communities. We cannot assume a person's gender based on their appearance, name, or pronouns. Keep in mind that not all trans clients will identify as men or women; it is important not only to avoid reinforcing the gender binary but also to create space for clients to express themselves if they have nonbinary identities. Additionally, there are people who identify as men or women and do not (or no longer) identify as having a "trans" identity. Table 2.1 shows terms that are no longer considered affirming in describing gender identities, as well as alternatives that are more inclusive and respectful.

### Table 2.1. Terms to Describe Gender Identity

| Instead of: | Use these terms: |
| --- | --- |
| Biological male<br>Natal male<br>Male-bodied<br>Bio-male, bio-man, bio-boy<br>"Born" as a man | Assigned male at birth (AMAB)<br>Designated male at birth (DMAB) |
| Biological female<br>Natal female<br>Female-bodied<br>Bio-female, bio-woman, bio-girl<br>"Born" as a woman | Assigned female at birth (AFAB)<br>Designated female at birth (DFAB) |
| "Real" man or woman | Cisgender man, cisgender woman |

| Opposite sex | Another sex |
| | A different sex |
| Both sexes/genders | All genders |
| Both men and women | People of all genders |
| MTF, male-to-female | Transgender woman |
| | Trans woman |
| | Trans feminine person |
| | Woman |
| FTM, female-to-male | Transgender man |
| | Trans man |
| | Trans masculine person |
| | Man |

Counselors who use paper intake forms can easily modify their forms to be culturally appropriate for trans clients. When using an electronic health record, it is likely that the counselor will have little to no control over the demographic questions. For this reason, even if you use an electronic record, you may want to use paper intake forms that can be uploaded to electronic systems.

## Quick Tips for Discussing Gender Identities

- Use the affirming terms suggested in table 2.1, but listen for and mirror language that clients use to refer to themselves.

- Refrain from assuming a person's gender identity based on appearance.

- When asking about someone's assigned sex, try to pause and ask yourself if and why the question is relevant. If it is out of curiosity, this is not an appropriate reason to ask. If it is for a legitimate reason, such as needing to determine appropriate medical care, it is important to ask in a sensitive, caring manner. We advise caution here, as there are actually few situations in which this question is legitimate, useful, or medically relevant.

# Greetings and Terms of Address

Many of the common ways that people great each other in society are gendered, and this can be alienating for trans people or people who do not identify with a binary gender. Even when you know the person you are addressing is comfortable with a gendered greeting, this can signal non-inclusivity to a trans person. Using inclusive, gender-neutral terminology reduces the harm that could result in inaccurate assumptions based on one's appearance and takes out the guesswork about a person's gender (and sometimes age). For example, someone perceived as a woman might be called "Miss" or "Ma'am" depending on how old the person appears. The speaker in this case is making two assumptions: one about gender and one about age.

We understand that some people were taught that using gendered terms of address is an expression of respect (e.g., "Yes, sir!"), and many of these gendered terms of address are grounded in cultural practices (e.g., demonstrating respect to elders). De-gendering one's language can be challenging and take a great deal of intention and willingness to experience discomfort. Nevertheless, we advocate that readers embrace this change process, both in their professional practice and in everyday life, as well as encourage others to do the same in order to make all environments more trans-inclusive. Table 2.2 provides examples of non-affirming greetings and terms of address along with gender-neutral alternatives.

## *Table 2.2. Inclusive Terms of Address*

| Instead of: | Use these terms: |
|---|---|
| Ladies and gentlemen… | Hello everyone. |
| Hey ladies! Hey girl! | [Use the person's name.]<br>Hey everybody!<br>Hey folks!<br>Hey friends! |
| Yes, ma'am! | Sure! I can do that! |
| Miss, ma'am, sir | [Use the person's name.] |
| Dear Mr. Smith, | Dear Jesse Smith, |
| You guys | You, you all, y'all |

## Quick Tips for Greeting People

- Adopt gender-neutral ways of greeting or addressing *all* people.

- Refrain from assuming you know the composition of a group of people. For example, avoid generalizations such as "There are no men in the room."

- Change demographic forms or salutations in letters; incorporate gender-neutral ways of addressing others.

- When referring to a person whose name you do not know, it is appropriate to say, "the person in the blue shirt."

# Describing Aspects of Transition

Transition is a process in which a person shifts aspects of their gender expression, physical appearance, or social identity; this often involves moving away from a gender expression, physical appearance, or social identity that is associated with their sex assigned at birth. Transition is a multifaceted process that some, not all, trans people go through. Many people think transition means "the surgery" or "a sex change surgery." However, there is no single medical procedure that changes someone from one gender to another. Nor is transition solely a medical phenomenon. There are many pathways that a trans person can take in order to improve well-being. Some people seek medical care so that their bodies or external appearance feel more aligned with their gender identity, or the internal sense of who they are (man, woman, both, neither).

Some people choose to have chest reconstructive surgery (often referred to as "top surgery") but never have genital reconstructive surgeries. Other people may desire multiple surgeries to feel affirmed in their authentic gender. Some who want to access gender-affirming medical care cannot because they do not have health insurance or economic means to do so, or because they have medical conditions that make medical interventions risky.

Other trans people do not desire medical transition but wish to socially transition. There are many aspects of social transition, including but not limited to changing one's name and/or pronouns, using different restrooms, and living in a gender role or having a gender expression that differs from what is expected based on sex assigned at birth.

If it is appropriate to ask someone about transition (e.g., you are in the role of providing a letter for a surgeon), do so in a way that does not communicate that transition (medical, social, or legal) or a certain transition trajectory is an expectation. For example, when someone discloses being trans, it is not uncommon for them to be bombarded with questions about whether they have started taking hormones or have had surgery, or plan to do either. This is a reflection of a societal fixation on the medical aspects of transition to the exclusion of other aspects of transition, such as emotional, spiritual, and relational aspects.

## CASE EXAMPLE. The Impact of Non-affirming Assumptions: *Working with Sam*

*Sam (he/him/his) is a twenty-six-year-old Filipinx client who grew up as a tomboy. Sam reports being accepted by friends, family, and teachers in the Philippines as a boy from a young age. His name was gender neutral, and Sam reports he felt free to dress in a more masculine way. Sam also shares that others generally perceived him as a boy or man. When he came to the United States at age eighteen, he learned that he had access to gender-affirming medical services and decided to pursue chest reconstructive surgery.*

*Sam goes to a trans clinic for mental health assessment and referral for surgery. The counselor, Liz, asks when he came out to others and started socially transitioning. This question is confusing to Sam, as he does not feel that coming out or socially transitioning were clear, discrete events in his life. He reports, "I've just always been this way." Liz seems hesitant to accept Sam's answer, which makes Sam wonder if he has somehow given a "wrong" answer that will cost him his chance to get surgery.*

In this example, Liz is struggling to integrate a new, different experience into her limited view of transition. She is stuck believing that prior to medical transition, trans clients must socially transition toward a gender that is different from a previous gender expression. Liz does not center Sam's gender experiences or reported needs in their interaction. This causes a therapeutic rupture at a basic level; at a larger level, it furthers the understandable distrust that trans communities have of mental health providers.

## Quick Tips for Discussing Trans Clients and Transition

- Don't assume that all trans clients relate to the concept of transition. For example, some human resources policies ask trans employees to name a "start date" of their transition, one in which they will officially be recognized in their affirmed gender. This request may have legal and ethical uses, and may even aim to protect the rights of trans employees. However, some trans people consider their transition (including the initiation of it) as a process rather than an event.

- Don't assume that all trans clients want to medically transition or have access to transition-related health care.

- Remember that medical information and histories are sensitive and may not be relevant to your work with the client.

- If you wouldn't ask a cisgender person about their genitals or medical/surgical history, then do not ask a trans person about this sensitive information either.

- Avoid using terms like *post-op* or *pre-op* when describing a trans person's gender identity. This perpetuates the expectation that all trans people want to or will eventually have surgery.

**Examples of non-affirming usage:**

- "Have you had *the* surgery?"

- "Is she pre-op or post-op?"

**Examples of affirming usage:**

- "What forms of transition are part of your path?"

- "Are you interested in a medical transition?"

## Describing Bodies

It is important to be sensitive when discussing trans people's bodies, which are often scrutinized or called into question as soon as the person states they are trans. It is intrusive and disrespectful to casually discuss another person's genitals or other private body parts, yet trans people encounter this kind of microaggression all the time.

It is important to respect others' freedom to decide how to refer to their own bodies, and whenever possible use gender-neutral language (Deutsch et al., 2013; Spade, 2011). Terms that feel affirming should be used over what is considered "anatomically correct." Above all, it is important to ask yourself whether it's necessary or relevant to discuss body parts, especially if your client does not initiate this discussion.

Table 2.3 provides examples of affirming ways to discuss bodies and body parts. These are general recommendations; above all else we recommend following the client's lead and mirroring the language they use to describe their bodies.

*Table 2.3. Trans-Affirming Terms to Describe Bodies*

| Instead of: | Use these terms: |
| --- | --- |
| Breasts | Chest |
| Penis, vagina | Genitals, private parts |

| Female reproductive organs, male reproductive organs | [Name specific organs, such as uterus or testes, and mirror the language of the client.] |
| --- | --- |
| Beard | Facial hair |
| Women (e.g., in the case of preventative health screenings) | People with cervixes, ovaries, uteruses |
| Men (e.g., in the case of preventative health screenings) | People with penises, testes, prostates |

## Quick Tips for Respectful Communication About Trans Clients' Bodies

- If discussing bodies or body parts is *relevant* to the client's concerns, make every effort to use gender-neutral language.

- Never ask a trans client about their genitals unless you have a legitimate reason to do so. It's equally inappropriate to ask any trans person *unless the person brings this subject up and indicates wanting to talk about it.*

- It can be more respectful to refer to body parts (especially genitals) using "the" instead of "your" (e.g., "the cervix" instead of "your cervix").

- Be mindful that discussing body parts can be emotionally upsetting or cause a trauma response in some clients. When in doubt, ask what language is most affirming or least distressing for clients.

- Pay special attention to how sex-specific medical information is recorded in electronic medical record (EMR) systems. Notice whether it allows for the complexity that is sometimes introduced when a trans person has socially or medically transitioned but may still need medical care associated with their birth-assigned sex. Be mindful of automatic preventative health alerts and how EMR systems may make inappropriate prompts (e.g., prompts for prostate exams for trans men).

---

**Examples of non-affirming language used to describe body parts:**

- "All women need to have pap smears."

- "I hear that you want to have surgery to remove your breasts."

**Examples of affirming usage to describe body parts:**

- "I want to respect how you would like me to talk about your body. What words would you like me to use to refer to your genitals?"

- "It is important for people with ovaries and uteruses to have a gynecological exam regularly."

- "I hear that you want top surgery."

---

# The "Passing" Police: Avoiding Gender and Body Appraisal

Trans people's bodies are often scrutinized by others, and this can be disempowering for those who want to be seen and affirmed for how they perceive themselves. Body appraisal can occur in interactions with well-meaning professionals who wish to validate a trans person's gender. Consider the following two examples.

## CASE EXAMPLES. Making Gender Assumptions: *Working with Osamu and Alana*

*Osamu (he/him/his) is a twenty-eight-year-old Asian American trans masculine client who feels insecure about whether others perceive him as a man. He talks to his provider about this in one of his first counseling sessions. His provider, Dr. Tatum, says to him, "You look great! I definitely see you as a man." Although this is well intentioned on Dr. Tatum's part, it is not an appropriate response, as it reinforces the idea that gender is determined by others' perceptions and that trans people need to be validated or reassured by others in order to be taken seriously. Additionally, it reveals Dr. Tatum's personal opinion or perception rather than a clinically informed and useful response. It would have been more helpful if Dr. Tatum had noticed her discomfort with Osamu's fears and instead created a safe space for Osamu to explore his fears. Dr. Tatum could also have reflected on her own desire to be seen as an ally or to save Osamu from discomfort.*

*Alana (she/her/hers), a thirty-nine-year-old Caribbean trans woman, meets with a medical team at a trans health clinic to discuss her options regarding genital reconstructive surgeries.*

*During this intake appointment, her provider says to her, "You would also be a very good candidate for facial feminization surgery. It would help you to pass a lot better." Alana likes the way her face looks, and she has never desired facial feminization surgery. Hearing this from her provider is difficult because she feels that the inherent message is that she does not look enough like a woman according to standards that are not only very binary but also come from a White, Western ideal of femininity.*

In these two examples, the counselor makes inaccurate assumptions about the client relative to how and whether they conform to expectations of gender expression. This is one example of how a counselor's biases about gender can adversely impact the client's self-conception.

The concept of "passing" is pervasive in discussions about trans people and is closely related to body appraisal. Clients themselves will use this term in relation to their own experiences with others. For some clients, it is important that they have a gender that is legible to others perceiving it from a binary framework. However, it is not every client's goal to "pass" as anyone other than who they are. The word "passing" can be used to communicate whether a trans person has been "successful" at approximating a cisgender person's appearance, and often it is used in a way to reinforce the gender binary, sexism, misogyny, racism, and ageism, among other oppressive systems. In the film *Diagnosing Difference*, activist and counselor Adela Vázquez states, "Passing is a word that discriminates [against] us immensely. Not everybody can pass. And passing is something that the doctors will tell you to do… How about empowering me as the transgender woman that I am?" (Ophelian, 2009). Passing is not the one and only goal of all trans people, and providers should be careful not to assume that their trans clients hold passing as an objective or priority.

At the same time, we do not want to minimize how the goal of passing may be connected to not only gender affirmation, but also safety. Some clients express that a desire to pass is about avoiding anti-trans bias and violence rather than wanting others to perceive them correctly. For trans people of color, who are already more vulnerable to stigma and harm based on racism, there may be more pressure to avoid calling undue attention to themselves. As a result, trans people of color may experience more pressure to "pass." Our aim is not to deny passing as a goal that some trans people have, but to encourage clinicians to think critically and to support clients in thinking about what passing means to them and why.

There are times when clients directly solicit advice or feedback on their appearance. Though it may seem benign to engage or comment on the client's appearance because the client is requesting it, we think it is important to remain clinically grounded and instead take the approach of exploring the motivation or meaning of this request. There may be useful clinical information about the client's internal process and how they are relating to you and others in their environment. For example, the client may be seeking reassurance from you, and this relational dynamic may be clinically rich and worth exploring. By responding in a way that centers the client's thoughts and feelings, you can reaffirm the client's sense of empowerment and self-determination.

# Recovering from Mistakes

When working with any clients, mistakes are to be expected, which can bring up difficult feelings, including guilt and shame, for clinicians. When you make a mistake, we encourage you to prioritize correcting it first and then later getting support in dealing with challenging feelings you may have. When you are able to acknowledge having made a mistake, it takes the pressure off your client to correct you or take care of your feelings, and it also keeps the client from having to wonder whether you are aware of the error. When a client chooses to let you know that you have made a mistake, we recommend listening, responding from a place of humility, and acknowledging or repairing the harm. Overall, following the client's lead requires a great deal of listening and suspending or challenging your own assumptions.

# Conclusion

In this chapter, you learned about basic terminology and skills for clinicians seeking to interact respectfully with trans clients. You also explored ways of demonstrating respect and allyship by using language and communication appropriately, in order to uphold client self-determination as the pillar of affirming work with trans clients. In chapter 3, we will utilize a social justice lens to explore the cultural landscape in which trans clients live.

# Going Deeper:
# Questions for Clinicians and Clients

## Questions for Clinician Self-Reflection

1.  What theoretical frameworks or techniques do I apply most often in my work with clients? What, if any, are this theory's perspectives on trans clients?

2.  How might I need to adapt my theoretical approach to make it affirming of trans clients across a wide spectrum of gender identity?

3.  How might my role with trans clients be similar to or different from my role with cisgender clients?

4.  How do I feel about the concept of self-identification? If I struggle with it, what deeply held beliefs might inform this?

5.  How good am I at respecting others' pronouns, including gender-neutral pronouns that I did not learn early in life? What about when I am talking about the client in third person when the client is not present? What am I willing to do to practice respecting my clients' pronouns?

6.  What do I tend to do when I make a mistake with someone's name, pronoun, or gender? Is this strategy effective in helping that person feel respected or affirmed? Or do I get defensive or try to explain myself?

7.  Do I greet others in gendered terms? What changes can I make to be more inclusive and gender neutral?

8.  In what ways do I notice body appraisal occurring in my environment? How do I participate in body appraisal of the people I encounter in my life, and how might this affect my interactions with trans clients?

9.  What would I do if a client directly asked me whether she "passes" or if I perceive her as a woman?

## Questions for Client Exploration

1.  What name would you like me to use to refer to you?

2.  How do you identify in terms of gender?

3.  (If a client uses a term for their gender or some other marker of identity that you're not familiar with:) I am not familiar with that term and do not want to

make any assumptions about what it means for you. Would you be willing to share what it means for you?

4.  (*If a client uses a term for their gender or some other marker of identity that you're familiar with:*) I am familiar with that term, but I do not want to make any assumptions about what it means for you. Would you be willing to share what it means for you?

5.  What are your pronouns? How would you like for me to refer to you?

6.  What actions, words, and attitudes from others help you feel the most affirmed in your gender?

7.  How do you feel or respond when people do not refer to you with your correct name, pronouns, or gender?

CHAPTER 3

# Understand Cultural Landscapes of Gender Diversity

As noted in chapter 2, gender diversity exists within a multicultural and social justice context. It is impossible to look at gender without considering other cultural markers of identity. Therefore, clinicians should be prepared to explore the cultural landscape of trans people's lives. This preparation can vary across clinicians and depends on factors including the type of graduate training a person receives (e.g., clinical, counseling), the extent of the multicultural focus in their graduate program, and that person's lived experiences. However, there are certain basic skills that clinicians of all disciplines can use. In this chapter, we talk about the importance of multicultural and social justice approaches in trans-affirming practice. We give specific attention to the intersection of social identities for trans people, and we also discuss the roots of trans experiences to inform trans-affirming perspectives in counseling.

## History of Gender Diversity Around the Globe

One of the major foundations of trans-affirming counseling is having an understanding of the history of trans people around the globe (Singh & dickey, 2016). Many people believe that being trans is a recent trend—or even a fad—but in actuality, trans people, experiences, and communities have existed for a long time across diverse cultures (Roberts & Singh, 2014). For instance, the *hijra* (trans people of South Asia) have existed across India, Pakistan, and other South Asian countries for hundreds of years. These communities were long involved in sacred rites and rituals related to births, weddings, and other cultural events in South Asia, and though many hijra communities were decimated due to British colonization practices that pathologized trans identities within South Asian cultures, hijra people remain active in these roles today (Roberts & Singh, 2014). This history is not limited to the Asian continent. Gender diversity and variance is expressed among the *mahu* of the land now called Hawai'i, the *muxe* of Mexico, and the *kathoey* of Thailand. The *two-spirit people* of North America also have a long history of gender fluidity within indigenous groups. Essentially, trans people (both those who would be considered "trans masculine" and those who would be considered "trans feminine" today) were considered an important fabric of society across many diverse cultures, yet due to Western colonization and hegemony, these experiences were not recorded or included in historical accounts. In addition, it is important to avoid artificially conflating all Western and European histories of gender variance, as this centers whiteness over the diverse ethnicities and experiences in those parts of the world.

Although it is tempting to view bias and discrimination against trans people within a purely modern-day context, once you know that trans people have existed for hundreds of years in many different countries and continents, as a clinician you begin to view anti-trans bias differently. For instance, ancient stories of trans communities existing throughout the world serve not only to validate the long legacy of trans people across the continents, but also to demonstrate how trans communities often held sacred and important roles during religious ceremonies and important rites and rituals related to weddings and births. Knowing this history also helps clients take a wide-angle view of trans communities as resilient and existing over the ages across diverse gender identities and expressions as well as diverse cultures. This view of trans resilience is crucial as trans communities have faced decimation and challenges from mostly Western practices of colonization.

This wider-angle lens afforded by trans histories—or "t-stories," as we like to call them—can help you contextualize the challenges that trans people face across the globe. Many trans people who present for counseling certainly experience immense barriers, as you will read about in chapter 8. However, they also have the opportunity to develop resilience to navigate these challenges, as we will discuss in chapter 9. Integrating a trans-historical perspective in your counseling approach is one way you can counter clients' barriers and increase client resilience. This perspective should be introduced within the counseling session in a measured and tactful fashion, so as to avoid overwhelming clients who are accustomed to seeing trans identity from a Western lens of being a "recent experience" and only as perpetually marginalized. Rather than providing an extensive history of trans communities to clients who may not be aware of the legacy of their gender identities across time and culture, you can weave the existence of diverse trans communities within the counseling process as a method of empowerment. Consider the following examples of how the legacies of trans communities might be integrated in counseling sessions.

## CASE EXAMPLES. Integrating a Trans-Historical Perspective: *Working with Julian and Dorothy*

*Julian (he/him/his) is a fifty-three-year-old Chicano American trans man who seeks counseling for depression. He shares that his life has "lost all meaning." He also reports feeling "alone and different" because all of the trans people he knows are White. His family and friends have also told him that they think his trans identity is a "White people thing," which increases feelings of isolation. During the intake session, Julian's counselor assesses how much Julian knows about the history of trans people in Mexico and the Americas. Julian expresses he knows very little. His clinician shares a few stories of the muxe—the trans people of Mexico—and how in current times, the muxe are celebrated with festivals and integrated within society. Julian's eyes light up, as he says he is "interested in learning more" and it feels "good to know [he is] not alone."*

*Dorothy (they/them/their) is a sixteen-year-old multiracial, genderqueer client. Their parents bring them to counseling, as Dorothy has suddenly "started getting bad grades." Over a few sessions, the clinician assesses Dorothy for mental health issues such as depression and anxiety, as well as their experience of overt or covert discrimination. In the fourth session, the clinician asks Dorothy which classes they are struggling with, and they share that English and History are their least favorite. Dorothy shares that they are "tired of reading about White cis people" in these classes. The clinician asks if Dorothy would be more interested in these classes if the long and rich global histories of trans people were included, such as the hijra of South Asia or the sangopas of Africa. Dorothy expresses surprise at hearing trans communities existed around the world and wants to learn more about their history.*

These are just two examples of how you might integrate the long histories of trans people across diverse cultures, especially when clients are struggling with isolation or lacking trans models. You will want to keep in mind that some of this information is readily available online; however, a tremendous amount of trans history has been lost or destroyed by colonialism.

## Multicultural and Social Justice Counseling with Trans Clients

Having knowledge of trans histories is an important multicultural and social justice foundation of trans-affirmative counseling. In addition, it can be helpful for clinicians to understand some of the history underlying multicultural and social justice approaches to counseling.

Multicultural approaches within the helping professions date back to the 1980s. Early multicultural approaches focused on issues of race/ethnicity and binary gender, as well as how to attend to the needs of clients across cultural backgrounds or respond to clients' preferences for working with clinicians with certain identities. Gender identity and trans people were not yet included in discussions about gender.

Traditionally, there have been three hallmarks of multicultural competence: developing awareness of one's attitudes and beliefs about a culture, gaining knowledge about a culture, and building the skills needed to provide culturally responsive counseling with a group (Sue, Arredondo, & McDavis, 1992). In the revision of the multicultural competencies by Sue et al. (1992), a fourth domain of clinician "action" was added to emphasize the connection that multicultural competence has with social justice advocacy (Ratts, Singh, Nassar-McMillan, Butler, & McCullough, 2016). Clinician action refers to your ability to reflect on your privileged and marginalized identities, the privileged and marginalized identities of your clients, and how these identities intersect with one another.

# Social Identities of Trans People

Aside from gender identity, trans people may have numerous other social identities. Social identity refers to how people define themselves in terms of group membership, such as by:

- Age

- Race/ethnicity

- Education level

- Gender (including identity and expression)

- Sexual orientation

- Socioeconomic status

- Emotional, physical, and developmental ability

- Immigration status

- Religious/spiritual affiliation

- Relational/relationship status

These are just some examples. Other social identities might include those related to experiences (e.g., being a fat activist or being a member of the leather community), practices and belief systems (e.g., veganism, political affiliation), or occupational identities (e.g., artist, veteran).

The multiple identities trans people have can range in terms of salience as well. For instance, an African American trans woman may find more salience and meaning in her race/ethnicity than in her gender identity. This may be for many reasons. She may have grown up with a sense of belonging and similarity in an African American community that supersedes her identification with other trans women. She may feel racial/ethnic pride, but she may also have had repeated experiences of racism that have increased this salience. The following two examples demonstrate how trans people can experience social, multicultural identities very differently.

## CASE EXAMPLES. Exploring Social Identities:
### *Working with Bai and Toni*

*Bai (he/him/his) is a forty-six-year-old Chinese American trans man whose family has been in the United States for two generations. He presents for counseling two years after beginning social and medical transition. He shares that he is experiencing stress because of new attractions toward cisgender men. Bai was formerly dating lesbian women, and he reports feeling fearful of sharing his emerging sexual orientation identity not only with his community, but also with his parents. He says his "transition was already hard enough" for his family, and he is worried they will not accept him as a gay man.*

*Toni (they/them/their) is a White, fourteen-year-old genderqueer youth. They report feeling solid in their gender and sexual orientation identities. Toni asked their parents if they could go to counseling. When Toni speaks with you during the intake session, they share that they have been recently getting involved with youth activism and have begun exploring their racial/ethnic identity as a White person. They report feeling "stressed out" about this exploration because they are realizing they have White privilege. Toni gives you a few examples, such as recently going to a restaurant with Black friends and the server only addressing Toni instead of addressing the group as a whole, and on another occasion noticing the White members in a trans support group were "taking up a lot of space." Toni shares that they are learning "so much, so fast" about White privilege, and sometimes this brings up feelings of guilt.*

As the two cases indicate, different social identities are salient for Bai and Toni. Bai's sexual orientation is a prominent presenting concern, whereas Toni is experiencing more salience in their racial/ethnic identity. It is important to keep in mind that at different developmental or life stages, the identities that are most salient for a given person may shift. This shift is not necessarily an indication that a trans person has made or is considering a shift in their trans or gender identity.

## Exploring Client Privilege and Oppression

The term *privilege* refers to the advantages that people may have that are unearned and based on social identity (McIntosh, 1991), whereas *oppression* refers to the lack of those advantages related to social identity (Ratts et al., 2016). Privilege and oppression are closely linked, not only to individual social identities, but also to larger systems (Israel, 2006). Table 3.1 provides just a few examples of the connections between social identities, systems of oppression, privileged groups, and marginalized groups.

Social identities of privilege and oppression can shift throughout one's life. Within the system of sexism, trans men may gain male privilege. This shift in societal perception provides a very different experience from their previous gender socialization in an oppressed identity (i.e., perceived as women). On the other hand, trans men who are not perceived by others as men, or who are perceived as men some of the time and not others, may experience a range of contrasting privilege and oppression experiences. Even these generalizations within the system of sexism become more complex and nuanced, as the racial background of the person will have bearing on how that person is treated, regardless of their being perceived as a man. No matter how much society perceives and accepts a trans man of color as a man, he will still have to contend with the impacts of racism.

## Table 3.1. Social Identities and Systems of Oppression

| Social Identity | System of Oppression | Privileged Groups | Marginalized Groups |
|---|---|---|---|
| Age | Ageism | Young to middle adults | Youth, older adults |
| Race | Racism, White supremacy | White skinned, people with lighter skin | People of color, mixed race, darker skin |
| Socioeconomic class | Classism | Owning and ruling class, formal education | Poor and working class |
| National origin | Xenophobia | U.S. born, U.S. citizens | Immigrants, Native Americans |
| Religion and spirituality | Anti-Semitism, Islamophobia, etc. | Christian | Atheist, agnostic, Muslim, Jewish |
| Sex | Sexism | Males | Female, intersex |
| Gender identity | Transphobia, cissexism, misogyny | Men or cisgender men, binary identities | Trans, nonbinary, gender nonconforming |
| Sexual orientation, sexuality, attractionality | Homophobia, heterosexism | Heterosexual, allosexual, monogamous | Gay, bisexual, lesbian, queer, asexual, polyamorous, kink/BDSM |
| Disability | Ableism | People without disabilities | People with disabilities |
| Size | Sizeism, fatphobia | Thin people | Fat people, people considered "overweight" or "obese" |

Clinicians can seek to understand the complexity of trans people's experiences related to privilege and oppression and how they influence the client's mental well-being. See the next case for an example of exploring privilege and oppression in the intake session.

# CASE EXAMPLE. Exploring Client Privilege and Oppression Experiences: *Working with Charlene*

*Charlene (she/her/hers) is a twenty-five-year-old White trans woman who grew up in a working-class family in a rural area. Her family rarely had money to buy enough clothes for her to go to school, and she frequently experienced the "lights being turned off" because there was not enough money to pay the bills. Charlene presents for counseling and shares that she recently moved from a rural to an urban area so she "could finally be [herself]." Charlene is having difficulty finding work, and she reports fearing that she will not be able to finance her transition. The counselor notes Charlene's areas of privilege (e.g., White) and areas of oppression (e.g., trans, woman, working class) in order to identify the trans-affirming resources she may need access to (e.g., low-cost medical care, job placement, and career development). The counselor decides to structure their work together so as to help Charlene secure as many of these resources as she can.*

In this case, we see how Charlene's socioeconomic status impacts her ability to feel secure in her identity and choices. As clinicians, we can take responsibility for valuing and exploring client needs related to their trans identity and overall well-being. You can use a privilege and oppression framework to help clients gain a better understanding of the challenges they face. Although a client's presenting issue may not always be related to gender identity, it is not uncommon for clients to report challenges related to anti-trans bias in their lives. You can then collaboratively explore resources that can help them navigate anti-trans bias. Having a clear assessment of the relationship between social identities and current concerns can help you focus your interventions when anti-trans bias is at play.

# Addressing Clinician Privilege and Oppression

In addition to exploring client social identities of privilege and oppression, it is important to interrogate your own social identities, how they intersect with one another, and how they may relate to your client's identities. This is true for clinicians of all genders (i.e., whether you identify as a man, woman, nonbinary, cisgender, transgender). The four domains of multicultural and social justice competence—awareness, knowledge, skills, and action (Ratts et al., 2016)—are useful here. Consider the following questions related to cultural domains:

- What is my *awareness* of my own privileged and oppressed identities and how they might intersect with those of diverse trans clients?

- What is my *knowledge* of my own privileged and oppressed identities and how they might intersect with those of diverse trans clients?

- What are my *skills* in recognizing and reflecting on my own privileged and oppressed identities and how they might intersect with those of diverse trans clients?

- What are the *actions* I can take considering my own privileged and oppressed identities to advocate for the needs of diverse trans clients?

When you reflect on these four domains, you can develop accountability for ensuring your work with trans clients is grounded in multicultural and social justice. The complexity of multiple identities that both you and your clients hold can lend richness to the clinical experience. The next case demonstrates how these four domains can be brought into the counseling session.

## CASE EXAMPLE. Applying Multicultural Competence: *Working with Nomi*

*Sheila is a twenty-seven-year-old, cisgender, White, master's level clinician. She is working with Nomi, a forty-year-old Thai American trans woman who presents with concerns about her spirituality and her gender identity. In terms of awareness, Sheila has continually assessed her biases as a White cisgender person when working with trans people. Sheila is mindful that although spirituality is not integral to her identity, as she is an atheist, it is an important part of Nomi's life. With regard to knowledge, Sheila has had formal training in trans-affirming counseling and has worked with many trans women of color. However, she has less knowledge of the issues influencing trans people and their spirituality, especially in a Thai cultural context. Sheila brings up this case in her peer consultation group, where there is a clinician named Anthony who specializes in spiritual concerns. Anthony advises Sheila to identify specifically how her own identity as an atheist influences how she views Nomi's coping and resilience as a trans person. In terms of skills, Sheila decides to attend a workshop on spirituality and counseling to develop her skills in this area. In the course of working with Nomi, Sheila also researches the spiritual supports available in her community for trans people of color; a few sessions into her work with Nomi, she has found several. Sheila decides to take action and shares this resource list within the trans-provider listserv of which she is a member.*

As the example of Sheila and Nomi demonstrates, the four domains of multicultural and social justice competence are quite interrelated. Each is uniquely important and builds upon the other, and is most effective when consultation and supervision practices are employed. There are several free resources available to guide you in developing multicultural and social justice competence, especially as you explore your own identities (see appendix B).

# Conclusion

In this chapter, we discussed the importance of gaining knowledge of trans histories across diverse cultures. We also reviewed social identities related to systems of oppression, as well as how privilege is assigned within these systems. We discussed the four domains underlying multicultural and social justice competence and explored how you can incorporate these domains into your practice. In the following chapter, we will examine the history of trans health care in the United States.

# Going Deeper:
# Questions for Clinicians and Clients

## Questions for Clinician Self-Reflection

1.  What do I know about the history of trans people around the globe, and how can I learn more?

2.  Did my graduate training emphasize a power analysis when discussing race, gender, or other cultural identities? Was this in single courses or infused across the curriculum?

3.  Did I receive training across many different aspects of cultural identity, or was it focused on certain aspects of identity (e.g., race, gender) to the exclusion of others (e.g., gender identity, ability)?

4.  What are the implications of the disconnection of trans communities from their histories for mental health and overall client well-being?

5.  How can I integrate historical perspectives into work with trans clients?

6.  How can I understand the intersection of identities for trans clients with whom I work?

7.  How will my own identities related to privilege and oppression influence client assumptions and treatment?

8.  What are the gaps in my multicultural and social justice training, and how can I address them so as to be more clinically competent in these areas?

## Questions for Client Exploration

1.  How much do you know about trans histories over time and across cultures?

2.  How does it feel for you to work with me as a [insert practitioner-salient identities; e.g., race/ethnicity, disability]?

3.  In order to develop a trusting and affirming environment, what do I need to know about the identities that are important to you?

4.  Trans people can have multiple experiences of discrimination related to gender and other identities like race/ethnicity, disability, and class. What experiences of discrimination have you faced based on your identities?

5.  If someone followed your life for one day, what values would they notice are important to you? How do these values support or challenge your gender identity or gender expression?

# CHAPTER 4

# Know the History of Trans Health Care in the U.S.

As awareness of trans people and their medical needs has gained attention in the media due to recent events and legislation, providers can be misled to believe that trans medicine is a new endeavor in the United States, rather than one that has a long and complicated history. It is important for clinicians who interact with trans clients to understand and learn from the history of trans health care in this country; doing so can inform forward progress and prevent repeating previous mistakes.

Medical interventions have existed in many countries for centuries (Stryker, 2008). This chapter focuses on gender-affirming health care practices dating back to the 1950s that are most directly linked to current practice in the United States. A more detailed account of the history of trans people in medical literature is discussed in *The Transgender Studies Reader* (1st and 2nd editions; Stryker & Aizura, 2013; Stryker & Whittle, 2006). We have highlighted a few aspects of this history so that you can better understand the context of your work with trans clients. We encourage you to take note of themes woven throughout this history and how they affect current practice, including power differentials and the ways in which language is shaped by the environment.

## "Psychopathia Transexualis" and "The Transsexual Phenomenon"

Perhaps the first instance of writings about trans people in medical literature is an article published in 1949 by American sexologist David Cauldwell. Cauldwell wrote about the phenomenon of "psychopathia transexualis" and used language from the field of eugenics to suggest a "poor hereditary background" and a "highly unfavorable childhood environment" caused this "condition." He referred to people afflicted with this "condition" as a burden to society (Cauldwell, 1949). From its inception, the concept of being "transsexual" was pathologized. Trans identity was viewed as a deviation from an otherwise normal society rather than an expression of human diversity, and both genetics and environmental influences were to blame. Unfortunately, the basic philosophical under-pinnings of Cauldwell's ideas are still pervasive in trans health care, especially among providers who lack current training in gender identity.

The next major development in the history of trans identity in a Western context occurred in 1966, when Harry Benjamin, often credited as the first physician to treat trans people in the United States, published *The Transsexual Phenomenon: A Scientific Report on Transsexualism and Sex Conversion in the Human Male and Female*. In it, Benjamin conceptualized gender and sex as different constructs, and he differentiated gender identity and sexual orientation, which had been conflated by the work of earlier sexologists (Benjamin, 1966).

Although some of Benjamin's ideas were progressive for his time, he was overly fixated on determining a singular narrative for all trans people. As an attempt to identify the "true transsexual," Benjamin devised a rating scale to measure gender variance, sexual orientation, and desires to alter one's body. From this scale, he developed seven categories that factored in sexual attraction and the degree to which a person desired surgery. Benjamin proposed that the "true transsexual" must express a desire for genital surgery and report something akin to being a "man trapped in a woman's body" or a "woman trapped in a man's body." This was just part of a singular medicalized narrative that developed at that time and still influences society's view of trans people. Unless they espoused this narrative to medical professionals, trans people were not afforded access to hormone therapy or genital reconstructive surgeries.

In many ways, the medicalized narrative and "rules" for trans people trying to access gender-affirming medical services still govern medical providers' decision making, even unconsciously or unquestioningly. We encourage clinicians to reflect on and challenge their biases about trans people that are based on antiquated narratives. For example, as we've said, some trans people do not desire any kind of medical intervention. For others who do not relate to the idea of being "trapped in the wrong body," there are specific medical interventions that would help them to feel more comfortable in their bodies.

# Public Awareness: Christine Jorgensen and Media Attention

Christine Jorgensen was the first person in the United States to have a visible and public transition. After seeking medical care (i.e., surgeries) in Denmark in 1951, as well as undergoing hormone therapy supervised by Harry Benjamin, her transition spread quickly in the news. Jorgensen became an early public icon whose transition made other trans people aware that surgery and hormones were a possibility. Many trans people wrote to their doctors to inquire about these medical interventions.

What is little known about the publishing of the first news article about Jorgensen is that the public nature of her transition was without her consent (Jorgensen, 2000). After that, Jorgensen accepted exclusive rights to write about her own story. Accounts of Jorgensen's life suggest that she did not want to be a spokesperson for trans people, but she felt a responsibility to educate the public about her experience. Though the media portrayed Jorgensen simply as a spectacle and source of public amusement, Jorgensen wrote about the challenges trans people faced during her time, which resemble the struggles of trans people today. Those challenges "made me more determined than ever to fight for th[e] victory" of a successful transition, she wrote. "The answer to the problem must not lie in sleeping pills and suicides that look like accidents, or in jail sentences, but rather in life and the freedom to live it" (Jorgensen, 2000, p. 90).

We can consider Jorgensen's story as an example of the ways in which the popular conception of trans people has been overly fixated on surgeries (i.e., genital surgeries), how trans people are depicted as caricatures and stereotypes, and how trans people have been robbed of the power to choose if and when to disclose their being trans. Many of the ideas about trans people that manifest in Jorgensen's case have carried over and continue to affect access to care.

## The Rise of University Gender Clinics

In 1966, the same year that Harry Benjamin published *The Transsexual Phenomenon*, the Johns Hopkins Gender Identity Clinic announced its program to perform sexual reassignment surgeries. This was the first of over forty gender clinics, mostly university-based, that opened in the late 1960s and early 1970s (Meyerowitz 2009). Although some argue that the opening of gender clinics was a positive direction in the treatment of people who sought medical interventions for gender affirmation because it increased access and awareness of the need for such interventions, the approach that these early gender clinics took—which relied heavily on Harry Benjamin's conceptualization of a "true transsexual" (1966)—set the stage for gatekeeping and limiting the possibilities available for trans people. Clinics were extremely selective and treated a low number of individuals.

Compounding matters was the fact that most people who were determined to be eligible for treatment at the university gender clinics were White. People of color were explicitly excluded. Treatment options were for people on the trans feminine spectrum, as even the few medical providers who knew anything about trans identities did not know how to treat trans masculine people. People who were too high functioning, who had an affinity for the gender roles or behaviors associated with their sex assigned at birth, who had no report of childhood "cross-gender" identification, who had a history of successful heterosexual relationships (who would then be considered lesbians after transition, as they would be women in relationships with other women), and who had children (used as evidence of heterosexuality prior to transition) were often excluded from treatment (Denny, 2002).

## Eligibility Criteria Used by the University Gender Clinics (Denny, 2002)

- Detailed intake assessments (lasting five hours or more) performed only by "opposite-sex" clinicians

- Extensive psychological testing

- Interviews of significant family, friends, and partners/spouses (lasting four hours or more)

- Long-term psychotherapy, usually lasting several years

- "Passing" sufficiently as the gender the client was reporting to be; in fact, some clinicians reported that they used their sexual interest or attraction as a way to determine whether a trans woman was convincing enough as a woman (Kessler & McKenna, 1978)

- Exclusive preference for "opposite-sex" childhood toys

- Early childhood "cross-gender" identification

- Dissolution of preexisting marriages

- Participation in longitudinal research

You can see how important it is that clinicians be aware of the unreasonable standards that have been imposed on trans people seeking care and the ways that these standards still affect current care models. For example, many of the questions that are embedded in assessments for medical interventions are aimed at determining whether a person is truly transgender. You will read throughout this book that it is not a medical or mental health provider's task to determine a person's "true" gender; the best way to figure out a person's gender identity is to ask and listen to what they say about themself. Some parameters for determining eligibility for care are based on unfair standards that cisgender people would not be asked to meet; for example, a cisgender person needing a lifesaving or quality-of-life-improving surgery would not be asked to be in perfect mental health in order to access this care.

## Privatization of Trans Health Care

In 1979, Johns Hopkins University closed its gender clinic, reporting little evidence that gender-affirming surgeries were effective in treating trans people. It based this conclusion on the fact that after having undergone surgeries, trans patients still reported problems, such as gender dysphoria (i.e., distress related to gender or gendered aspects of one's body). That same year, the Harry Benjamin International Gender Dysphoria Association

(HBIGDA) was founded, and its first task was to create and approve standards of care. As the last of the university gender clinics closed in 1989 and as trans health care moved toward privatization, the HBIGDA standards provided guidelines to help independent practitioners (i.e., surgeons, endocrinologists, and mental health professionals) make decisions about eligibility for services.

The HBIGDA Standards of Care have come to be known as the WPATH (World Professional Association for Transgender Health) Standards of Care—guidelines to help determine the course of treatment and care for trans people seeking gender-affirming medical care. These standards named requirements, such as certain benchmarks, that trans people had to meet before being determined "ready" or "appropriate" for receiving medical interventions such as hormones or surgeries. Since its conception, the WPATH Standards of Care perpetuated the idea that gender variance was pathological, that trans people must be closely monitored, and that medical professionals must maintain control over trans people's transition trajectories (e.g., require a certain order of attaining gender-affirming medical care, such as a certain minimum length of time in therapy or time on hormones before surgery). In order to access transition-related or gender-affirming care, trans people would coach each other on what to say to doctors who had expectations of a uniform medicalized narrative (Spade, 2000; Stone, 1991), and without this universal narrative, care was likely to be denied.

The privatization of trans health care limited who could access gender-affirming medical care. Only people who could afford to pay out of pocket the huge costs of hormones or surgeries, as well as the medical visits associated with the assessment and referral process (e.g., at least six months of psychotherapy according to Standards of Care at that time), could access this care. In 1989, Medicare officially excluded what it termed "transsexual surgery" from its coverage. This exclusion remained in place for over twenty-five years as a barrier for many trans people who desired access to surgeries.

# Gender-Related Diagnoses in the DSM

Though homosexuality as a mental health disorder was removed from the *Diagnostic and Statistical Manual of Mental Disorders* (DSM) in 1973, gender identity disorders were introduced around this time. The diagnosis of transsexualism first appeared in the DSM-III (American Psychiatric Association, 1980) and was later changed to gender identity disorder (GID) in the DSM-IV-TR (text revision; American Psychiatric Association, 2000). These diagnoses required clinicians to determine the extent to which a person's gender identity was "disordered" or pathological, as well as whether the person wanted to transition or seek medical interventions. In 2013, with the publication of the DSM-5 (American Psychiatric Association, 2013), the diagnosis of gender dysphoria replaced gender identity disorder. This is the current diagnosis applied to trans people and often justifies medical necessity for gender-affirming medical care. It is important to keep in mind that DSM-5 diagnoses typically correspond with diagnoses in the *International Classification of Diseases, 10th revision,* (ICD-10; World Health Organization,

2016), so when considering diagnosis (or diagnosis reform), both of these documents must be considered.

Although many consider gender dysphoria an improvement over GID, as the focus is on distress rather than identity, there are many criticisms of the gender dysphoria diagnosis. Though some argue that there must be a diagnosable disorder to justify the necessity of medical interventions, others raise the concern that this does not allow for the existence of a disorder-free or healthy conception of trans experience (Winters, 2013). In addition, there are trans people who do not fit the diagnostic criteria for gender dysphoria. For example, they may meet the criterion of having the desire to be treated as a gender different from the one associated with their sex assigned at birth, but they may not report clinically significant distress. These people may be denied the gender-affirming medical care they desire if they do not tailor their gender histories or experiences to match diagnostic criteria.

In 2018, it was announced that in the next version of the ICD (ICD-11), the diagnosis of gender dysphoria will be referred to as gender incongruence, and it will be moved out of the chapter of the ICD that addresses mental disorders and into the chapter on sexual health. As the change will not go into effect until 2022, it remains to be seen how this change in diagnostic categorization will affect trans people and their access to care. It is worth noting that the diagnostic criteria rely on the concept of "gender incongruence"; the measure or expression of this incongruence may vary across individuals, and what constitutes incongruence is often based on the idea that the gender binary is and should be the norm. Although some trans people may consider their bodies to be incongruent with their affirmed genders, there may be others who feel congruent in a body that does not fit cissexist expectations or ideals.

In a model of trans health that relies on pathology in order to justify treatment, trans people can be afforded gender-affirming health care only if they desire to move *away from* something negative rather than wanting to move *toward* something that feels more authentic or affirming for them. In chapters 9 and 10, you will learn more about the role of diagnosis in assessment and referral for gender-affirming care.

# Current Approaches to Trans Health Care

It is important to note that there is no singular approach to working with trans clients, and there is still a great deal of controversy in terms of what approaches are deemed the most efficacious for trans communities. There are several resources that clinicians can use as recommendations for best practices, some of which are described below.

Many medical and mental health professionals who work with trans clients follow the World Professional Association for Transgender Health Standards of Care, Version 7 (WPATH SOC7; Coleman et al., 2012). The SOC7 states readiness criteria according to medical services or procedures. For example, a client seeking hormone therapy or chest surgery is required to provide one letter from a mental health provider (Coleman et al., 2012). Those seeking genital surgeries are typically required to obtain two letters from mental health providers. There are also requirements related to transition pathways. For example, "living full time" in one's reported gender for one year is often required before accessing genital reconstructive surgeries (formerly referred to as sex reassignment surgeries).

Informed consent models for trans health care—models that propose that clients should be able to make their own choices regarding health care as long as they understand the risks and benefits—sprang up in the late 1990s to early 2000s, beginning with the Tom Waddell Clinic in San Francisco and later adopted by other community health centers such as Fenway Health in Boston, Callen-Lorde in New York, and Howard Brown in Chicago. Informed consent models deemphasize the role of the provider in gatekeeping or evaluating whether a trans client has sufficiently met expectations as laid out in the WPATH SOC and attempt to give power and autonomy back to trans individuals. Many institutions use an informed consent model for hormone therapy; however, this model is not widely used for surgeries. The Informed Consent for Access to Trans Health Care (ICATH, n.d.) is a document that describes and advocates for an alternative to the more formal WPATH SOC. The ICATH was developed by advocates, allies, and providers with the intention of creating a treatment approach that reflects the importance of providing trans people with the power to access the care they need with or without a mental health diagnosis (e.g., gender dysphoria).

In addition to the WPATH SOC, several publications set forth by professional organizations guide clinicians in addressing the needs of trans people, such as the American Psychological Association (2015) guidelines and the American Counseling Association (2010) competencies. A list of these publications is included in appendix B and can also be downloaded from the website for this book, http://www.newharbinger.com/40538.

# Insurance Coverage

The landscape for trans health care in parts of the United States shifted around 2013, as some insurance companies started to include gender-affirming health services in their coverage plans. The Patient Protection and Affordable Care Act (2010) played a key role in the expansion of coverage. The gender-affirming services that are covered by insurance plans vary greatly depending on a person's geographical location and corresponding laws and policies. For example, in 2013 the Department of Managed Health Care (DMHC) in California ordered the removal of any blanket exclusions on trans health and ruled that these exclusions were discriminatory. As a result, many health insurance plans in California started to include gender-affirming care under their base benefits plans. However, in many states, insurance coverage for gender-affirming care does not exist. At a national level, the Medicare exclusion originally set forth in 1989 was lifted in 2014. This meant that people with Medicare coverage could request gender-affirming surgeries on a case-by-case basis. Though this was a huge triumph for trans people, there have been problems with the implementation of this change, such as a lack of surgeons who accept Medicare insurance and are trained to perform the requested surgeries (dickey, Budge, Katz-Wise, & Garza, 2016).

Insurance plans vary in coverage for gender-affirming medical care. One major question is how medical necessity is determined. This is where mental health providers play a significant role in diagnosing gender dysphoria as a prerequisite for trans people seeking hormone therapy or surgery. Health insurance companies who provide gender-affirming services continue to struggle with questions of how to differentiate coverage for the same procedures for different populations (trans versus cisgender people). Many of these questions have been harmful to trans people, as their desires and needs have been called into question as "cosmetic" when in fact they are medically necessary. It is not appropriate to use the same evaluation tools for cisgender and trans people accessing care that should be considered separate and distinct. Another question insurance companies have dealt with is which services will be covered for different trans people. For example, chest reconstructive surgeries for trans masculine people are covered by a number of insurance plans, while feminizing mammoplasties (breast augmentation surgeries) are not. There are erroneous assumptions that certain medical procedures are sought for the same reasons regardless of the patient's goals, concerns, or motivating factors. Just because cisgender women seek augmentation surgeries for cosmetic reasons does not negate the true medical necessity associated with feminizing mammoplasty for trans women. This raises concerns about discrimination, as access differs based on gender identity.

Finally, it is important for clinicians to remember that though more trans people have access to gender-affirming medical services through their insurance plans, many others continue to remain uninsured. In fact, one out of every five trans people and one out of every three Black trans people are uninsured according to a national survey (dickey, Budge, et al., 2016; Grant et al., 2011). Although a positive trend occurred in increased health insurance coverage for trans people between 2014 and 2016, many questions exist about how viable coverage will remain under the U.S. administration at the time of this writing. At this time, trans health care is highly susceptible to changes based on the political climate. In our collective experience, reports of anxiety and fear rose significantly among our trans clients due to an increasingly vocal, anti-trans sentiment from both political figures and the media. As changes occur and access is granted or denied, you will find that your clients will appreciate having a space in which they can discuss their feelings and reactions. In your role, you may be able to identify opportunities to advocate for the rights and needs of trans clients at an individual, institutional, or policy level (see chapter 20).

## Lessons Learned from Trans History

The brief historical review discussed in this chapter serves to provide context and help clinicians understand and learn from historical approaches to treatment and care of trans people. Here is a summary of key lessons to integrate into your practice:

- Trans people have not always had a choice about when and how to disclose being trans. It is a matter of respect, as well as safety, to allow trans people to decide if, when, and how they disclose being trans. Clinicians should refrain from pressuring trans people to "come out," especially before they are ready and have adequate support.

- The history of trans health care in the United States is rooted in a tradition of gatekeeping, medicalization, and the perspective that trans people are not capable of making decisions about their health and bodies. This sets the stage for health care providers, including mental health professionals, to take responsibility for the health care decisions that trans people are capable of making for themselves. An affirming approach is to share responsibility with trans people and to employ a collaborative model of care.

- The media, society, and trans health care system have been overly fixated on genitals as determining a person's gender and on medical transition as trans people's only concern. It is important for clinicians to be aware of the bias this creates and to let trans clients guide the discussion about what is important to them and how they conceptualize their gender and medical needs.

- Gender diversity has been pathologized, while a binary, cisnormative view of gender has been viewed as normal. Clinicians must challenge this socialized conception in order to provide affirming care to trans clients.

- People who don't fit the medicalized narrative are not seen as trans or taken seriously, and this gets in the way of access to medically necessary health care. Clinicians should challenge any notions that trans people are more legitimate if they fit certain narratives of what it means to be trans.

The following case example serves to illustrate ways in which the barriers imposed by antiquated models of understanding gender and assessing appropriateness for medical interventions can harm trans clients and how biases can obstruct clients from accessing necessary care.

## CASE EXAMPLE. Understanding Differential Health Care Access: *Working with Nadine*

*Nadine (she/her/hers) is a sixty-eight-year-old African American transgender woman who presents at a trans health clinic requesting genital reconstructive surgery (vaginoplasty). Nadine socially transitioned and started hormones early in her life, and she has lived happily as a woman for over forty-five years. She has a supportive husband and reports having a successful and rewarding career. Nadine reports that she first sought out surgery at a university gender clinic in the early 1970s, but she was told that the clinic was not performing surgeries on women of color. She reports that she struggled for many years with not being able to access surgery, but over time she became resigned to the fact that she would probably never have surgery.*

*With changes in health care, Nadine's insurance now covers genital reconstructive surgeries. She reports being "overjoyed" but "a little in shock" at being able to access surgery. The mental health provider Nadine works with, aware of the history of bias and gatekeeping in the university gender clinics, took time to talk to Nadine about her feelings and the adjustment she was making in recovering a lifelong dream that she felt she had no chance at realizing. Her therapist explored what it was like in the early days of her transition and her attempts to get the health care she needed. Nadine appreciated being able to tell her story to someone who affirmed her experiences and explored how those experiences might impact her current needs.*

This example highlights the importance of mental health providers' being aware of the history of trans health care so that they may be sensitive to their clients' experiences and concerns.

## Conclusion

In this chapter, we summarized some key points in the history of trans health in the United States, including knowledge of different waves of access to gender-affirming medical services, to provide you with the context for your work and role with clients. We also highlighted mistakes that have been made by health care providers as opportunities to learn and provide more affirming care to trans clients. In chapter 5, we explore aspects of gender and sexuality in greater detail, giving special attention to nonbinary identities.

# Going Deeper:
# Questions for Clinicians and Clients

## Questions for Clinician Self-Reflection

1. How much have I educated myself about the history of trans health care, including the role of mental health professionals?

2. How does learning more about this history affect how I see my role?

3. Do I recognize ways that my views about trans health care have been influenced by outdated conceptualizations of trans people?

4. In what ways might I adjust my practice so that I do not repeat harmful mistakes of the past?

## Questions for Client Exploration

1. What has allowed you to access the care that you need from medical and mental health providers?

2. What obstacles have prevented you from getting medical care?

3. What has your experience been like with providers who have held the power to make decisions about your health care needs and access?

4. Given that most people, health professionals included, have heard only one version of what it means to be trans and what trans people want in terms of medical services, how are you able to speak your truth about your story?

5. How, if at all, have changes in access to gender-affirming health care affected your identity or health care decisions?

# CHAPTER 5

# Consider Diverse Genders and Sexualities

The gender binary is a cisgender-normative categorical system in which there exist two mutually exclusive genders (male/man and female/woman) and immutable ways of expressing those genders. A person is considered either a man or a woman or masculine or feminine. There are no options in between these polar concepts, and a person must declare and adhere to the associated expectations. In this chapter, we will emphasize nonbinary identities, including the erasure of nonbinary people in popular discourse. We will also discuss the many ways that trans people may experience and express their sexualities and intimate relationships.

## Understanding Nonbinary Identities

The existence of nonbinary identities is not a new phenomenon; nonbinary people have existed throughout history, dating back centuries across many continents. Unfortunately, colonialism had a great influence in erasing these identities from popular discourse or the recording of history. It is important to keep in mind that not all people who have defied gender identity or expression norms used the label *transgender* for themselves, as this is a relatively recent term used to differentiate trans and cis people. This differentiation has its limitations, as it is a somewhat artificial binary in the context of gender variation and expression.

As a modern movement within the United States, nonbinary people became more visible beginning around 2002. The popular term used at that time was *genderqueer* (Nestle, Howell, & Wilchins, 2002), whereas today the term *nonbinary* is more popular. There are many different labels or descriptors under the nonbinary umbrella. As a clinician, it is more important that you respect your clients' identities and listen rather than attempt to memorize the definitions of each term.

## Examples of Nonbinary Identities

- Androgyne
- Bigender
- Demiboy
- Demigirl
- Gender diverse
- Genderfluid
- Gender nonconforming
- Gender variant
- Genderfuck
- Genderqueer
- Mixed-gender
- Multigender
- Neutrois
- Nonbinary
- Omnigender
- Pangender
- Stud

## CASE EXAMPLE. Supporting Nonbinary Identities: *Working with Ethan*

*Ethan (he/him/his) is a biracial (Native American and Asian), twenty-year-old college student who was assigned female at birth. Ethan started hormones six months ago, and as a result he has grown facial and body hair that he feels proud of. Hormones are the only medical intervention Ethan has sought. Because he lives in the Midwest, he has decided that the pronouns "he/him/his" are the best to use as he feels less at risk for harm; however, he does not identify with the gender binary as others would assume based on his pronouns. Although he uses male pronouns, he identifies as "genderfuck." Ethan alternates his appearance on a regular basis. Some days he wears a dress or other "feminine" clothing and continues to wear a beard. On other days, he presents in "masculine" attire and makes no effort to bind his chest. Ethan enjoys this flexibility in how he presents from one day to the next. He doesn't mind the confusion this creates for others; in fact, he enjoys using the confusion of others as a moment for education about the variations of being trans. As stated earlier, his decision to use "he/him/his" pronouns is about personal safety, and therefore he is especially careful about whom he chooses to educate.*

*Ethan sees a counseling intern named Abigail (she/her/hers), a thirty-four-year-old biracial, heterosexual, cisgender woman. Ethan is Abigail's first trans client. After completing an intake, Abigail seeks supervision. Abigail is confused about Ethan's history and also concerned about how his story clashes with her values. Abigail was raised in a politically and socially conservative family. As such, Abigail knows little about trans people and believes that "they do not deserve special protections." She learned in her abnormal psychology class that trans people should be diagnosed with a mental health disorder. In supervision, Abigail was encouraged to do some research about trans people and was provided with resources to understand affirmative practice with trans clients. Abigail completed the research as suggested; however, this did not change her opinions.*

*In the second session, Abigail begins to inquire about what Ethan meant when he said he was "genderfuck." Abigail is clearly confused and alarmed about Ethan's reported identity. She asks Ethan if it is acceptable to use the term genderfuck. Ethan can see that Abigail is uncomfortable and having a hard time with the conversation, and he begins to doubt whether he can get the support he needs. He challenges Abigail in the third session and states that he does not feel supported in his identity and wonders why Abigail hasn't attempted to educate herself.*

In this example, Ethan could have had a more affirming experience if Abigail had taken time not only to educate herself but also to understand the ways in which her values and biases might be different from her client's. Further, had Abigail explored her own ideas of gender (as addressed in chapter 1), she may have come to see how she was imposing her values on Ethan.

When considering more contemporary nonbinary identities, one will notice that there is often little adherence to the gender binary. It is not accurate to say that people with nonbinary identities are androgynous. This may be confusing for members of the general public, because it is the way in which they have been able to make sense of people who do not clearly appear to be either male or female. People with nonbinary identities may feel some identification with aspects of being a man or a woman; for example, those who identify as genderfluid may identify with both binary genders and move fluidly between them. Others may identify as both, neither, or as having a "third" gender that is not defined in terms of adherence to or rejection of the gender binary.

# Sexual Identity

Sexual identity, sometimes referred to as sexual orientation, is often conceptualized as having three components: identity, attraction, and behavior. Sexual identity is a separate, but sometimes interrelated, concept from gender identity and expression (American Psychological Association, 2015; Chandra, Copen, & Mosher, 2011). All people have a sexual orientation, even if that includes not feeling sexual attraction toward others, as is the case for some people on the asexual spectrum. Sexual identity is the process by which a person comes to understand this orientation and may also be used as an alternative to sexual orientation.

# Examples of Sexual Identity Labels

- Aromantic

- Asexual

- Bicurious

- Bisexual

- Demiromantic

- Demisexual

- Dyke

- Gay

- Graysexual/Gray

- Heterosexual

- Lesbian

- Pansexual

- Queer

- Questioning

- Straight

Although many consider sexual orientation immutable over one's lifetime, research has indicated this is not the case (Diamond, 2009). In fact, sexuality may be fluid for some people. For nonbinary people, the commonly known labels of lesbian, gay, bisexual (LGB), and straight are confining as they are based on the gender binary. If a lesbian or a gay man is sexually or affectionally attracted to someone of the same sex or gender, what then is the same sex or gender for a nonbinary person? For this reason, it is not uncommon for trans people, especially those with a nonbinary identity, to identify as queer, as it is a useful umbrella term that does not require one's sexual orientation to be relative to their assigned sex or gender identity.

Historically, the term *queer* has been used as an epithet toward LGB people. The term has been reclaimed and is a source of pride for many people, especially younger LGBTQ (lesbian, gay, bisexual, transgender, queer) individuals. This term can still be offensive to older LGBTQ people (e.g., baby boom generation) whose lived histories include the term being used as a derogatory slur against them. By using terms like *queer* and other inclusive terms (e.g., *pansexual*) to describe one's sexual identity, trans people are able to express their sexuality without having to conform to the gender binary or even disclose their gender or the gender of those to whom they are attracted.

Some trans people experience shifts in their sexual identity or attraction as they transition (Chang, Singh, & Rossman, 2017). There are no definitive reasons why this shift might occur. A person may feel more comfortable in their body, in the ways in which they express their gender, or in the new ways in which they respond to others on romantic and sexual levels. For clinicians, it is important to remember that the client defines their sexual identity. Just because a person experiences a shift in sexuality does not mean that they will change the label used to identify their sexuality. Further, this shift is not an indication that a person's sexual identity can be changed through therapeutic interventions, often called reparative or conversion therapy. Jordan's story highlights the concept of sexual fluidity.

## CASE EXAMPLE. Affirming Sexual Fluidity and Asexual Identities: *Working with Jordan*

*Jordan (they/them/their) is a thirty-eight-year-old Native American, nonbinary person who began exploring their gender after having come out as a lesbian in high school. Jordan initially felt their sexual orientation was why they felt so different from their peers. Jordan began seeing a counselor, Michael (a thirty-five-year-old Native American), after a difficult breakup. It was through Jordan's work with Michael that they came to realize their gender identity. Jordan felt affirmed as a lesbian by Michael's validating, humanistic stance; this later allowed Jordan to start exploring gender concerns.*

*As Jordan focuses on exploring what it means to them to have a nonbinary identity, they slowly realize that they are no longer sexually attracted to women. To Jordan's surprise, they find they are attracted to cisgender men. This is surprising for Jordan as this is a completely new experience. Over time, Jordan dates cisgender men but is never in a significant or committed relationship.*

*Jordan decides to take a low dose of testosterone, while still in counseling with Michael, for the primary reason of ceasing their menstrual cycle. This is effective for Jordan and helps them to feel less distress about their gender, but they stop taking testosterone after a couple of years. This decision is related to health concerns that Jordan wants to address without adding medications to their daily routine. One of the things Jordan notices is that their libido diminishes. Jordan begins to identify as gray (this is one way to identify as asexual). In Jordan's mind this helps them to explain that their interest in sexual experiences is not a significant part of their identity. In fact, Jordan has little to no interest in having a sexual experience. Instead, what Jordan experiences are emotional connections with other people.*

This example illustrates the point that some trans clients experience fluidity or shifts in attraction in relation to shifts in their gender identities, and for some, sexuality or attraction can be more or less salient at different times in their lives.

# Relational Structure Diversity and Kink/BDSM

Some trans people's relationships are similar to those that are considered mainstream or in line with dominant cultural expectations (e.g., heterosexual, monogamous). Other trans people may choose to structure their relationships in ways that are nontraditional. Most of this chapter has focused on aspects of sexuality that are about attraction or direction of attraction. However, there are other dimensions of sexuality and relationships that are also important for you to be knowledgeable about and respectful of when working with trans clients.

One such dimension is the way in which people form relationships. We term this *relational structure diversity*, and we affirm that there are varying degrees to which a person may subscribe to or reject monogamy. While some trans people are monogamous or choose to be in monogamous relationships, others engage in consensual nonmonogamy or polyamory, meaning they may choose to have more than one romantic and/or sexual partner at a given time. Some clients have attractions to more than one kind of person and find that consensual nonmonogamy is a way of being in a relationship that allows for greater need fulfillment. Nonmonogamous clients may choose to structure their relationships in many different ways, including the extent to which they relate sexually or emotionally and how they negotiate boundaries.

People who are nonmonogamous or polyamorous face a great deal of stigma from society. We want to underscore that consensual nonmonogamy is just that—consensual, with all parties knowing about the nature of sexual interactions or relationships that are occurring. It is different from cheating or infidelity. Just as many of your trans clients may seek therapy for reasons unrelated to gender but still need to know that you are culturally competent in regard to gender diversity, polyamorous clients may not always seek therapy related to polyamory, but they will want to know that you are culturally competent with regard to polyamorous relationships or communities. If this is an area of practice that is new or unfamiliar to you, we recommend seeking consultation so as not to impose biases or communicate rejection or disapproval. We encourage you to educate yourself about the many ways in which clients may engage in nonmonogamy. Helpful books on this topic can be found in the "Further Reading" list in appendix B, which is also available on the book's website, http://www.newharbinger.com/40538.

Another dimension of sexuality and relationships you will want to be familiar with is engagement in kink/BDSM practices or communities. There are many different definitions and facets related to involvement in kink/BDSM, but one definition is "the knowing use of psychological dominance and submission, and/or physical bondage, and/or pain, and/or related practices in a safe, legal, consensual manner in order for the participants to experience erotic arousal and/or personal growth" (Wiseman, 1996, p. 10). A great deal of stigma exists around being "kinky" or involved in BDSM, so clients may be hesitant to disclose much about their involvement if they are not sure you are affirming and open to these sexual practices (i.e., sex-positive). There are also many misconceptions related to kink/BDSM, such as assumptions that these practices are inherently unhealthy, dangerous, or reenactments of trauma. If you are unfamiliar with these practices or communities, it will be helpful for you to familiarize yourself with them so as not to assume a pathologizing stance.

Some clients will engage in gender play in the context of kink/BDSM or fantasy, and this may or may not inform the client's gender identity on a day-to-day basis. For example, some people find that "playing" with gender in a kink/BDSM context allows them freedom to explore gender and get closer to being able to socially transition (if they are trans). However, other people who engage in gender play are not trans, and this is simply a part of the realm of sexual fantasy. If this is something that a client talks about, be careful to not make any assumptions about whether gender play is part of their identity. As always, you will want to listen to the meaning of different behaviors or gender expressions according to the client.

## Conclusion

Trans communities and movements have varied across time, and this has affected our understanding of diverse genders and sexualities. Rather than being pathologized or considered "confused," deviations from or fluidity within the binary gender system can be considered normal variations of human experience. Open discussions about gender and sexual identity, including nontraditional relationship structures, can be useful in deepening clients' understanding of themselves. In part 2, we discuss the skills that are a foundation to trans-affirming practice, beginning with a discussion of the mental health provider's role in chapter 6.

# Going Deeper:
# Questions for Clinicians and Clients

## Questions for Clinician Self-Reflection

1. Do I conduct a thorough sexual history of my clients when this is relevant to the clinical conversation?

2. How comfortable am I asking clients about their sexual history, orientation, or behaviors?

3. In considering my own life, how did I come to define my own sexual identity or orientation? Is this an area that needs additional exploration?

4. How do I conceptualize gender? What messages do I send to clients that reify the gender binary?

5. What is my concept of "healthy" sexuality, and how might this bias my work with clients (e.g., bisexual, asexual, nonmonogamous, kink)?

6. Have I encountered clients with fluid or shifting sexualities, and, if so, what feelings did it bring up for me?

7. What judgments or biases might I have about sexualities that are considered "alternative" to the dominant culture, including LGBQ identities or practices in consensual nonmonogamy, polyamory, or kink/BDSM?

## Questions for Client Exploration

1. What were you taught related to norms in sexual orientation, behavior, and identity, and how has your own experience fit in with or disaffirmed previous beliefs or messages? How has your understanding of sexuality shifted based on your own experiences?

2. How do you relate to the gender binary? In what ways do or don't you identify with expectations based on the gender binary?

3. What stressors do you experience regarding your affirmed gender identity? Your affirmed sexual orientation?

4. What are the things that you appreciate about your experiences related to your gender and sexuality?

5. Have you experienced fluidity regarding your gender or sexual identity? How did you make sense of this shift? Was it important to do so?

6. If your experience of gender and sexuality has shifted over time, what are the things that you need from sexual and/or romantic partners or others in your life?

7. What support do you need from a mental health provider to feel seen and heard in your affirmed gender or sexual orientation?

# PART 2

# FOUNDATIONS FOR AFFIRMING MENTAL HEALTH CARE

# CHAPTER 6

# Understand Your Role as a Mental Health Provider

When working with trans clients, your role as a mental health provider may be varied and multifaceted. It is essential that you view clients as existing within a social system, but also understand how you are part of this system and influenced by the social and political climate that dictates how care is conceptualized and provided. Gender-affirming work cannot exist or occur within a vacuum, as powerful influences of the social world, especially oppressive systems such as cisgenderism and trans-prejudice, are ever present in our trans clients' lives. In this chapter, we will discuss the mental health provider's roles, from basic affirming care to advanced gender specialist training.

## Acknowledging Trans Clients' Needs: An Ethical Responsibility

In 2009, the American Psychological Association Task Force on Gender Identity and Gender Variance surveyed psychologists and psychology graduate students. Of those surveyed, less than 30% reported familiarity with issues that trans people experience. Research suggests that mental health professionals who have limited training and experience in affirmative care with trans and gender nonconforming clients may cause significant harm (Mikalson, Pardo, & Green, 2012; Xavier et al., 2012). In addition, many trans people have had negative experiences with medical and mental health providers, with 28% avoiding going to the doctor out of fear of discrimination and 19% having had the experience of being refused care due to being trans (James et al., 2016).

Mental health professionals must abide by the codes and principles set forth by their governing licensing boards, which vary depending on the type of degree and licensure (e.g., psychologists, marriage and family therapists, social workers, licensed professional counselors). We encourage you to revisit the ethics codes that apply to your degree and discipline. For example, the American Psychological Association (2017) Ethics Code states that psychologists should provide services only within their boundaries of competence and that when there is a gap in knowledge related to cultural factors, psychologists should seek training and consultation.

If we integrate ethical principles with the information we know about the lack of education in the field about gender identity and serving trans clients, as well as the high rates of discrimination that trans people encounter when seeking medical and mental health care, the fact that most mental health professionals do not receive even basic information about trans people puts trans clients in a vulnerable position (American Psychological Association, 2015). Not all clinicians can or will want to become specialists in working with trans clients and communities, but it is important that they at least cultivate a basic breadth or foundation of knowledge in working respectfully with trans clients.

# Breadth Versus Depth of Training

Whereas some trans clients seek mental health care for reasons related to gender or transition, others are simply seeking care from a clinician who has adequate awareness and skills concerning trans identities and experiences so that they can get support in working to address other life concerns. The role of the clinician will vary based on each client's presenting needs. A useful framework for understanding the appropriate role of the clinician is considering breadth versus depth. Breadth pertains to the ability to deal with the broad spectrum of identities and concerns that trans clients may present, while depth pertains to the particular skills and competencies a clinician will need to develop if they're involved in deeper, more complex aspects of trans mental health or assessments for gender-affirming medical interventions.

## Breadth: Culturally Responsive Care

We believe that there is a need for all health care professionals to have basic cultural competency and an ability to respond skillfully when interacting with trans people. We consider it an essential and ethical responsibility of training programs to provide—and clinicians to acquire—this **breadth** of knowledge. This is what is most closely related to the previously referenced ethics codes. The goal of acquiring this dimension of competency is to ensure that *any* trans patient or client entering *any* health care office or department, even when not related to gender concerns, is treated with utmost respect and affirmation. Training for this must be broad and address every touch point of service (e.g., from receptionists to medical assistants to surgeons and everyone in between). Here is an example to illustrate the need for breadth of training.

## CASE EXAMPLE. Boundaries of Competence:
### *Working with Scout*

*Scout (they/them/their) is an eighteen-year-old Laotian person who identifies as agender, asexual, and on the autism spectrum. During their first semester of college, Scout sought counseling to assist with setting boundaries and communicating their needs as a neurodiverse (a* term often used to refer to people on the autism spectrum) person in a neurotypical setting. Scout, considering their main challenges to be related to others' reactions to their neurodiversity, sought out Dr. Vu, a Vietnamese American psychologist in private practice who specializes in working with people on the autism spectrum.

Scout is frustrated when Dr. Vu, upon learning that Scout is agender, immediately starts asking inappropriate questions about Scout's "transition," even though this is not a term that Scout relates to or used in describing themself. Dr. Vu asks a series of intrusive questions, including about Scout's genitals and childhood preference for gendered toys. Scout feels overwhelmed by these questions and does not know how to communicate that this is not why they are seeking counseling services. As a result, Dr. Vu incorrectly assumes that Scout is confused about their gender. Dr. Vu further deduces that Scout does not truly have a gender "issue," but rather that Scout's gender is a manifestation of a "stereotyped interest" (a symptom ascribed to people on the autism spectrum).

After determining that Dr. Vu is not a good fit for them, Scout meets with Isabelle, a Hmong, heterosexual, cisgender clinician in a community mental health center. Isabelle does not specialize in autism spectrum disorders or gender concerns. However, she has basic cultural competence working with trans clients from reading books and taking a continuing education course on working with trans clients. Isabelle knows from her training that not all trans clients seek therapy for reasons related to gender, and this helps her to hear Scout's concerns. Isabelle, knowing that she does not have a lot of experience working with people on the autism spectrum, works with a consultant who helps her formulate and address ways of helping Scout to communicate and set boundaries with their professors. Isabelle also takes it upon herself to read the available body of literature on the intersections of gender diversity and autism so that she can be sure she is not missing an important piece of Scout's clinical presentation. Scout is able to have a space to express their frustrations as well as learn concrete skills they can apply to their challenges with school.

In this example, Dr. Vu demonstrated not only an inappropriate fixation on Scout's gender (when it was not the presenting concern in treatment), but also a lack of competence concerning gender identity that got in the way of giving Scout the help they needed with their current life stressors. Isabelle, though not an expert, took responsibility to ensure she was working within her competence, sought necessary consultation, and acted as an ally in centering Scout's experience. She was able to do this because of her commitment toward cultural humility and her ability to listen to and respect experiences different from her own.

## Depth: Transition-Related Care

In addition to having a breadth of knowledge, in some cases—especially when it comes to transition-related or gender-affirming medical care—clinicians must have a **depth** of knowledge and skills. Competency in depth of knowledge seeks to ensure that providers who are involved in transition-specific care have the advanced, specialized training necessary to perform accurate assessment, differential diagnosis, and treatment. When assessing for appropriateness for medical interventions, it does not suffice to have basic familiarity with the concerns that trans people face or even to consider oneself a supporter or ally. Professionals in this position must have a specific skill set and ongoing investment in staying current with an ever-evolving field.

Without adequate training of professionals providing transition-related care, clinical care is greatly compromised (Mikalson et al., 2012); thus, there may be times when a clinician must acknowledge the limitations in the scope of their practice and expertise and refer clients to practitioners with advanced training. Keep in mind, though, that inadequate training should not be a reason to avoid acquiring basic cultural competency knowledge and skills in order to provide optimal transition-related care to other clients in the future.

## Multifaceted Roles as Mental Health Providers

You may provide a wide range of services and function in a number of roles with various clients or in different circumstances with the same client. These include counseling or psychotherapy (individual, couples, family, and group); collateral visits (e.g., with your client and significant other or family member); training and education of other professionals; interdisciplinary consultation and collaboration; advocacy; and assessment, letter writing, and referral. In all of these clinical situations, you may provide psychoeducation on behalf of your clients to lessen the burden that they feel in having to educate people about gender-related concerns.

### Counseling or Psychotherapy

Like other clients, trans clients seek counseling or psychotherapy for a variety of reasons. There is no single "right" way to provide psychotherapeutic services to trans clients. Above all, we support a gender-affirming approach; a general respect for and responsiveness to the client's identity and needs forms the basis of effective, supportive, or healing work with trans clients. Counseling or psychotherapy may occur within a variety of structures, including individual counseling, couples or relationship counseling, family therapy, or group therapy. Counseling may range from supportive to exploratory to deeper grief or trauma recovery work. It may be related to gender concerns, adjacent or intersecting concerns, or concerns entirely unrelated to gender or trans identity. In part 4, you will learn more about different modalities of providing care, including individual counseling, couples and family therapy, and group and peer support.

### Collateral Visits

There are times when it may be helpful to invite a friend, family member, or loved one to attend a session with a client. In collateral or collaborative visits, the individual is maintained as the primary client; however, other people in the client's social system are included with the acknowledgment that they can contribute significantly to a more positive outcome for the client. The clinician is often in the role of an educator or translator in that they can help significant others better understand what the client is experiencing. Utilizing family therapy skills, the clinician can also create a space in which all involved parties may express their feelings and practice improved communication.

## Training and Education

Many mental health providers do not receive even basic education on working with trans clients. Those who have familiarity with this work often have opportunities to provide formal training and education to their colleagues and communities, such as by teaching a course on trans concerns or providing supervision to a trainee who is working with a trans client for the first time. They may be in a position to provide professional education to coworkers of varying backgrounds. For example, mental health providers working in university settings may be asked to provide basic trans cultural competency training (often referred to as a "Trans 101" training) to campus communities.

Mental health providers may also engage in training and education in more informal, less structured ways, including sharing resources (e.g., books, articles, professional guidelines) with other health professionals, clients, family members, friends, teachers, clergy, administrative staff, and more. Because awareness of trans people and communities is increasing yet still limited in society, mental health providers may find countless opportunities to educate others and provide information that can challenge widely held myths and stereotypes about trans people.

Complex considerations are involved in identifying who is best situated to provide training and education about trans people and communities. Efforts to involve, empower, and center the voices of trans people should be prioritized, and trans people should be recognized and compensated for the time, work, and emotional labor involved in educating others. Cisgender providers who engage in training and education are encouraged to acknowledge their own position and privilege in speaking about or for a demographic group to which they do not belong. One way to do this is to begin trainings or presentations by acknowledging their relationship to trans communities in the context of systems of power. If you are a cisgender clinician, you can say something like the following:

> I am here to talk about issues related to transgender health. I want to acknowledge that I am a cisgender person with cisgender privilege, and even though I work with trans clients, I do not assume that I am an expert or truly understand what it is like to be trans or gender nonconforming.

In an ideal world, trans people would be respected just as they are; however, because of trans-prejudice, there are times when cisgender providers may be better situated to promote attitudinal changes about trans people. For instance, in a group of cisgender parents who have just learned that their child is transgender, it may be better for someone with this lived experience (i.e., being a parent of a trans child) to provide education or information. In this situation, the group members may need the freedom to ask questions or express feelings or concerns without a trans person present. An additional consideration is that the burden of educating others cannot rest solely on trans people, so cisgender providers may aid in this endeavor. Educating others and promoting accurate and respectful representations of trans people and communities can be a demonstration of allyship.

## Interdisciplinary Consultation or Collaboration

Mental health providers are often in positions to consult or collaborate with other service providers—including but not limited to primary care providers (e.g., physicians, nurses, physician assistants), surgeons, OB/GYN physicians, psychiatrists, chaplains, pastoral counselors, nutritionists, social workers, career coaches, and career counselors—and a systems approach in working with trans clients is often crucial in helping your clients receive the care they need. Other health professionals who are unfamiliar with trans clients' needs or experiences may look to mental health providers for expertise and assistance. See chapter 13, where we provide an in-depth description of interdisciplinary collaborations.

## Advocacy

Advocacy for trans clients may take many forms. In the National Association of Social Workers Code of Ethics, Section 6.04 (d) on Social and Political Action states that social workers should act to prevent and eliminate domination of, exploitation of, and discrimination against any person, group, or class, including on the basis of gender (Workers, 2008). As stated in the *Guidelines for Psychological Practice with Transgender and Gender Nonconforming People* (American Psychological Association, 2015), psychologists' clinical practice can include endeavors to reduce systematic impact and promote positive social change. See chapter 20, where we describe the important role of being a strong advocate in trans-affirming mental health care.

## Assessment, Letter Writing, and Referral

Clinicians are often in the role of assessing trans clients for appropriateness and readiness for gender-affirming medical services and recommending clients for surgical evaluations. Letter writing may occur as part of an existing counseling process, or it may be a freestanding service that clinicians offer. We emphasize that **psychotherapy is not a requirement for receiving gender-affirming or transition-related medical care**. Psychotherapy can be recommended or highly encouraged, but it should never be used as a barrier or requirement for clients who are otherwise appropriate candidates for medical services. Assessment and letter writing related to gender-affirming medical interventions is covered in greater depth in chapter 12.

# The Need for Gender Therapists or Specialists

A clinician may identify as a *gender specialist*—a term that has been used to refer to health care providers with expertise in trans health, partially due to its inclusion in the WPATH SOC. We opt for the term *gender therapist*, as we think it is a more respectful way to position oneself in relation to trans clients. It is questionable when any mental health professional specializes in a demographic population, especially one who does not belong to that particular group. We acknowledge that depending on context, there are times when the term *specialist* may be useful or necessary in helping clients and health professionals (who base their information on the WPATH SOC) to locate qualified mental health providers. As with so many issues related to language in this field, we encourage providers to develop a nuanced understanding that is informed by humility and respect for trans communities.

## Gender Therapist Qualifications and Characteristics

Gender therapists are trained and licensed mental health professionals who have advanced knowledge and experience in working with trans clients and communities. Ideally, gender therapists are professionals with a sophisticated understanding of the profound impact that social and medical transition has on a person's physical and emotional well-being. They understand that their role is not to determine the validity of anyone's gender identity or expression, but rather to assess informed consent about the services requested that might aid a person in socially, legally, or medically transitioning and the potential risks and benefits. In order to maximize the potential for a life-affirming transition experience, gender therapists need to aid their clients in understanding the complexities of gender transition, developing clarity and self-awareness regarding the appropriateness of transition for themselves, and making necessary preparations including the establishment of a stable support system and adequate coping skills.

People who consider themselves gender therapists should have sophisticated knowledge about and clinical skills related to:

- Gender identity and factors that affect its formation

- The wide spectrum of gender identities and expressions that exist, including nonbinary identities and expressions

- Cultural factors that inform the experience of gender identity and/or trans experience

- The complex ways that gender and sexuality interact

- The complex and specific concerns that arise for those who are considering or are undergoing some form of medical, legal, or social transition

- The physical effects of hormone therapy

- In-depth knowledge of gender-affirming surgeries, including risks, benefits, and possible complications

- Assessing informed consent

- The diagnosis and treatment of gender dysphoria

- The evaluation of common psychiatric concerns, including suicide and depression, and how they interact with gender dysphoria and affect trans people's lives

- The social context in which trans clients exist, including high rates of discrimination, violence, and trauma, as well as disparities in health care, housing, employment, education, incarceration, and access to public accommodations

- Interdisciplinary practice

- Local and national resources geared toward trans people and their communities

## Lack of Training: Red Flags and Common Pitfalls

In our collective experience working as gender therapists, we have encountered some disconcerting examples of problems that can arise when untrained providers are in the role of assessing and treating trans clients seeking gender-affirming, transition-related medical services. These examples strongly support the need for advanced training of gender therapists:

- denying a referral for gender-affirming medical care based on the existence of well-managed mental health symptoms (e.g., anxiety, depression) and the insistence that these symptoms be alleviated before the client is ready for referral;

- using outdated standards of care, such as requiring a minimum number of psychotherapy sessions before making a referral or recommendation for transition-related care;

- requiring trans patients to live "full time" in their affirmed gender for one year before starting hormone therapy;

- refusing to recommend a trans or gender nonconforming person with a nonbinary identity for transition-related care;

- not respecting trans clients' self-identified names or pronouns even after being corrected;

- having no knowledge about the medical procedures that a trans client may seek and how to assess psychosocial considerations related to goals, preparation, and recovery;

- overemphasizing or scrutinizing a trans client's gender history or physical appearance as measures of appropriateness for gender-affirming care (e.g., whether the person played with certain toys, or whether the person "passes" or is considered attractive in their affirmed gender);

- lacking awareness of the WPATH Standards of Care (though not all competent gender therapists choose to follow the WPATH SOC, it is important to be familiar with them and the ways that they inform care and coverage);

- referring/recommending a client for gender-affirming care without having necessary conversations related to informed consent; and

- engaging in reparative or conversion therapy techniques in an effort to deny trans identity and reinforce a cisgender identity (e.g., assuming that a trans client who has questions or concerns about their identity really isn't trans and just needs to be convinced of their cisgender identity, or believing that a gender-fluid child needs to learn to play with toys and behave in ways that are consistent with the sex they were assigned at birth).

In order to maintain an up-to-date skill set in the midst of a rapidly changing field and society, gender therapists should consider engaging in continuing education, getting involved in professional organizations devoted to trans health care, and obtaining clinical consultation from more experienced clinicians, especially if they are new to the field of trans health. Attendance at professional conferences focused on trans identities is highly encouraged.

# Managing Dual or Multiple Relationships in Work with Trans Communities

Because trans communities are often highly interconnected, especially due to the Internet, clinicians working within these communities often face the challenges of navigating dual or multiple relationships. It may be that your clients know each other, that you have overlapping social circles with your clients, or that you are a member of trans communities. Special attention to ethical guidelines and clinically informed decisions is required to balance the needs of the larger trans community in your local area, the needs of each individual, and your own needs as a community member. This issue, which is further discussed in chapter 21, may be especially salient for trans clinicians.

Dual or multiple relationships are not inherently unethical. Standard 3.05 in the American Psychological Association (2017) Ethics Code states that multiple relationships should be avoided if there is reasonable belief that they would cause impairment in your objectivity, competency, or effectiveness as a clinician or if there is a risk of exploitation or harm. If you do not have such suspicions, you may well be clear to proceed. There are times when multiple relationships simply cannot be avoided. For example, if you are the only therapist in your town who works with trans clients, many of your clients will likely know each other. You will want to have intentional conversations about privacy and confidentiality, sometimes repeatedly, and invite an exploration of your client's feelings about dual or multiple relationship dynamics.

## Conclusion

In this chapter, you learned about the many facets and roles of mental health providers who work with trans clients. You explored ethical considerations regarding trans clinical competency and scope, the difference between breadth and depth of training, and the characteristics and recommended training of those who consider themselves gender therapists or specialists. Finally, you learned that multiple relationships are common and sometimes unavoidable when working with trans communities. Chapter 7 is focused on how to apply assessment and diagnostic skills in an affirming way with trans clients.

# Going Deeper:
# Questions for Clinicians and Clients

## *Questions for Clinician Self-Reflection*

1.  What does it look like for me to practice within the scope and limits of com-petency with trans clients? What do I need to expand this area of expertise?

2.  How do I see myself in terms of breadth and depth of competency in working with trans clients?

3.  How do I relate to the concept of being a gender therapist or specialist while taking into account my own gender and cultural identities?

4.  What does it mean to specialize in working with a group to which I do not belong? Or a group to which I belong or feel a great sense of identification?

5.  What am I willing to invest in order to stay current in the field of trans health?

6.  What experiences do I have in navigating multiple relationships or working in small communities? What feelings or hesitations might this bring up for me?

## *Questions for Client Exploration*

1.  What questions do you have for me about my background and experience working with trans clients?

2.  What are the things that you are hoping I am aware of as I work with you and trans clients in general?

3.  What role do you see me playing in your process of healing, growth, or transition?

4.  As you know, trans communities are often small or highly intertwined. It is possible that I know or know of people you may want to talk about here, or we may even have some overlapping social circles. How would you like us to navigate that? Are there any needs or requests that you have of me, such as wanting or not wanting to know when I recognize the name of someone you discuss with me?

# CHAPTER 7

# Develop Trans-Affirming Mental Health Diagnostic Skills

As a clinician, you may already be very skilled in assessing mental health concerns, diagnosis, and treatment needs. While many of those skills are applicable in working with your trans clients, you may have to alter how you conduct assessments and, in some instances, change your approach altogether in order to best serve your trans clients. This chapter, which focuses on mental health assessment and diagnosis, should be used in conjunction with chapters 10 and 12, which elaborate on mental health concerns and assessment and referral for gender-affirming medical interventions, respectively.

Assessment is a broad term, and there are many ways to define how it relates to your role. We intentionally use the word *assessment* because it is broader and more neutral than the word *evaluation*, which we feel emphasizes the power imbalance between clinician and client. We think of assessment as a process of gathering information in order to come to a conclusion about a client's needs and how we (or other providers) may help fulfill those needs.

This chapter will cover conventional and traditional assessment approaches and measures in terms of their applicability or limitations when working with trans clients. In addition, you will get a better sense of what areas of inquiry or investigation are appropriate when working with trans clients. You will also learn why the commonly used terms *gender assessment* and *gender history* ought to be approached with caution, intention, and consideration of when they are or are not relevant.

## Conventional Psychological Assessment Measures

Testing, such as administering a standardized measure, questionnaire, or checklist, is formal and discrete in nature. Examples of measures that address symptomatology include the Beck Depression Inventory (Beck, Steer, & Brown, 1996) and the Yale-Brown Obsessive Compulsive Scale (Goodman et al., 1989). You can probably guess that the norming of these tests does not typically include trans and gender nonconforming populations. Therefore, we recommend that you approach use and interpretation of these tools with caution, keeping in mind that binary gender designations (i.e., male or female) do not truly reflect trans clients or gender diversity (Keo-Meier & Fitzgerald, 2017).

Other tests are used to measure personality characteristics. Consider the Minnesota Multiphasic Personality Inventory–2 (MMPI–2; Butcher et al., 2003), a personality test commonly included in psychological batteries. This measure has been criticized for its gender biases, most reflected in Scale 5, the masculinity-femininity scale. If you learned how to use this measure in graduate school or have recently used it, you may recall that the first item on this true-false test is "I like mechanics magazines." Women who endorse this and other similar items related to stereotypical gender roles and preferences are deemed abnormally masculine. This masculinity-femininity scale has little clinical utility and does not take into account contextual gender variability that occurs in all people. The fact that it is still part of the test and is administered to many people perpetuates harmful gender stereotypes and actively pathologizes those who deviate from traditional gender norms.

In addition, as mentioned above, the normative samples used for developing these assessment instruments illustrate the lack of inclusion of trans people and thus the limitations of using traditional or commonly administered tests. Moreover, research about assessment is based on using standardized and normed tests, which further contributes to the problem of misrepresentation or lack of representation of trans people in the literature. The challenges in measurement when attempting to include trans people in research go beyond the scope of this book.

We provide the above examples because we encourage you to be cautious in using or interpreting assessment tools with trans clients. Having knowledge of trans populations and a critical awareness and analysis of psychological assessment tools is necessary in order to accurately and ethically interpret results from testing with trans clients (Keo-Meier & Fitzgerald, 2017). The choice, use, and interpretation of tests should be informed by an understanding of trans communities and the social factors that affect them.

# Clinical and Observational Interviewing

In contrast to formal testing measures, clinical and observational interviewing approaches are less formal and more continuous in nature. In this sense, assessment may begin with your first phone call with a client in which you are listening for the client's concerns and assessing whether your background, skills, expertise, and style may be an appropriate match. Should that person become an ongoing client, you are often continually assessing treatment needs and goals throughout the course of treatment. Tools that include open-ended questions that aid in conceptualization may be less biased than traditional standardized tests but must still be approached with a critical lens.

For example, if you work from an attachment-based perspective, you could use a set of interview questions about early attachment experiences when working with clients in ongoing individual or relational/couples counseling. These questions and conversations can help you understand clients' experiences in relating to the world and to people in their lives, as well as provide information that might help you tailor your approach and interactions within the client-therapist relationship. When using this tool, you can ensure that you are not comparing the clients with whom you work to what might be assumed "normal" for any particular gender experience or evaluating their gender in any way. Additionally, instead of using it solely as a diagnostic tool, you can center the focus on attachment and relational style. You might often learn more about clients' gender experiences and gendered dynamics with others through this interview and conversation.

Another example might be the use of clinical interviewing to inform a specific treatment protocol. For example, if you are using EMDR (eye movement desensitization and reprocessing; Shapiro, 2001) therapy or another trauma-specific approach, you may conduct a detailed trauma history and coping skills assessment before engaging in these approaches with trans clients (Chang, 2016). Getting a broad sense of clients' experiences of being hurt in the past and how they deal with current triggers of past trauma aids in creating a tailored plan of intervention, including the order in which you address different trauma targets. In doing so, it is important to ground your clinical interviewing in culturally informed practices. For instance, not all clients find eye contact comfortable depending on their cultural background and norms, and this may or may not be related to experiences of trauma in their lives.

As clinicians, we also gather information about our clients through observation. One such observational measurement tool is the mental status exam (MSE), which is typically part of an initial intake assessment. Electronic medical record systems and practice management software typically include the MSE in a client's chart. For example, the practice management software may use prompts for the completion of a mental status exam that includes comments about appearance, attitude, behavior, mood and affect, thought process and content, cognition, insight, and judgment. It is important to use this measurement tool with caution, as the "answers" can be highly subjective based on what the clinician deems normal or appropriate (which is often culturally biased). For clinicians who are unaware of their own anti-trans bias, descriptions in these domains may invite interpretations of trans people that are pathological and do not take into account cultural differences or what it means to deviate from societal expectations.

## Debunking the Concept of "Gender Assessment"

If you have worked with trans clients or within the field of transgender health for any length of time, you will have heard the term *gender assessment* as a standard component of working with trans clients. This term is misleading and a misnomer for any type of assessment that is clinically relevant and useful. It makes the assumption that, as a clinician, you have the power to "assess" or determine what someone's gender is. As is stated as a core theme throughout this book, one of the basic tenets of affirming care is respecting self-identification. Assessing someone's gender should consist of asking the client how they identify and believing them.

Unfortunately, this basic form of respect for the client's subjective report is not how some clinicians approach work with trans clients. Many clients have felt pressure, whether overtly or covertly, to "prove" they are trans or "trans enough" to receive gender-affirming care. They have been asked questions such as "What toys did you play with?" and

"How old were you when you *knew* you were not a boy/girl?" The subtext of all these questions is that there is one right way to be trans or to describe one's gender history. We want to underscore that if a client comes to you with a desire to discuss their gender history, it is appropriate to provide a safe container for that conversation and exploration (as you would for any other area of exploration that a client brings up). Clients do not necessarily "owe" a clinician the recounting of their gender history, so we recommend proceeding with care, intention, and respect for consent.

We have encountered a number of "gender assessment" tools that have been developed by (mostly) well-meaning clinicians and researchers. These tools are typically biased toward assessing the degree to which the client adheres to traditional, stereotypical, and typically White/Western ideals for femininity or masculinity. In addition, even asking our clients to fill out certain measures can communicate a reductionist and categorical approach to gender rather than listening to or exploring a client's unique experience and truth. To date, there is no standard assessment tool that can determine whether a person is trans; furthermore, there is no need for this tool if the client's voice is centered and respected.

Some clinicians opt to interview significant others and family members of trans people to verify that they have been accurately reporting their gender identity, gender expression, and related behaviors (e.g., living "full time" in their affirmed gender). We find this to be disrespectful, as it is centered on the outsider's perspective rather than the felt experience of the client.

You might be thinking, *If we aren't assessing gender, what are we assessing?* There are approaches that may be more clinically useful and relevant to take into account. The client's goals and the extent to which they are related (or unrelated) to gender is one consideration. If a client is coming to you for therapy because they are experiencing work stress, it would be useful to assess the extent to which this has anything to do with dealing with anti-trans bias or discrimination at work. However, we would never want to make the assumption that the stressor is gender-related. Your client may simply feel like their workload is too heavy or that they are not feeling stimulated enough with their job role or responsibilities. Most clients will be able to articulate why they are seeking your services and what their goals are. Some will clearly state that they are not coming to therapy for gender-related concerns. In view of the client's goals, you can come up with an appropriate plan and course for treatment.

When a client clearly states that gender is one of the topics they would like to address in counseling, it is important to assess whether and to what extent gender-related concerns affect the client's overall physical, emotional, social, and/or spiritual well-being. This is a situation in which it is appropriate to ask about past and current distress related to gender (whether the client endorses the term *gender dysphoria* or has a different way of describing the distress). Discussions may allow you to identify the ways in which you can support the client in gaining insight, learning new coping skills, managing interpersonal interactions, or making changes in order to improve a sense of well-being and empowerment. Although the formal DSM diagnosis of gender dysphoria may be useful, bear in mind the importance of discussing this with a client, especially if the client is seeking gender-affirming medical interventions (this is discussed later in this chapter). The client's own language and subjective report of their experience as trans or gender nonconforming should be respected and believed. In other words, we emphasize what is generative (coming from the client's own volition and lived experience) rather than prescriptive (the ways in which one tries to "fit" a client into a predetermined frame of reference).

As stated, formal measures to determine whether a client has gender dysphoria do not exist. As of early 2018, there are different ways in which practitioners and health care systems are establishing or documenting gender dysphoria as a symptom or a diagnosis, but these are specific to those particular systems.

## CASE EXAMPLE. Being Transparent with Diagnoses: *Working with Tessa*

*Tessa (she/her/hers) is a forty-year-old Japanese American trans woman. She is in counseling with Dru, a Latina trans woman, and her main presenting concern is social anxiety. After two months of working together, Tessa lets Dru know that she is interested in pursuing two different gender-affirming surgeries. Dru is aware that in order for Tessa to be considered eligible for these surgeries, she will need to be diagnosed with gender dysphoria. She decides it will be useful to set aside time to discuss the gender dysphoria diagnosis and whether it fits for Tessa.*

*At the next session, Dru reviews the gender dysphoria diagnostic criteria with Tessa. Tessa reports that she has not felt that dysphoria was the best term to describe her motivation or need for surgery, but that she relates to the criteria and thinks it accurately describes her. Dru does not take this diagnosis lightly; in fact, as a trans woman herself, she has complicated feelings about being in a position to diagnose other trans people. She takes time to explore Tessa's feelings and questions about having this diagnosis, potential benefits such as eligibility for surgery, and potential risks such as having this diagnosis on her medical record. Tessa feels respected by Dru in these interactions. While she does not completely agree that she should have to be diagnosed with a mental disorder in order to access medical care, as she feels that her main concern is social anxiety related to gender identity, she understands the ways in which having the diagnosis benefits her.*

In this case, Tessa and Dru have important conversations to determine together whether the gender dysphoria diagnosis may or may not fit for Tessa. Transparency is key in allowing Tessa to feel more included in her own care.

# Assessment of Mental Health Concerns and Treatment Needs

A proper assessment of clients' goals as they relate to reported concerns and symptoms can lead to more personalized, client-centered treatment plans. Just as you would assess mental health concerns and needs with any client, you can listen for the ways in which a client describes current stressors, struggles, or areas of growth. It is important to keep in mind that trans clients are frequently misdiagnosed, in part because their gender concerns often become such a focus of the work that other concerns are underreported or not addressed. Based on the assessment process, you can direct your treatment plan toward the possibilities discussed in chapter 11 on medical interventions, chapter 14 on individual therapy, chapter 15 on relationship and family therapy, or chapter 16 on group therapy and peer support.

## Gender Dysphoria as a Diagnosis

In chapter 4, you learned about some of the history of gender-related diagnoses in the DSM. In the DSM-5 (American Psychiatric Association, 2013), the broad criterion for a diagnosis of gender dysphoria in children as well as in adolescents and adults is "a marked incongruence between one's experienced/expressed gender and assigned gender, of at least six months' duration" (p. 452), with some variation in the specific criteria based on age. An important aspect of the diagnosis is that it is focused on distress and not on the person's identity.

Within the field of trans health, there are varying opinions as to whether there should be a gender dysphoria diagnosis and the utility of having it for children. Some trans clients do not relate to the concept of gender dysphoria, and others do. As with other mental health diagnoses, some clients may benefit from understanding that their experience is not unique, has a name, and is formally studied. There are individuals for whom having a formal diagnosis opens access to gender-affirming medical interventions (such as when a health care provider adheres to the WPATH SOC). Still others do not feel the need to be pathologized or considered "disordered" in order to seek and receive the care they need.

Because gender-affirming medical interventions are not a possibility for prepubertal youth, many argue that there is no need for a diagnosis of gender dysphoria or incongruence in childhood. There is a myth that if someone is trans, that automatically means they are mentally ill or emotionally unstable. **We believe that trans-affirming counseling recognizes that being trans in and of itself is not a mental illness.** To better understand relevant factors of diagnosis would require a lengthy discussion that goes beyond the scope of this book. We want to impart the idea that the gender dysphoria diagnosis is not an absolute or universal truth, but rather a lens or perspective that may or may not apply to each trans person.

## Assessment and the Gender Minority Stress Model

Minority stress (i.e., chronically high levels of stress experienced by members of marginalized groups) greatly affects the overall well-being of trans people, and it is important to take this factor into account when conducting any assessment of the needs, experiences, and challenges that trans people face. Minority stress may include *distal stress factors*, which refers to challenges that occur at higher rates in the population, such as discrimination, sexual assault, physical violence, and other forms of harassment; as well as *proximal stress factors*, such as the awareness and expectation that one is at risk for adverse experiences (Hendricks & Testa, 2012). Related to minority stress is the resilience that often develops as a result of facing adversity, as we will discuss in chapter 9. The Gender Minority Stress and Resilience Scale (Testa et al., 2015) is one of the few assessment tools that takes into account the sociocultural influences that affect trans people and how they may contribute to health disparities. It can be a useful tool for case conceptualization and a springboard for discussion to help you address these factors with clients.

## Conclusion

In this chapter, we explored topics related to assessment and diagnosis with trans clients, including the caution that must be taken when using conventional psychological assessment measures, the use of less formal tools to enhance clinical and observational interviewing, the problems inherent in "gender assessment," and the diagnosis of gender dysphoria, which in some cases may assist in accessing gender-affirming medical care. In the next chapter, we look at barriers and challenges that trans people face in the world and the ways they impact our work with trans clients.

# Going Deeper:
# Questions for Clinicians and Clients

## Questions for Clinician Self-Reflection

1.  In my role as a clinician, what am I assessing when working with trans clients? Do I know the difference between assessing mental health concerns and assessing a person's gender identity?

2.  What are my reactions to the diagnosis of gender dysphoria, and what is my approach to assessing for and discussing this diagnosis with my clients?

3.  How do my assumptions about assessment and diagnosis influence my practice?

4.  Am I willing to forgo the use of assessments that have not been developed or validated for use with trans clients?

## Questions for Client Exploration

1.  In what ways do concerns related to your gender affect your mental health or emotional well-being and vice versa?

2.  Have you been diagnosed with gender dysphoria or another gender-related diagnosis, and what does this mean for you? How accurately does this diagnosis describe you? How does it feel for you to have been diagnosed?

3.  How do you feel about my role and the power I have in giving you a diagnosis, even if it helps you to receive the medical care you need or desire?

# CHAPTER 8

# Identify Barriers and Challenges

Trans people face significant barriers and challenges that can limit opportunities for their lives. Access to affirmative health care, supportive family and friendship networks, and the sense of safety a person has in their environmental contexts can all influence and be influenced by these barriers. In this chapter, we explore the barriers and challenges trans people commonly face within the individual, immediate environmental, and larger systems, and how clinicians can assess the impact of these barriers and challenges on physical, emotional, financial, and spiritual well-being.

## The Individual Level

As discussed in chapter 3, the cultural or demographic groups to which a person belongs (and the ways that these intersect) have a great influence on that person's life experiences, access to resources, and the barriers and challenges they will encounter. These factors, or social determinants, can influence health or well-being in a positive or negative direction. Most at risk of suffering from these social determinants are people who hold one or more marginalized identities, such as gender identity, racial or ethnic origin, or disability status (White Hughto, Reisner, & Pachankis, 2015).

For trans people, a lack of economic resources can significantly limit access to health care and stable housing. Given that these are the most basic of human needs, it is not surprising that some trans people engage in coping strategies that may result in negative consequences (e.g., self-injury, substance abuse) or engage in street economies as a means of survival (e.g., drug trade, sex work). We encourage you to thoroughly, and thoughtfully, explore the ways that individual challenges impact your clients' well-being and discuss them as a regular part of your intake process. We encourage approaching these topics sensitively, in a way that is not shaming and that takes into account that unhelpful coping behaviors are often short-term means of survival.

Clinicians working with trans people often make the assumption that any doubt or intrapersonal difficulty that arises in the course of a social, medical, or legal transition is an indicator that the decision to make the transition was ill-informed. It is not uncommon for a client to begin to move forward in their transition process, in whatever way they define that, and have moments of difficulty, doubt, or grief. Doubt may take the form of experiencing emotions that, historically, have been interpreted as indicating a lack of readiness. Moments of nervousness or concern related to different aspects of transition can be part of any process of change and should not be perceived as evidence of not being "ready" to move forward. To complicate this, some clinicians have only exacerbated these concerns by assuming that these doubts are an indication that a person is not "really trans." We encourage you to normalize doubt or fear and convey that being able to have candid discussions can be helpful and validating. Being willing to explore challenging emotions as normal responses to any major life change or transition is important.

Another area of concern affecting trans clients at the individual level is the ways in which privilege can shift over the course of transition and have differential effects on trans masculine and trans feminine people. For trans feminine individuals, the loss of privilege associated with being perceived as male can be a stark awakening; this, of course, also varies depending on other aspects of identity such as race. For trans masculine people, a different process can occur. Rather than losing privilege, they may gain the privilege of being regarded as men in society. Much has been written about male privilege and the ways that plays out in the lives of trans masculine individuals (dickey, 2014). Others may suddenly assume that a trans masculine person must know what they are talking about simply because they are male, and they may express beliefs that a trans masculine person was socialized as a male and therefore holds belief systems similar to others with such socialization. For people who make a medical transition, the introduction of testosterone can be very powerful. Some trans masculine individuals undergo significant body changes (e.g., secondary sex characteristics and a flat chest) to the point where it may be difficult for the untrained observer to see that the person was assigned female at birth—a situation that can make the sudden possession of male privilege even more jarring. All of these experiences will vary, of course, depending on racial context, such as having White skin privilege or racialized gender stereotypes.

## CASE EXAMPLE. The Individual Level: *Geoffrey*

*Geoffrey (he/him/his) is a thirty-five-year-old White trans man. Prior to transitioning, while presenting as a woman, Geoffrey asked for—and was denied—numerous promotions at the company he worked for, called SomeCo. He was even told that he should be satisfied with the salary he was making, as this was more than most women make. While medically transitioning, Geoffrey was treated poorly by his employers, leading him to leave his job at SomeCo. Unfortunately, he was also treated poorly by employers at other companies he worked for during his medical transition. A couple of years later, when he was further along in his transition and had changed his legal name and gender marker, he decided to return to SomeCo to pursue career interests that were a good fit for him. This time, Geoffrey received three promotions, increasing his pay by a total of fifteen dollars an hour. Geoffrey had no reason to understand these changes as being related to anything other than his gender, as he had not acquired any further job training.*

Although he was pleased to receive promotions and pay increases, Geoffrey was left wondering how his gender transition had so significantly impacted his standing in the workplace. This exemplifies one of the ways that a trans masculine person might experience a shift in privilege.

# The Microsystem Level

There is strong evidence indicating that trans people who are supported in their identity within their immediate environments will have positive outcomes related to developing their sense of self, positive results in transition, and increased psychological capacity (American Psychological Association, 2015; Olson, Durwood, DeMeules, & McLaughlin, 2016; Travers et al., 2012). The microsystem—which contains the most immediate contextual influences for trans people, including family members, peers, places of employment, and schools—is where many people seek and experience this support. However, it is not always the case that one will receive support from one's microsystem. Consider a client who has come out to their parents. They may find one parent to be very supportive and the other to be hostile upon learning about their trans identity. The ways in which the client continues to engage, or not, with each of these parents may be influenced by the reaction the parent had. We encourage you to explore your clients' immediate and extended support systems.

Given the overwhelming evidence regarding the need for support, clinicians are encouraged to explore the ways they can advocate on behalf of their clients. There are a variety of approaches to advocacy. Trans people may need support in coming out to family members and friends. For trans children and adolescents, it may be necessary to work with administrators in their schools to ensure that the client (student) is being treated respectfully. This includes access to common restrooms that are consistent with the client's affirmed gender, the use of names and pronouns that match what the client uses, and policies that are enforced that establish a "no bullying" environment in the school. Trans students of color are especially vulnerable to bullying due to their race and gender. Schools must be established as safe and affirming spaces for all trans children and especially those who are adversely targeted.

Trans people may also need support in deciding how to relate to individuals with whom they are not comfortable enough to disclose. The process of "coming out" or disclosing one's gender identity may or may not be a priority for trans people. However, we think it is useful to attend to the ways in which a person feels safe or supported by others in their immediate environment. This may be especially complicated for people who come from families who hold conservative beliefs and values. Negotiating this process requires special attention to the ways in which your client needs support for emotional concerns that might develop as they navigate this process. We encourage you to help your clients develop positive coping skills (e.g., meditation, mindfulness, or relaxation techniques) that they can implement in those times when coming out, not just once but potentially many times throughout their lives, creates distress.

CASE EXAMPLE. Tension with Unsupportive Parents in the Microsystem: *Working with Sylvia*

*Sylvia (she/her/hers) is an eighteen-year-old Native American trans woman who lives with her parents. Although Sylvia's parents indicate support for Sylvia and her gender identity, they consistently use the wrong pronouns and name for Sylvia. Sylvia brings her father to a counseling session with you, during which you explicitly ask Sylvia to state what name and pronouns she would like others to use when referring to her. Sylvia's father is reluctant, stating, "This is very hard since I have known Marcus since he was an infant." Sylvia's expression indicates her frustration and disappointment.*

*In noticing how uncomfortable Sylvia appears when being misgendered and referred to incorrectly, you ask to meet separately with Sylvia's father for a segment of the session. When speaking to Sylvia's father, you validate that change can be difficult but affirm that respecting Sylvia's name and pronouns could make a big difference in easing tension and improving the relationship between the two of them. You also direct Sylvia's father to a few educational resources on using affirming language to demonstrate respect of trans identities. Sylvia's father is better able to hear the request coming from you, as a professional, and slowly starts to make improvements in using affirming language.*

In this case, you, as the clinician working with Sylvia and her father, were able to recognize the tension between Sylvia and her father due to the demonstrated lack of support. By meeting separately with Sylvia's father, you were able to appropriately intervene and encourage a more supportive stance, thus aiding in the preservation of Sylvia's relationship with her father. While it may seem simple, sometimes the most basic support demonstrated by a clinician can go a long way in helping family members to turn a corner in their capacity to offer support to their trans loved one.

# The Macrosystem Level

There are many larger systems of influence, sometimes referred to as macrosystems, that affect trans people by creating institutional barriers. These include laws, history, cultural norms (including those related to gender), and social and economic systems. Examples of institutional barriers are the challenges related to finding a safe restroom, changing one's gender marker on various forms of identification, and finding employment and housing in areas that protect trans people from discrimination. One reason trans people face these challenges is that they have little to no legal protection (Campbell & Arkles, 2016). Although some states, counties, and municipalities have laws in place that protect trans people, this is still far from ubiquitous in the United States. Depending on where a trans person lives and works, they may be at risk for discrimination in housing, employment, health care, and public accommodations. These risks, along with the emotional implications of living with such uncertainty, illustrate how the minority stress model can be applied to understanding the experiences trans people have in society (Hendricks & Testa, 2012). These distal, environmental stressors take an exacting toll on those who must deal with the everyday threat of discrimination and mistreatment.

There are a number of organizations whose primary mission is to dismantle systems of oppression that adversely affect trans people. The National Center for Transgender Equality (NCTE; http://www.transequality.org) focuses its work on addressing necessary policy changes at federal, state, and local levels. This includes health policy, voting rights, identity documents, and immigration. The Transgender Law Center (http://www.trans-genderlawcenter.org), based in California, works to change "law, policy, and attitudes so that all people can live safely" (Transgender Law Center, n.d., para. 1). One of the ways that the Transgender Law Center expands on the work of organizations like NCTE is by providing legal assistance to help address policy issues. The Sylvia Rivera Law Project (SRLP; http://www.srlp.org) provides legal and social services for trans people in New York. In addition to these services, SRLP is actively addressing the social determinants of poverty and homelessness in the community. We will discuss some of the larger systems that create barriers to the well-being of trans people.

## Asylum

In some cases, trans people are fleeing their country of origin because they are at risk of death or imprisonment due to their trans identity. Campbell and Arkles (2016) describe the asylum process and the ways that mental health providers might engage with these clients. One of the challenges faced by providers is developing a level of trust in which the client is willing to discuss the reasons for seeking asylum, while also being cognizant of time constraints. In some cases, the reasons for seeking asylum are related to trauma and abuse; unless a provider is able to document this mistreatment within the deadline for application, it is possible that asylum will be denied (Campbell & Arkles, 2016).

Violence does not necessarily cease for the trans person who moves to the United States to seek asylum. In addition to intimate partner violence, trans people who are seeking asylum are also at risk for violence from law enforcement officials and staff in detention and shelter facilities (Anderson, 2013; Goodmark, 2013). Reports of rape and violence in addition to being placed in "solitary confinement" are far too common for trans people who are seeking safety from their country of origin.

## Incarceration and Overrepresentation in the Prison-Industrial Complex

Trans people, and especially trans women of color, are overrepresented in the prison-industrial complex. Miss Major, a well-known and celebrated trans activist and community organizer, stated, "The abuses that [trans people] suffer in prison are tantamount to torture" (Nichols, 2016, para. 6). This inhumane abuse comes at the hands of fellow inmates and prison guards. If a trans person is placed in a more protective location, it is often solitary confinement and "for their own protection." This type of seclusion, especially when not a part of the person's ordered prison term, is cruel and unusual punishment. A trans person should not have to be removed from the general prison population as the only means of ensuring safety.

Miss Major (Nichols, 2016) relates her and others' experiences in prisons and jails. She speaks of experiences of having been beaten up and raped. She states that trans people have a role in prisons, as they are assigned as cellmates of angry, brutal prisoners. This is intentional and for the purpose of calming the cellmate down. The trans person becomes the victim of the cellmate's abusiveness and anger. The guards are deliberate in this assignment as it helps them to focus their attention in other places. It also allows them to not have to intervene when the abusive cellmate is interacting with others in the general population because they have already worked out their anger and aggression on the trans person (Nichols, 2016).

In 2012, the U.S. Department of Justice (DOJ) set out regulations that were designed to combat and ultimately eliminate the problems of rape in the prison system. These standards focus on detection, prevention, and elimination of prison rape. This guidance came after the passage of the Prison Rape Elimination Act (PREA), which was passed in 2003 (DOJ, 2012). To the extent that a prison facility is willing to adopt a culture that has zero tolerance for sexual violence among inmates or at the hands of guards, it is likely these regulations will significantly reduce the incidence of sexual violence in prisons.

As indicated above, another issue in prisons and jails is the use of solitary confinement (also known as administrative segregation or protective custody) from the main prison population as a means of ensuring the trans prisoner's safety (Arkles, 2009). Historically, solitary confinement was used as a means to "induce repentance and motivate prisoners to live a devout, socially responsible life" (Cloud, Drucker, Browne, & Parsons, 2015, p. 19). Currently, solitary confinement is used to punish prisoners, to ensure the protection of the general population from someone who has been deemed too violent to be housed in the general population, and to ensure the safety of a person who is thought to be at risk for violence from others in the general population. It is under this last area that trans people find themselves housed in solitary confinement. Arkles (2009) argues that rather than protecting the trans inmate, this puts the inmate at greater risk for harm. For a trans person this is an additive challenge in the same ways that intersecting identities impact trans people.

A final area of concern for trans people is the reasons they are incarcerated for supposed crimes they have committed, such as for acting in self-defense when being attacked by another person, for being assumed to be engaging in sex work due to profiling by police (particularly of trans women of color), and, finally, for simply using a restroom (Arkles, 2009). As noted earlier, some trans people will engage in survival sex work and other street economies, in part because of discrimination in the workplace (Burnes, Long, & Schept, 2012). As clinicians, it is important for us to understand these larger social contexts and refrain from judging or shaming clients who are making decisions based on survival. Additionally, the movement to decriminalize sex work acknowledges that not all sex workers are forced to engage in sex work; some choose it, and this choice should not be pathologized.

People who have been traditionally marginalized are at greater risk of incarceration, in part because they are more likely to be living in poverty. In fact, 29% of trans people reported living in poverty compared to 12% in the general population (James et al., 2016). This is in spite of the fact that trans people have a higher level of educational attainment (38% have a bachelor's degree; James et al., 2016) compared to the general population (33.4% have a bachelor's degree; Proctor, Semega, & Kollar, 2016).

## Media Representation

Mass media is a significant system of influence. The ways in which trans people are portrayed in the media can be quite inaccurate and damaging. Positive examples of trans people are often limited to White people who have overcome a challenge or have access to resources that make a social, medical, or legal transition more accessible. In contrast, trans people of color are often portrayed in a negative light, typically engaging in criminalized behavior such as sex work or the drug trade. Positive examples of trans people of color are nearly impossible to find in media representations. There are even fewer representations in popular media of trans masculine or nonbinary people. Being able to see oneself in another, whether that person is a mentor or a role model, can give a person hope about their future, in part because they realize they are not the only person with their gender expression. This can be especially salient for clients who are not well represented by depictions of trans identity (e.g., people of color, people who have disabilities, people who identify as gay or lesbian). When working with clients who are facing challenges in finding adequate mirroring, it may be helpful to identify and explore underlying needs and feelings, such as a sense of belonging.

## Chronological Factors

Trans people's experiences can vary greatly depending on the era or generation in which they were socialized or the time at which they start to become aware of their gender identity. As a clinician, it is important to keep in mind the ways that generational or social influences, such as environmental and historical events, have affected or are affecting your clients. A person who came out during a time in which greater protections were created for trans people (e.g., during the Obama administration) may have experienced a greater sense of security and protection from harm than someone who came out during more conservative political eras in which there were few to no protections for trans people.

## CASE EXAMPLE. Chronological Challenges: *Victoria*

*Victoria (she/her/hers) is a fifty-seven-year-old African American trans woman. She is a staff sergeant in the U.S. Army. Victoria remained closeted about her trans identity until a regulation was put in place that allowed trans military personnel to openly serve. In 2016, Victoria came out to her command and made a transition while serving on active duty. Victoria was pleased that her fellow soldiers were accepting of her identity, in part because her command made it clear that any intolerance or mistreatment would be sanctioned.*

*The regulation that allowed Victoria to serve has been rescinded, and now Victoria is deeply concerned for her safety. She is worried that because of regulatory changes, which often dictate what is considered acceptable, she will experience marginalizing treatment within her unit without any protection. Victoria is three years from being able to make a full retirement from the military, and at this time she is unsure if she will be able to serve that time—for fear of her safety and the risk that she will receive a dishonorable discharge.*

This case example elucidates the impact of time on a trans person's life. Victoria felt safe enough at one point in time to come out as transgender in the military, as the rules were in her favor. However, over time, those rules were rescinded and she now fears not only for her safety but also for her financial well-being in retirement. It is vital to be aware of current policies and social forces that affect your trans clients' sense of safety and well-being in the world.

# Conclusion

Trans people are at risk of facing a variety of challenges that have the potential to adversely impact their lives. Clinicians are appropriately situated to work with clients to address these concerns by identifying factors at different levels, from the individual level to immediate environments to the larger systems at play. Readers are encouraged to explore "Trans-Affirming Counseling Resources" in appendix B (also available for download at http://www.newharbinger.com/40538) to access the numerous resources available for them and their clients. In chapter 9, we will explore the ways that trans people demonstrate resilience in their lives.

# Going Deeper:
# Questions for Clinicians and Clients

*Questions for Clinician Self-Reflection*

1.  What are the stressors in my client's life at each level of the individual, intermediate, and larger systems?

2.  What are the ways that I can intervene on my client's behalf to dismantle the systems and policies that are contributing to the stressors?

3.  Considering my own life, in what ways does a parallel process exist for me? What, if any, stressors am I facing that are similar to those of my client? Might these be interfering with my clinical work, and, if so, should I seek supervision or consultation?

4.  What types of changes have occurred at the policy level that may adversely impact my client's well-being?

5.  (*For trans providers:*) How do changes in policy impact me in ways that make it difficult to remain objective with my client's concerns?

*Questions for Client Exploration*

1.  What sources of support do you have to help buffer the stressors that you are facing?

2.  How have you coped with similar concerns in the past?

3.  Are there any changes that you might make that could help to alleviate the pressures you are facing?

4.  Do you have any requests for the people or systems in your life to help alleviate the pressures you are facing?

5.  How have changing policies regarding the protection of trans people affected you on practical or emotional levels?

6.  What kinds of support and advocacy do you need at this time?

CHAPTER 9

# Cultivate Resilience

One of the most meaningful components of trans-affirming counseling is recognizing the incredible resilience reflected in trans people and communities. While you will commonly encounter high rates of trauma due to the microaggressions, macroaggressions, discrimination, and violence that trans people experience, it is vital to recognize the strengths that trans clients possess and the supports that can be expanded upon. Though trans clients have faced extensive and pervasive oppression, they often develop strong communities of support, live their lives as their true selves despite mounting odds, and find meaning in their genders that can affirm other aspects of identity or areas of their lives. There are ample opportunities to address resilience with trans clients in order to further aid them in coping, surviving, and thriving in their lives. You will want to be prepared to explore resilience throughout counseling, from intake to termination.

## Resilience and Trans Health

Resilience has been defined as the ability to "bounce back" from adverse times (Masten, 2015). From an individual perspective, resilience entails personal coping strategies that people leverage to move through tough situations. A White and Western perspective of resilience is limited to focusing on individual hardiness, strength, and grit (Singh et al., 2011) and fails to recognize collective or community resilience. Scholars have called for investigations of collective and community resilience to counter the previous sole focus on individualized strengths (Hartling, 2005; Singh et al., 2011). With your clients, you can explore both types of resilience. Collective or community resilience is a critical area of focus within trans-affirming counseling, as trans clients often turn to social support and community groups to help them throughout their gender identity development. This is especially important to consider for clients who come from traditionally collectivistic or community-oriented cultures.

### Individual Strengths

The exploration of individual strengths with trans clients is an important part of encouraging further development of resilience. As a clinician, you will want to understand the individual strengths that trans clients have as they face various forms of oppression. To some extent, you have probably already engaged in exploring strengths, coping, and resilience with your cisgender clients.

You may ask questions like:

- How did you take care of yourself when you faced _____?

- Which of your strengths have gotten you through _____?

- Do you have a supportive person you can talk to about _____?

In exploring these individual resilience questions, you can easily begin to introduce attention to gender identity and other salient identities that your trans clients have, as in the following examples:

- As a trans man, how did you take care of yourself when you faced _____?

- Which of your strengths have gotten you through _____ as a nonbinary person?

- Do you have a supportive person you can talk to about _____ in the context of being a trans person of color living with a disability?

Keep in mind that an individual focus may differ among clients depending on how collectivistic their cultural backgrounds and identities are. The examination of personal strengths may be more easily accessible to clients raised in a more individualistic and Western context—those who are used to thinking about the world with an individual focus. Clinicians should be cognizant of the cultural history a given client brings to treatment and moderate their reliance on an individual focus accordingly. Still, with clients who have collectivistic cultural values or backgrounds and have experienced marginalization, it can be helpful to raise questions about how they, as individuals or within their communities, have developed strengths and resilience as a result of difficulties.

Take, for example, a White, upper-class trans woman who engages in a social and medical transition later in life and describes difficulties with discrimination and prejudice. She may have been socialized within gender, ethnic/racial, and financial systems of privilege. Therefore, because of her experiences with privilege, this client may already have an idea of what "rights" she should have or what experiences she should be expecting as a human being in the world. At times this can even come across as entitlement. However, we caution you against the idea that being a trans feminine person in this world is in any way easy. There is a great deal of transmisogyny in the world that makes it difficult for trans feminine people to be taken seriously; therefore, self-advocacy is a sign of strength and resilience and should not be written off as "male privilege." It is not called male privilege when upper-class cisgender women engage in the very same behaviors (i.e., those that reflect entitlement). Further, if a person's life has been fairly easy based on having privileged identities, that person may not have developed the kind of resilience that comes from navigating or overcoming adversity. By contrast, a client who has multiple marginalized identities (e.g., disability, immigrant, queer) may not have as clear a sense of their rights and the treatment they're entitled to as a human being in the United States. Clients with marginalized identities may have multiple experiences of internalized oppression that can be addressed in the exploration of resilience. In addition, people with multiple experiences of marginalization may not expect much from clinicians, as they are used to mistreatment by society. An important clinical role can be to help such clients understand the expectations for affirming care they should receive as trans clients. Some trans clients have had significant experiences of trauma outside of the social marginalization from society (e.g., childhood sexual abuse). For these clients, exploring the ways that trauma has influenced their resilience is quite important—as important as helping them to identify and access healing from trauma.

Regardless of the privilege and oppression experiences that trans clients present with in counseling, you can introduce the construct of resilience to the counseling process and collaboratively discuss and explore resilience from the client's perspective. A helpful approach is to share some of the research on trans resilience and explore which aspects of this research apply to their life and which aspects are not as relevant for them. Some of these areas, identified by Singh and colleagues (Singh et al., 2011; Singh & McKleroy, 2011; Singh, Meng, & Hansen, 2013) in resilience studies across the lifespan, include self-definition of gender, intersectional identities of pride, personality factors, and self-advocacy. We will briefly discuss each of these aspects of trans resilience.

## SELF-DEFINITION OF GENDER

A key component of individual resilience is a client's ability to define or identify their own gender, as trans clients often hear constant trans-negative messages from others about their identities, which can easily be absorbed as internalized oppression. This internalized oppression can further disconnect clients from what they know to be true about themselves, and can therefore be a threat to their individual resilience. You can explicitly name a client's ability to define their own gender as a demonstration of their resilience against forces in their lives that aim to dictate and disrespect who they are. This self-definition is a crucial aspect of resilience and the development of pride in one's gender identity, across different contexts, which can lay the groundwork for self-acceptance, self-esteem, and strengths-based coping. Read about how a clinician supports Rohit in the development of his gender identity across multiple contexts.

# CASE EXAMPLE. Exploring Client Resilience: *Working with Rohit*

*Rohit (he/him/his), an eighteen-year-old South Asian college student who identifies as a trans man, is in counseling with Ella, a forty-two-year-old White, genderqueer clinician. Rohit presents with concerns about telling his family he is trans. Throughout counseling, Ella explores Rohit's resilience in many different ways, including Rohit's ability to define his own gender. Rohit shares that this has been difficult, but by this point he feels secure in his gender identity.*

*Ella also explores Rohit's experience of being a young, South Asian, trans man, and Rohit shares that he feels proud of his gender and culture when he is with queer friends; however, he gets anxious when in primarily South Asian spaces. Ella asks Rohit how he advocates for himself in these situations, and Rohit shares that he typically just leaves these spaces. Ella and Rohit explore different ways Rohit could assert his needs so he can feel comfortable in primarily cisgender South Asian spaces.*

*Ella, aware of how conversations about and with trans clients may overfixate on trauma or challenges to the exclusion of recognizing strengths, asks Rohit about his individual and collective experiences of resilience. Rohit reports that writing music and playing guitar is a key aspect of self-care, and Ella reflects that this is a form of individual resilience. Rohit also shares that he gets through hard times as a trans man by connecting with his friends on campus and that he participates in several student groups where he has disclosed being trans. With regard to community resilience, Rohit expresses missing his connections with his religious community back home, and Ella explores how he might feel accessing the Hindu student group on campus. In addition, Ella asks Rohit whether he would be interested in attending an in-person or online trans support group. Ella is able to provide information about local support groups and the range of people who attend them. She shares that she knows of a trans masculine support group that is facilitated by a trans man of color and that has regular attendance by other trans people of color. Rohit shares that he would not like to attend a support group right now, but he may be open to doing this as he shares more of his identity with his parents.*

In this example, we see the ways that Ella explores individual and community resilience with Rohit. Prior to offering resources, Ella explores the challenges Rohit is facing and connects Rohit's strengths to the concerns he brings to counseling.

## INTERSECTIONAL IDENTITIES OF PRIDE

Building on resilience in the form of self-definition of gender, resilience research has also noted that the development of pride related to self-definition is critical—especially as it relates to racial/ethnic pride and other intersecting identities. For instance, a Latino trans man may have pride in his trans identity, but may have internalized oppression related to his Latino identity due to the lifelong racism he has encountered. Clinicians have an opportunity to explore resilience related to not just trans identities, but also other salient identities. In doing so, clients can develop intersectional identity pride, which can help them negotiate some of the impacts of oppression. Clients can use identities they are more comfortable or secure with to come to terms with ones with which they still struggle. When trans clients begin to consolidate pride not only in their gender identity but also in intersecting identities, their resilience and ability to cope with adversity is multiplied. Clinicians can join with clients in exploring which identities they feel pride in as a way to leverage identity pride with respect to other identities.

When exploring the development of intersectional identity pride, you may find the following questions useful to reflect on yourself or ask of a client:

- Which identities does this client feel most pride in?

- What are the intersections of identities for this client where they struggle to be resilient and/or experience more intensity of oppression?

- If this client feels pride in one or more of their identities, how did they develop this pride? Who helped them in this process? What did it entail? At what point in their life did this pride develop and why? What were the challenges they faced and supports they used to develop this pride?

## PERSONALITY FACTORS

Clinicians have long focused their attention on personality factors within counseling. Personality styles and types can influence how clients engage their resilience (e.g., advocating for rights and needs) and how they manage threats to resilience (e.g., discrimination at work, violence). Keeping in mind that oppression can influence personal development and expression, typical explorations of personality, such as a tendency toward introversion or extraversion, should be coupled with potential influences of marginalization. For example, clients who initially present as introverted (preferring to spend time alone or few a few amount of people) may become more extroverted after being able to claim and express their gender identity.

## SELF-ADVOCACY

Personality styles and types can also be related to the resilience that clients have or do not have related to self-advocacy—the ability to stand up for themselves in tough situations and ask for what they need when facing injustice. Self-advocacy can take many forms, including speaking out against oppression, advocating for trans-affirming environments, seeking legal aid when experiencing discrimination, and advocating for other trans clients or social justice movements. Self-advocacy might also entail connecting with trans communities or events (e.g., Trans Day of Visibility), but it is often subtler than this. Ultimately, self-advocacy entails the degree to which trans clients are aware of what they should expect in terms of respectful and humane treatment at any given moment in any given interaction. This awareness is something clinicians can foster. And, when you guide clients to recognize what they should expect, you can encourage them to act so as to have those rights respected. Self-advocacy is a skill as much as an ability, and it can be learned. For instance, if a client reports that there are no all-gender bathrooms in their workplace, you can explore how they can advocate for this or seek allies to advocate on their behalf in their work setting.

# Collective and Community Resilience

Collective and community resilience refers to skills related to the strengths of a group that help people to "bounce back" from adversity (Masten, 2015). Many aspects of individual resilience can be linked to collective and community resilience (Singh et al., 2011). For instance, strong and resilient trans communities can foster social support and connections to resources, especially for those who are newer in identity development.

You can explore collective and community resilience with trans clients by creating a map of the types of communities trans clients are connected to, as well as by identifying gaps in social support and interests in community building.

As important as collective and community resilience can be, keep in mind that for a variety of reasons, not all clients want to access community support. Some trans clients may have had bad experiences within groups, such as in-fighting within a group or being treated as an "outcast" or feeling like they didn't "fit in." Or, you may work with a highly introverted trans client or someone with an autism spectrum diagnosis, which can sometimes make group settings more challenging to access. In these cases, the client may feel more comfortable accessing online support. These areas of potential support are discussed below.

Clinicians can tend to value in-person community connections over online support. There are valid reasons for this. Research has long noted the powerful influences that human connections can have on coping and resilience. Trans clients who are at a certain point in their transition may be in need of in-person support from others having similar experiences. However, clinicians should be mindful that the multiple and intense experiences of oppression can influence the extent to which trans people feel comfortable attending an in-person support group or reaching out to another person at all. Some online forums tend to be more populated by older White trans women, and younger trans people of color may not feel "at home" in these groups. Younger trans people of color may feel more connected to community via social media (e.g., Twitter, Tumblr, Instagram) due to the intersections of their race/ethnicity, age, and gender. Clinicians should carefully explore these concerns with clients and consider the timing of such recommendations.

Online and in-person support groups and communities can all be fraught with a diversity of perspectives and tensions (dickey & Loewy, 2010). For instance, some support groups may predominantly cater to individuals who have children and are partnered, while others may have members who are dealing with the loss of partners and rejection from adult children. These groups can evolve and change rapidly in terms of members and needs (dickey & Loewy, 2010); you may want to gather information to help ensure that clients have similarities or points of connection with people who are in the group. In essence, no matter the source of community support you are proposing or exploring with clients, it is helpful to explore some of these tensions that trans clients may face when they think of support options. You will certainly be proposing these options to help increase their resilience, but they may see certain support groups as threats to resilience.

It is important for clients to be aware of the immense diversity that exists within the trans community. In this regard, in order to have helpful explorations of support groups with clients, you can ask the following questions:

- Are you aware of the types of online and in-person support groups that exist locally and nationally—and even globally?

- When you think of attending a support group, what feelings come up?

- Would you feel better about accessing an online or in-person support group if you had a supportive person to accompany you?

- There are some online support groups where you can anonymously post questions and receive answers about a range of topics. How would that feel to you?

We find it helpful to ask clients if we can continue to check in with them about their desires with regard to accessing support groups, as interest and desire may change depending on identity development or situational factors.

## Resilience Assessment

In this section, we discuss some of the ways you can assess aspects of resilience, including coping skills and strengths, in the intake sessions and throughout counseling with trans clients. A trauma assessment and resilience assessment pair naturally and can provide helpful information about how to respond to your client's concerns.

Even if you are meeting with a client for a single session, a resilience assessment is important and can be introduced in the following manner: "I know I am just meeting you for a one-time session for a referral for hormones. I will be asking some questions about your resilience—or how you cope with difficulty—to help us both remember the strengths you have to move through the next steps of your social and/or medical transition."

The following resilience questions can be included in the different sections of an intake assessment to integrate a strengths-based perspective:

- (Assessing sources of resilience:) What helped you "bounce back" or cope from [name experience]?

- (Assessing threats to resilience:) What made it hard to cope with [name experience]?

- What were the times when you found it difficult to bounce back?

- During these times, what helped you to recognize this difficulty and move forward?

- If I were to ask a close friend of yours to tell me your strengths, what would they say?

When assessing resilience, we begin by introducing the concept, which might sound like this: "Next, I would like to explore your sources of strength, and what you believe helps you bounce back from the bad things that we know can happen in society to trans people. Understanding these areas will help me to gain insight about your natural sources of resilience and strength—and how to support you when these sources of resilience are challenged or depleted."

Then, we explore sources of and threats to resilience, by asking questions such as the following:

- How do you feel about your gender identity?

- What have been the challenges to feeling positive about your gender identity?

- What do you need to feel more positive about your gender identity?

- What types of support have been helpful to you as a trans person?

- Who are your trans mentors or role models that you look up to? Do you have other mentors who are not trans? What is it about these people that is supportive of your needs?

With regard to assessment of trauma, a standard trauma assessment can be used that assesses potential experiences of trauma (e.g., abuse, neglect, sexual trauma, natural disaster). This initial (and ongoing) assessment is critical to be able to support trans clients in the most effective and helpful ways.

## CASE EXAMPLE. Assessing Client Resilience: *Working with Antonio*

*Antonio (they/them/their), a thirty-seven-year-old Latinx, genderqueer client, is working with Lily (she/her/hers), a twenty-nine-year-old African American, cisgender counselor. During the intake assessment, Lily explores resilience with Antonio, asking questions such as "What has helped you 'bounce back' or cope from traumatic experiences?" As they answer these questions, Lily deepens this exploration of resilience to Antonio's intersectional identities. When she nears the end of her intake assessment, she tells Antonio that she would like to explore their sources of strength.*

*Lily explores how Antonio feels about their gender identity and learns that Antonio has many skills related to being genderqueer. They have explored resources and have social support that has helped them to do this. When exploring what Antonio needs to feel more positive about their gender identity, Antonio shares that their cisgender partner does not understand their gender identity. Lily explores how Antonio copes with this, and Antonio shares they have referred their partner to some websites to read about being genderqueer. As Lily explores whether Antonio has trans mentors or role models that they look up to, Antonio says they follow some genderqueer folks on Instagram, but most of the genderqueer people they know are White. Lily asks if they would like to expand this area of resilience, and Antonio says yes. When Lily asks Antonio to use three words to describe their natural strengths in coping with hard times, they respond that their sisters, activism, and self-belief help them in these instances. As Lily explores what others in Antonio's life would say in describing their natural strengths in coping with hard times, Antonio is unable to identify what others might say. They share that even though they have social support, they sometimes don't let their friends and family "see" how hard it can be as a genderqueer person. Lily explores whether Antonio would like to address this in counseling, and they agree. This last question relates to the next resilience question Lily explores with Antonio: "When does 'bouncing back' from hard times get more challenging?" Antonio continues to self-reflect that they would probably have even more significant support as a genderqueer person if they took a risk to share more of their vulnerability with their friends and family.*

In this example, Lily's exploration of Antonio's resilience and strengths cuts across several areas of Antonio's life. As a result, Lily gains insight about how the resilience in one area of Antonio's life can be leveraged to address concerns in other areas of their life.

Resilience assessment should be ongoing throughout the counseling experience, beyond the intake and the assessment of everyday coping. The key to affirmative care with trans clients is to assess resilience to trans discrimination. This has two main benefits. First, it can be very empowering for clients not only to be introduced to the concept of resilience but also to explore resilience within themselves as an important part of being trans. Clients may not be aware of the sources of strength and coping they already have; this assessment will help them to gain insight about this. Second, clinicians can track resilience in order to bolster client coping and strengths of self-advocacy, self-affirmation, and social support in the face of everyday external challenges, given the reality of trauma in the lives of so many of their clients.

## Conclusion

In this chapter, we described the critical importance of exploring both sources of and threats to resilience. Clinicians can explore resilience—including individual as well as collective and community strengths—during the intake assessment and throughout counseling. In chapter 10, we discuss mental health concerns that trans people commonly face either distinct from or in conjunction with gender-related concerns.

# Going Deeper:
# Questions for Clinicians and Clients

*Questions for Clinician Self-Reflection*

1. What do I know about resilience in general when working with clients?

2. How might individual and collective (or community) resilience arise when working with trans clients?

3. How do my personal experiences of resilience influence what I might or might not identify as resilience?

4. What are the considerations I should think about related to multiple identities and resilience?

5. How do I integrate resilience into each part of the counseling process, even if I have just one session with a client?

6. How do I assess for both trauma experiences (e.g., everyday microaggressions, intimate partner violence, mistreatment from medical providers) and the resilience that may have developed that increases clients' ability to cope with these traumas?

*Questions for Client Exploration*

1. Resilience refers to how we get through hard times. As a trans person, what sources of resilience do you have? What areas of resilience do you think need more attention and development?

2. When you face hard experiences as a trans person, what helps you deal with those experiences?

3. When you spoke up for yourself about [insert challenging experience], what helped you to overcome this [insert challenging experience]?

4. Are you aware of the trans-affirming counseling and community supports that you can access in person or online?

# CHAPTER 10

# Assess Mental Health Needs

It is not uncommon for trans people to have mental health concerns that may or may not be related to their gender identity. Assuming that all mental health concerns are intrinsic to a person having a trans identity is problematic. These concerns (e.g., depression, anxiety, substance abuse) are more likely to be related to the discrimination and violence experienced by trans people. This chapter provides an overview of various mental health diagnoses along with factors to consider when working with trans clients with these presentations.

## Mental Health Diagnoses and Concerns

Trans people, like cisgender people, may present in counseling with a number of mental health concerns. In this section, we will review some of the key considerations in assessing mental health symptoms and disorders that trans people experience or that can be present alongside gender dysphoria. Differential diagnosis can be challenging, as many symptoms that appear with mental disorders may overlap at times with gender dysphoria or one's experience of living in a world that does not allow for a trans person's freedom of experience. It is important to keep in mind that trans people may be especially vulnerable to mental health problems and substance abuse (Carmel & Erickson-Schroth, 2016).

When a trans client's mental health symptoms are negatively impacting their well-being—whether it be physical, emotional, or spiritual—we can draw from harm-reduction and strengths-based approaches to reduce their suffering and increase their positive life experiences. As with all clients, it is important for you, as a clinician, to be aware of your expectations for what "mental health" looks like and how this relates to a client's "readiness" to make changes in their lives. There are clinicians who require trans people to be free of mental health symptoms before they believe the clients to be trans or before they refer them for medical interventions; this is unethical practice. There is only a need for the clinical concerns to be reasonably well controlled before pursuing medical interventions. It is important to keep in mind that medical interventions are often mental health interventions in that a client's anxiety, depression, or self-medicating substance use decrease as a result of being granted access to medical interventions.

# Mood Disorders

The lifetime prevalence of depression in trans communities is estimated as being between 50% and 67% (Clements-Nolle, Marx, & Katz, 2006; Nuttbrock et al., 2010; Rotondi et al., 2012). You will likely hear a great deal about depressive symptoms from your clients. You may be faced with the question, either in your own reflection or directly from your client, "Is this depression or gender dysphoria?" This may be an impossible question to answer, as it is difficult to truly and certainty establish a clear separation of the two. Some clinicians may attempt to determine which came first in order to make a differential diagnosis, but this is not a reliable way to make this determination. A more useful way to approach the question is, "In what ways does gender dysphoria manifest itself as depressive symptoms, and how can my understanding of how to treat depression inform treating this particular client's symptoms? Also, in what ways can dysphoria be addressed to alleviate some aspects of depression?"

Experienced clinicians know that it can be difficult to determine whether psychotherapeutic interventions, medical interventions, or both are warranted when treating mental health symptoms. This is a matter of balance and needs to be considered on a case-by-case basis. If there is a need for medication to treat mood symptoms, it is important to consider the timing of this in the context of whether or not the client is on hormone therapy. For example, it is generally not recommended to start hormone therapy and psychotropic medications at the same time because it is then difficult to discern what effects are from which medication. In addition, recovery from surgery requires that someone be able to physically care for themself; therefore, any significant barriers to self-care as a result of depression will need to be addressed before surgery to ensure safety in recovery. Consider the following two cases of trans clients diagnosed with bipolar disorder.

## CASE EXAMPLES. Addressing Mood Disorders: *Working with Nick and Kayla*

*Nick (he/him/his) is a twenty-two-year-old Native American trans man who presents in a trans health clinic requesting an assessment and referral for chest reconstructive surgery. He reports no prior history of counseling and does not endorse any mental health symptoms other than gender dysphoria. Nick's counselor does a thorough assessment and decides to write a letter that will support him in having surgery. Nick is then referred to have a consultation with a surgeon.*

*Two weeks later, the surgeon's office calls to report that Nick did not show up for his consult visit and is not returning calls to reschedule. A few more weeks pass with still no response from Nick. One day, the case manager at the clinic notices new documentation in the electronic medical record indicating that Nick has been hospitalized, has a new diagnosis of bipolar disorder, and has just started to take mood stabilizers. After getting out of the hospital, Nick calls the trans health clinic and asks for his surgery date.*

*The interdisciplinary team at the clinic debated the next course of action. Although the recent incidents in Nick's life do not make him ineligible for surgery, it is clear that he could use more support if he is to safely complete surgery and recovery. The team does not consider this a "hard stop" for Nick; rather, they work together to ensure that Nick is referred to a psychiatrist who can manage his new medications. Nick is frustrated by these delays; however, he is frightened at having been hospitalized and reluctantly agrees that it makes sense to take some time to gain more stability in his life and with his health before having surgery. He is referred for consultation with the surgeon and is given a surgery date that is three months later than originally planned. Nick meets with a counselor during this waiting period and learns to adjust to and manage his new bipolar diagnosis. Nick stabilizes within a couple of months and moves forward with top surgery.*

*Consider a different example of a client named Kayla (she/her/hers), a thirty-four-year-old Black trans woman who is interested in starting hormones. Kayla was diagnosed with bipolar disorder in her early twenties, and, after a couple of difficult years, she found a combination of psychotropic medications and herbs allowed her to stabilize her mood symptoms. She reports having mild depression and anxiety at times, but none of this significantly interferes with her daily life. Kayla meets with a doctor who prescribes hormones for her and asks that she call the doctor immediately if she starts to notice any negative effects of hormones on the management of her mood symptoms.*

Nick's case is difficult in that the mental health concerns that came up for him do not negate the fact that he has gender dysphoria that needs to be treated. However, in looking at Nick holistically and in the context of a new mental health diagnosis, it was prudent to offer support in helping him to stabilize and to establish ongoing care with a medical team before surgery. In Kayla's case, her mental health symptoms are reasonably well controlled, and her diagnosis of bipolar disorder does not influence whether she is considered an appropriate candidate for hormone therapy.

## Anxiety Disorders

As with depression, there may be an overlap between gender dysphoria and anxiety, and it is typically not possible to draw a clear line between the two. One study found that 26% of trans people have an anxiety disorder (Hepp, Kraemer, Schnyder, Miller, & Delsignore, 2005). Your clients may struggle with worry or fear, some directly related to gender (e.g., worry about whether there will be an accessible, inclusive restroom; fear of losing a job) and some unrelated (e.g., worry about getting good enough grades; fear of flying on airplanes). As a clinician, it is important to keep the client's gender-related experiences in mind as a possible contributor to anxiety while not assuming that just because a trans client is anxious it is related to gender.

Social anxiety is quite common among trans people, as social interactions carry great potential to be invalidating of one's identity or experience. It makes sense that if a person receives negative attention or experiences gender-related microaggressions when in social situations, avoidance of these situations may increase. You may find some of your clients can name specific kinds of anxiety they carry with them related to social interactions. For example, some people have a heightened sense of awareness regarding whether others will use the correct name or pronoun to refer to them, whereas others may have significant self-consciousness about their voice or their facial features. Typical exposure-based approaches to treating social anxiety can be helpful for some clients; but for others, simply increasing the amount of interaction they have with others will not be effective and may create more distress and avoidance. Other cognitive behavioral approaches that challenge negative cognitions may also be invalidating of a trans client's reality (i.e., the fact that the world really is treating them differently). In these cases, we recommend challenging the negative self-referential cognitions (e.g., "I deserve to be treated badly") rather than the client's reality (e.g., "People are staring at me in public"). You can work with your clients who experience social anxiety to create "safer" spaces, for example by identifying specific settings, situations, or people that are associated with positive or affirming experiences and then strategizing with your clients to increase those kinds of resilience-building experiences.

Transition, in the broad sense of the word, is change, and change of any kind can create stress. The process of coming out to oneself and others, as well as undergoing changes in one's body, relationships, or ways of relating to the world, can come with significant stress and anxiety. Some amount of anxiety can be healthy, informative, optimal, and motivating in that it tells the person that a change is needed. Therefore, sharing with clients that even positive, invited life changes can increase a sense of stress can be helpful. This knowledge can give them permission to have a mixed or paradoxical experience, such as being relieved to finally be getting a surgery they want while also feeling overwhelmed with the amount of preparation and aftercare that is involved.

You can work with your clients to discern what is a reasonable or even adaptive experience of anxiety and what forms of anxiety they may want to work on reducing through building coping skills and social support. The integration of the seemingly contrasting concepts of "acceptance" and "change," which are present in both dialectical behavior therapy (DBT; Linehan, 2014) and acceptance and commitment therapy (ACT; Hayes, Hayes, Strosahl, & Wilson, 2012), can be a useful tool to use in discussing anxiety with your clients. There are times when it is appropriate to simply feel the feelings of anxiety (and trust that they will pass) and times when it is more useful to try to shift one's emotional experience through contrary action or healthy distraction.

## Trauma, Dissociation, and PTSD

Reports of trauma, dissociation, and posttraumatic stress disorder (PTSD) are common among trans people, as would be expected for any group that experiences societal marginalization. Prevalence rates of PTSD in trans populations are estimated to be between 18% and 61% (Rowe, Santos, McFarland, & Wilson, 2015; Shipherd et al.,

2011). One study estimates that almost 10% of trans women have PTSD (Reisner, Biello, et al., 2016). There is a strong relationship between experiencing everyday discrimination—ranging from gender-related microaggressions to assaults—and endorsing PTSD symptoms, even when adjusting for prior trauma experiences (Reisner, White Hughto, et al., 2016).

Because there are disproportionately high rates of trauma in trans communities, it is crucial that any interactions and treatment approaches serving trans clients be trauma-informed. According to the Substance Abuse and Mental Health Services Administration (SAMHSA; 2014), a trauma-informed approach is one that realizes the widespread impact of trauma; understands potential paths of recovery; recognizes the signs and symptoms of trauma in clients and their systems; responds by integrating knowledge about trauma into policies, procedures, and practices; and actively resists retraumatization. A trauma-*informed* approach is differentiated from those that are trauma-*specific* (e.g., EMDR, exposure therapy, somatic experiencing). One aspect of trauma-informed practice is understanding that trans clients may be understandably guarded when meeting with health care providers; this can be a reflection of healthy protectiveness and resilience. As clinicians, we cannot demand politeness or trust from clients before we have proven our trustworthiness.

Dissociation is a symptom that is often associated with trauma, and it can exist along a spectrum. Some forms of dissociation are considered normal or common (e.g., daydreaming, getting immersed in a book, automatic driving), while others, such as those consistent with a diagnosis of dissociative identity disorder (DID), are more pathologized. Because rates of trauma are high in trans communities, rates of dissociation may be higher than in the general population. It is important to familiarize yourself with dissociative symptoms. There are scales that measure dissociation, and we have found that these can often be helpful for discussion with clients rather than for determining a diagnosis. As with other mental health symptoms, you will want to assess whether dissociative symptoms interfere in a significant way with a person's overall functioning, sense of well-being, or capacity to care for themself.

Dissociative symptoms, a full diagnosis of DID, or a report of a multiple or plural system (e.g., different parts, alters, distinct identities) should not be used as a barrier to clients' having their trans identities respected or accessing medically necessary interventions. For clients living with DID, questions often arise regarding whether all alters, parts, or distinct identities need to consent to treatment or medical interventions. We recommend educating yourself about DID, as well as remaining open to learning about and respecting people who report having a multiple or plural system, before making assumptions of pathology or determining that this presentation is a barrier to affirming care. Seeking supervision and consultation is also essential if you do not have training in working with people living with DID. You may talk with clients about whether distinct parts or people are co-conscious and in communication; the goal may not be "integration" but rather a shared understanding, open communication, and an agreement that next steps (whether they be regarding therapy goals or gender-affirming medical interventions) are in the best interest of most of the system.

When working with trans clients, it is important that you feel comfortable conducting a trauma and resilience assessment, which we described in detail in chapter 9. By conducting this kind of assessment, you will be able to assess the level of trauma and whether you or another professional will be best equipped to provide trauma-specific treatment. We receive referrals from therapists who work with trans clients but report that they do not work with trauma. This is challenging, as we believe any clinician who chooses to work with trans clients needs to have a strong grounding in the symptoms and signs of trauma and how to offer tools to manage the symptoms or provide deeper trauma recovery work. If you are interested in working with trans clients and do not feel comfortable with or competent in working with trauma or dissociation, it is important to seek training and consultation. A lack of training or knowledge in this area could pose major barriers to affirming care and result in client retraumatization.

## Nonsuicidal Self-Injury

Nonsuicidal self-injury (NSI) refers to self-inflicted wounds that are not intended to be lethal (Muehlenkamp, 2005). NSI includes cutting, banging, or hitting oneself; interfering with wound healing; severe scratching; biting; pulling hair; sticking oneself with needles; and swallowing dangerous substances. Culturally sanctioned body modifications such as piercing or tattoos are not considered to be NSI. Prevalence rates of NSI in the clinical population of cisgender people range from 4% to 37%, whereas nonclinical rates are 1% to 4% in adult populations and 13% to 23% for adolescents (Jacobson & Gould, 2007). dickey, Reisner, and Juntunen (2015) found that almost 42% of trans people in their study had a history of NSI. Nonbinary participants had the highest rate (48%), followed by trans masculine people (45%); trans feminine people had the lowest rate (27%).

NSI has traditionally been thought of as having intra- or interpersonal purposes. People may use NSI as a means of pushing people away from themselves or as a means of managing interpersonal distress. NSI can be a challenging clinical concern, and DBT has proven to be very effective in treating NSI by teaching clients skills to tolerate distress and regulate intense emotions that may lead to NSI (Linehan, 2014).

More research is needed to understand the trajectory of NSI and the ways in which trans people use these behaviors. dickey and colleagues (2015) found that 95% of trans people stopped engaging in NSI within two years before and five years after the initiation of a transition (as self-reported). It is unclear why the other 5% of people had not stopped, nor how the initiation of a transition impacts the cessation of NSI or whether it is simply a developmental process that leads to a person's stopping NSI behavior.

## Eating Disorders

There is a high occurrence of eating disorders in trans communities. In 2015, a large survey of college students ($N = 289,024$, with 479 transgender participants) found that trans people were more likely to have received a diagnosis of an eating disorder than cisgender people (Diemer, Grant, Munn-Chernoff, Patterson, & Duncan, 2015). In fact, almost 16% of trans participants reported being diagnosed with an eating disorder within the last year, compared to 1.85% of cisgender heterosexual women and 0.55% of cisgender heterosexual men. An additional finding was that trans participants endorsed engaging in compensatory behaviors (e.g., compulsive exercise, purging) more than cisgender participants. Unfortunately, a limitation of this study is that "transgender" was a single category and there is no information about specific subgroups (e.g., trans feminine, trans masculine, nonbinary).

Concerns regarding food, body image, and weight are embedded in the context of diet culture. What is considered "normal" or "desirable" is highly biased, fatphobic, ableist, classist, misogynistic, and racist. Therefore, how people feel about their weight and appearance is highly susceptible to societal influences and ideals as well as familial and cultural factors. Like everyone else, trans clients are susceptible to prescribed ideals for masculinity and femininity, and these are not unrelated to gender.

When discussing and assessing food and body concerns with clients, it is important to listen for and mirror back the language that they use. Keep in mind that for some clients and in some instances, eating concerns are highly related to gender or gender dysphoria, whereas for other clients or in other instances, they are not. It can be difficult to discern weight dysphoria from gender dysphoria, and because they overlap it may not be possible to state that concerns or behaviors are one or the other. A thorough history of eating concerns and related thoughts, feelings, and behaviors can be useful.

As with any psychological work, we need to check our own biases and the ways in which internalized fatphobia and sizeism operates within us. We never want to assume anything based on how a person looks. For example, we cannot decide whether a person is "healthy" or "unhealthy" by simply looking at them or knowing their weight. We will want to be mindful of the insidious ways that value judgments based on diet culture can come out in conversation. You may want to reflect on these questions:

- Do you categorize foods as "good" or "bad"?

- Do you tell people they "deserve" to eat certain food?

- Do you categorize bodies as healthy based on weight?

- Do you say things like, "Oh, just start again tomorrow" or "It's okay to cheat!"?

- Do you use words like *obese* or *morbidly obese* without a critical lens of what this means?

- Do you promote "clean eating" or "fitness"?

Trans clients with eating disorder concerns may not be diagnosed because their symptoms may not fit a stereotype or because the conversation about bodies may be so focused on gender that important information is missed. Therefore, it is important to become familiar with the ways that eating disorders or body image concerns may manifest in trans clients, such as:

- Atypical anorexia nervosa, in which food restriction is present but the person is considered to be at a "normal" weight

- Restriction in order to have a smaller body size or fewer curves

- Binge eating without meeting diagnostic criteria for frequency or duration of binges

- Binge eating to manage stressors related to dysphoria or anti-trans bias or discrimination

- Purging in the absence of binge eating

- Night eating syndrome, in which excessive food is consumed late at night or in the middle of the night

- Compensatory behaviors such as purging or overexercising to combat hormone-related weight gain

- Intentional weight gain as a strategy to hide one's body when it appears "too masculine" or "too feminine"

- Negative body image and preoccupation with feminine or masculine cisnorma-tive ideals

- Negative body image and comparison with visible trans people who do meet feminine or masculine cisnormative ideals (e.g., YouTube sensations or celebri-ties who document their transitions)

Causes, reasons, or motivations related to eating disorders within trans communities may be similar to or different from those related to cisgender populations. There are several hypotheses as to why there may be a higher risk or prevalence in trans communi-ties. One hypothesis is that trans people are not only subjected to the feminine and masculine ideals (typically White, Western ideals) that all people are subjected to, but they are also expected to achieve an even higher standard of beauty. In other words, trans people may be scrutinized or objectified more than cisgender people because they are expected to "prove" themselves as being "man enough," "woman enough," or "trans enough." Another hypothesis is that greater body dysphoria in general and a sense of overall powerlessness (related to one's body, the medical establishment, or anti-trans bias) may lead to behaviors that provide a sense of control or influence over one's body size or shape. Sometimes these behaviors, such as restriction, overexercising, or purging, may feel more accessible or actionable than convincing a medical provider to grant access to necessary medical interventions. Another possibility is that minority stress increases eating disordered behaviors as it does other medical and mental health problems. Gender-affirming medical interventions, which decrease body dissatisfaction, may be key in pre-venting or reducing eating disorder symptoms in trans populations (Testa, Rider, Haug, & Balsam, 2017).

A common message in society as well as in eating disorder treatment and recovery communities is "Just accept yourself as you are." Although this may be an ideal or goal to strive toward regarding body size and weight acceptance (e.g., Health at Every Size movement; Bacon, 2010), this message can be misapplied in a distorted and harmful way to trans people. It can suggest that trans people should just learn to accept and live in accordance with the gender identity associated with their sex assigned at birth. Therefore, we suggest being attuned to the nuances and complexities attached to the concept of acceptance. A useful framework for examining these complexities is the dialectic of acceptance and change that is integral to mindfulness-based approaches such as ACT (Hayes et al., 2012) and DBT (Linehan, 2014).

## CASE EXAMPLE. Affirming Trans Clients with Disordered Eating: *Working with Charla*

*Charla (she/her/hers) is a twenty-two-year-old Latina trans woman who reports having engaged in eating disordered behaviors around the time of puberty while presenting as a boy. She reports that she started overexercising to gain muscle, restricting food intake, and occasionally purging (without binge eating). She reports, "I didn't know it at the time, but I think it was my way of dealing, or actually not dealing, with my gender dysphoria." Charla reports that she no longer overexercises or purges, but she still engages in food restriction. She reports that she feels anxiety because her weight and height place her in the "normal" body mass index (BMI) range for males but the "overweight" BMI range for females. Additionally, Charla reports being anxious and ambivalent about her desire to start feminizing hormone therapy. She reports that she would like to have a curvier figure that is more in line with her identity as a woman, but she is also scared that being "curvy" will mean that others will perceive her as overweight.*

*The clinician Charla meets with, Tobias, recognizes that although she may not meet full criteria for an eating disorder diagnosis, her concerns indicate a subclinical eating disorder. He uses a motivational interviewing approach to assess Charla's stage of change regarding her restriction and body concerns. He knows that it is useful not to try to designate Charla's concerns as either an eating disorder or gender dysphoria, but rather as both or an interaction of the two. He invites Charla to explore her feelings and concerns about hormone therapy. They speak about the challenges of the BMI rating system and the gendered classifications of what typifies a "normal" or "healthy" body. Charla appreciates that Tobias is not trying to pigeonhole her as having either gender dysphoria or eating disorder concerns, but rather sees that she is experiencing the complexity of both in a social world that has expectations for what bodies are "supposed" to look like.*

In this case, the clinician takes a cautious but informed approach to working with Charla. As such, Charla is able to explore her eating concerns as being intricately informed by her gender questions and vice versa.

# Autism Spectrum Disorders

There has been growing awareness about the intersection of trans identities and autism spectrum disorders. Although the research on this intersection is limited, there is some evidence of a higher prevalence of autism spectrum disorders in youth with gender dysphoria (Shumer, Reisner, Edwards-Leeper, & Tishelman, 2016). In addition to increasing attention paid to the overlaps between these clinical concerns in the field of trans health, an unfortunate event that was covered in the media prompted even greater awareness. This event was the killing of Kayden Clarke, a twenty-four-year-old trans man in Arizona who was shot by the police in February 2016. The police were called to perform a wellness check on Clarke, who had a history of mental health concerns in addition to being diagnosed as being on the autism spectrum. This story highlighted the ways in which people with autism are not well understood, and there is little room for people who deviate from "normal" expectations for social interaction or communication.

The misunderstanding of trans people who are on the autism spectrum or otherwise considered neurodiverse extends to those who are seeking mental health services, whether the request is related to gender-affirming medical interventions or not. For example, some people on the autism spectrum are not believed when they express they are trans or a gender different from what others perceive. As we mentioned in the case example of Scout in chapter 6, sometimes people's trans identity is written off as a "stereotyped interest" (which is one of the diagnostic criteria for autism spectrum disorder). Some providers have difficulty with the idea that a person may be both autistic and trans, be autistic and not trans, or be trans and not autistic. There may additional bias and ableism embedded in the assumption that autistic people cannot make decisions on their own behalf related to their bodies and genders.

There are some special considerations to make when working with trans clients on the autism spectrum. In discussing medical interventions, you may have to be mindful about framing information in a concrete way. You may also have to take more time to assess informed consent; it is important to check with your client to ensure they have an understanding of the information you provided and can reflect it back to you. You may find some, though not all, of your clients on the autism spectrum may have difficulty understanding and answering abstract "what if" questions. Although some people on the autism spectrum have a rich fantasy life, exploring possibilities that are not imminent may be challenging. Collateral or collaborative sessions with family members or other supportive people in your client's life may be especially helpful in establishing a solid plan for surgical preparation and recovery. Finally, you will want to resist the stereotype that people on the autism spectrum do not have access to emotions. Many people on the autism spectrum experience a great deal of emotion internally that is often overwhelming and not visible to others.

# CASE EXAMPLE. Affirming Trans Clients Living with Autism: *Working with Melody*

*Melody (she/her/hers) is a forty-two-year-old trans woman with an autism spectrum disorder diagnosis. She lives in an assisted living facility and relies on social services for transportation and help with medical concerns. She comes to a trans health clinic to talk about her desire to have genital surgery (vaginoplasty). In talking about her desire for surgery, Melody does not make eye contact. She is quite talkative, however, and it is clear that she has done extensive research on the risks and benefits of the surgery. Melody does not have much information about what recovery entails. Melody's parents, who live nearby, have expressed a desire to support her through surgery (including having her stay with them while recovering), but they do not understand her gender as she seldom wears clothes that they perceive as "feminine" enough for her to be a trans woman. Melody is very direct in stating, "I don't want to be denied surgery just because I'm autistic."*

*The clinician assigned to meet with Melody is mindful of the bias that can work against trans clients who are on the autism spectrum and is careful to focus on informed consent, not whether Melody fits stereotypes of what it means to be trans or articulate a trans identity. Over the next couple of sessions, the clinician works with Melody on providing more information about surgery recovery and care planning. The clinician has Melody's parents attend one of the sessions and is able to educate them about the differences between gender expression and gender identity, which helps them to better understand the way Melody presents herself in the world. A solid care plan is set in place and Melody is able to have her surgery scheduled.*

In this example, the provider is able to focus on the client's clinical needs and not assume that because the client is diagnosed as being on the autism spectrum she is not trans. The clinician also engages in advocacy with the client's parents to ensure they have a good understanding of their daughter's identity.

## Substance Use Disorders

Substance use and abuse occurs at higher rates in trans communities (James et al., 2016). Trans people may use substances for any number of reasons. Substance use may help people to cope with and survive oppression and violence (e.g., anti-trans bias, racism, ableism) and may help in temporarily reducing or managing unwanted feelings or mental health symptoms. Despite its potential negative impact on one's health or well-being, substance use can provide short-term relief and, in some cases, keep people alive. Substance use can also be a way to connect socially or enhance pleasure or enjoyment. We do not want to assume that motivations for substance use are the same for everyone, and therefore it is important to listen to clients about the reasons, meaning, benefits, and drawbacks of their use.

Conversations about substance use in trans populations can be controversial and complex, as substance use can negatively impact recovery from surgeries and can become a barrier to or reason for withholding medical treatment. In some cases, medical providers, surgeons, or insurance plan policies require patients to eliminate all substances before surgery as a way to mitigate risk. At this time, there is limited knowledge of how different substances affect surgical outcomes (for any surgeries, not just those that are gender-affirming), and there are no clearly stated best practices. We discuss substance use and surgery in greater detail in chapter 12.

Substance use is often underreported, regardless of whether a person has a problem with substances. This is likely due to the social stigma and criminalization associated with being a substance user; in other words, this is yet another way that bias can contribute to negative health outcomes. For many trans clients, there may be little incentive to report substance use accurately compared to the great incentive to minimize use in the context of accessing necessary services for survival. However, not discussing substances or having an accurate report of use could jeopardize the client's health. Real conversations about substance use from a nonjudgmental stance can increase knowledge, safety, and self-care for your clients.

Given that substance use is so prevalent in trans communities and is often a way of coping with anti-trans bias and related stressors, relying solely on abstinence-only models for all substances can stop important conversations. Harm reduction is a set of practical strategies aimed at reducing the negative consequences of drug use, and specific approaches or interventions can be tailored in accordance with the needs of specific individuals or communities. Harm-reduction strategies exist along a spectrum and may range from safer use of substances to abstinence. The harm-reduction approach is regarded as a social justice movement that advocates for respect and the rights of people who choose to use substances. A harm-reduction approach recognizes that substance use is a reality and does not ignore or condemn (or shame) those who use substances. Informed consent regarding substances (i.e., making a conscious choice about substance use based on available knowledge about the substance's effects) is an important consideration. We do not know all the risks associated with particular substances, but in general we can support clients in making the best possible or most informed choices to minimize harm and optimize recovery. This is especially relevant when substances interfere with consciousness, sensation, or sensing danger, which are all relevant to surgical recovery.

For our clients who identify as being in some form of recovery from substance use or addiction, we will want to be active in communicating and developing safety plans in the case of cravings or triggers for regression into past unhelpful behaviors. We can discuss risk factors for use, such as feelings of isolation or difficulty being vulnerable and asking others for help. We can discuss the fact that past use can still affect a person's body and response to different aspects of care (e.g., anesthesia, pain management). Assessing a client's coping strategies and resilience can help to strengthen the development of their internal resources and skills that can be helpful as a person undergoes medical interventions (e.g., assertiveness, boundary setting, relaxation). Some clients will benefit from help in creating a concrete safety plan, which could include asking a loved one to hold and administer pain medications at prescribed intervals or setting up times to check in with a recovery support system (e.g., a sponsor or friend also in recovery).

Finally, for trans clients who are actively struggling with substance use or addiction and are motivated to seek professional help, it is important to be careful about the referrals we make. We recommend doing research about local (or national) treatment options to determine whether the care provided is trans-affirming. For example, you may want to call local chemical dependency treatment centers to inquire about awareness of or policies related to gender (e.g., sex-segregated treatment groups, residential accommodations, protocols for supervised urine drug tests).

## Harm-Reduction Strategies for Trans Clients Undergoing Surgery

- Considering periods of abstinence from substances during critical preparation and recovery windows

- Considering periods of moderation or reduced frequency or amount during critical preparation and recovery windows

- Changing mode of administration for a substance

- Making intentional choices about substances based on medical information, such as using substances that have less of an interaction with anesthesia or recovery

- Reducing negative impacts of substances, such as by engaging in self-care (e.g., hydration, rest)

# Conclusion

Many factors must be considered in making an accurate assessment of trans clients' mental health and wellness. Being aware of common co-occurring mental health concerns is necessary in order to make a differential diagnosis or determine the best course of treatment. In the next part of the book, we address transition-related care. We begin in chapter 11 with descriptions of the differences between social and medical transition and the kinds of care that clients may be seeking.

# Going Deeper:
# Questions for Clinicians and Clients

*Questions for Clinician Self-Reflection*

1.  What level of skill do I possess in making a differential diagnosis?

2.  What are my beliefs about trans clients with mental health concerns?

3.  What is my experience with clients with eating disorder symptoms?

4.  What is my experience with clients on the autism spectrum?

5.  What are my biases about substance use? How might it vary among different substances?

*Questions for Client Exploration*

1.  In what ways do concerns related to your gender affect your mental health or emotional well-being and vice versa?

2.  In what ways do concerns related to your gender affect your coping strategies?

3.  Have you been diagnosed with gender dysphoria or another gender-related diagnosis, and what does this mean for you? How accurately does this diagnosis describe you? How does it feel for you to have been diagnosed?

4.  Are there other mental health concerns of which I should be aware?

5.  What is your history with substance use?

# PART 3

# TRANSITION-RELATED CARE

# CHAPTER 11

# Know Options for Social, Medical, and Legal Transition

In this chapter, you will learn basic concepts regarding the pathways that trans clients may consider related to transitioning gender identity and/or expression. We will present common clinical themes and challenges and outline approaches you can utilize when working with trans clients who are considering or undergoing a transition process.

## Transition Broadly Defined: One Size Does Not Fit All

As mentioned in previous chapters, the dominant narrative around transition has been a medicalized one. The ways in which trans people choose to express themselves related to their gender can be different from one person to the next. Media portrayals of transition tend to be overly focused on a medical transition and ignore the social aspects of transition. Therefore, trans clients and clinicians may not always have a complete understanding of the ways that transition can be defined or delineated for a given person.

For example, transition is often described or portrayed as a monolithic event rather than a process that occurs over time, which is often highly individualized. To illustrate, the trans people portrayed in the media are often ones who present initially as one gender (usually as a man), disappear for a period of time, and then suddenly reemerge as a brand-new person (usually a woman) with little trace of the person they were before. The transition, which is often referred to as a "sex change," is not discussed or explained in any way (including any reference to the wealth or financial resources involved), and there is an air of magic around the situation. Rarely depicted in these narratives are the transitions of trans masculine people, people of color, people with nonbinary identities, or people without wealth.

The real-life narratives that conform to this model—of the privileged, often White person achieving an instantaneous "sex change"—garner the most attention. The reality for most trans people is not consistent with these stereotypes. Different aspects of transition, including social, medical, and legal, are distinct but interrelated realms. As a clinician, you may play a role in helping clients with realistic and concrete planning within these realms. Although for some people, medically transitioning using hormone therapy and surgical interventions is necessary to achieve a sense of comfort in one's body and gender expression, others desire to transition socially without any medical or physical changes. Still others who want to transition face barriers that make it difficult if not impossible to do so, such as lack of financial resources, limited access to trans-affirming health care providers, or health challenges that interfere with medical interventions.

Within society, including among health care providers, there is a persistent assumption that trans people with more binary identities will desire medical transition, while trans people with nonbinary identities will be comfortable existing in a liminal space without a medical transition. This is an inaccurate distinction, as there are people with binary identities who do not desire medical transition and people with nonbinary identities who do. Regardless of whether a person has a binary or a nonbinary identity, the desire to have or not have medical interventions differs from one person to the next. Rather than automatically grouping gender by a set of physical attributes, it is useful to think about the ways that people would like to present themselves, or be perceived, and how this may determine a transition pathway.

Although there is no single, correct way to transition, there are some common aspects of transition—certain social, medical, legal, and other elements that many individuals who are navigating a transition will contend with—and it is useful to be aware of and familiar with these aspects to effectively work with trans clients undergoing or considering transition. It is also necessary to examine and challenge your own past and present beliefs and feelings about gender and people who choose to transition (see chapter 1). You may have feelings, conscious and unconscious, that could affect how you discuss transition issues. The clinician's role and stance will be discussed later in this chapter.

# Common, But Not Universal, Transition Pathways

This section will provide an overview of social, medical, legal, educational and vocational, and relational aspects of transition. These broad categories are descriptive yet not exhaustive and may overlap. In other words, there are other ways that trans people describe and characterize their transitions, and often this is culturally based or defined. These categories will give you a broad base from which to work to cultivate and refine your understanding of transition among clients of all kinds.

## Social Aspects of Transition

Social transition typically refers to the ways in which a trans person may shift gender identity, expression, or role, usually in relation to others or society. For some trans people, coming to terms with one's own gender identity (sometimes referred to as "coming out to oneself") may be the first step in socially transitioning. Coming into awareness about one's gender identity and how it does not fully align with sex assigned at birth may motivate a person to start expressing this to others—for example, by letting others know how they would like to be addressed (e.g., names, pronouns) or by choosing to wear clothing that is more in line with their gender identity.

## SELF-AWARENESS

There is a longstanding misconception that all trans people knew from a young age, such as early childhood, that their gender identities were not in line with sex assigned at birth (e.g., "being born in the wrong body"). This misconception is characteristic of what is known as the "medicalized narrative" of trans experience (Vipond, 2015), a narrative that does not fit for all trans people. In reality, there is a great deal of developmental diversity when it comes to the ways in which trans people come to understand their own gender identities and start to communicate this to others. Self-awareness regarding gender identity may be sudden or gradual. For some people, this is not so much a coming out process but an inherent knowing.

Many clients, both trans and cisgender, report having had a sense of freedom of expression at a young age (e.g., early toddlerhood or before starting school) because gender roles and expectations were not as fixed. For clients with this experience, therapy or transition may be a matter of regaining or returning to this sense of freedom and comfort with oneself. Some clients report they had a felt sense about their authentic gender as children, but a lack of recognition or validation of this pushed them to conform to gender-role expectations based on the sex assigned at birth or to push their authentic gender identity out of awareness for the purposes of survival or belonging.

## GENDER EXPRESSION AND ROLE

Social transition may involve exploration of gender expression, either privately or publicly. This can include wearing different clothing or accessories and changes in hairstyle or makeup. Some people may find ways to have their bodies appear more in line with their affirmed gender, such as binding their chest or tucking their genitals. Clinicians working with people in early transition may want to discuss physical safety and direct clients to resources that can educate and support them as they are exploring or making changes to their gender expression. Many trans clients report feeling that the expectations of them based on sex assigned at birth do not feel authentic or natural to them. Social transition often involves clients exploring and expressing themselves in ways that feel more fitting to them. Some people continue to pursue interests, professions, and roles that they had prior to initiating social transition, while others find that these things change significantly and in unexpected ways after transition.

There are a number of ways in which trans people may engage in exploration in the realm of gender expression. Some people explore varying their gender expression in the context of drag, while others may change their online social presence (e.g., avatars) to get a sense of how it feels to be perceived differently by others. Cosplay, which came out of the anime culture and community, involves dressing up as a fictional character. For some trans people, this provides a safer space to freely explore presenting as a character that has a different gender expression.

## FORMS OF ADDRESS: NAMES AND PRONOUNS

Names, pronouns, and other forms of address constitute a component of social transition. Some people will choose a new first (and sometimes last) name that is more affirming of their gender identity, while others may feel comfortable with their given or birth-assigned names. For some trans people, their close friends or clinicians may, at first, be the only people who know about and address them by their affirmed name. Some people will want to try different names before choosing one that feels like a good fit for them, and it's important to use whatever name your client uses, regardless of the person's "legal" name.

Because pronouns in many languages, including English, are rooted in gender, they may become of great importance to trans clients and often signal whether they are recognized, perceived, or respected in their affirmed gender. At the outset of counseling, it is helpful to ask clients (of any gender, trans or not) what pronouns they use. Even better is to ask the question on intake paperwork, which serves to not only get information about the client but to also communicate to the client an awareness that pronouns are best not to be assumed by others. As noted in chapter 2, "preferred gender pronoun" (sometimes abbreviated as PGP) is often used as shorthand when asking about a person's pronouns. However, we encourage you to avoid using the term *preferred* because for most trans people, their pronouns are not a preference. Rather, using correct pronouns is a crucial sign of respect and affirmation. It can be helpful to check in with clients periodically about their pronouns, as this can change over time. In addition, some people use different pronouns depending on the day, how they are feeling, or their environmental context. Other clients will specify that they are comfortable with more than one set of pronouns (e.g., "I go by he/him/his and they/them/their").

## NAVIGATING RESTROOMS AND OTHER SEX-SEGREGATED SPACES

Sex-segregated spaces, such as restrooms, locker rooms, and fitting rooms, can be challenging for trans people to navigate, especially if they do not fit a binary gender presentation. Trans people will want the freedom to use the restrooms that are affirming of their gender, but often this can be a challenge that creates significant fear and stress (Herman, 2013). This concern is not unfounded, as many trans people experience anti-trans bias, misgendering, and even violence in restrooms. Laws vary considerably from state to state regarding policies and protections related to restroom access for trans people. Regardless of the rights afforded or withheld by a given state, this aspect of transition can be extremely stressful for people to navigate day-to-day. You will want to explore how much these experiences impact your clients' physical and emotional health. It may be helpful to collaborate with clients in creating safety plans (e.g., when going through airport security, when starting to use different restrooms), which may maximize a sense of agency and resilience.

## Medical Aspects of Transition

This section provides a brief, basic overview of medical transition. Some of the more pertinent points that concern the clinician's role are discussed in chapter 12. Before we begin to describe components of medical transition, however, we must establish the importance of avoiding the view of medical transition encouraged by the medicalized narrative of trans experience. In 2014, Katie Couric interviewed trans media figures Carmen Carrera and Laverne Cox (McDonough, 2014). The lesson from this conversation is representative of the problems associated with assuming trans people are committed to a medical transition.

Laverne Cox, a well-known African American trans actress and activist, and Carmen Carrera, a trans model, appeared on the Katie Couric show in January 2014. Instead of discussing the guests' careers or social justice concerns, Couric launched the interview by asking the women about their genitals and whether they have had surgery. Carrera simply stated that she did not want to discuss the issue, as it was personal. Cox replied:

*I do feel there is a preoccupation with that. The preoccupation with transition and surgery objectifies trans people. And then we don't get to really deal with the real lived experiences. The reality of trans people's lives is that so often we are targets of violence. We experience discrimination disproportionately to the rest of the community. Our unemployment rate is twice the national average; if you are a trans person of color, that rate is four times the national average. The homicide rate is highest among trans women. If we focus on transition, we don't actually get to talk about those things.*
(McDonough, 2014)

Katie Couric's interview of Laverne Cox serves as a reminder of society's fixation on trans people's bodies, genitals, and medical transitions, leading people to ask trans people questions that would never be asked of cisgender people. This is quite damaging and dehumanizing. Trans people do not want their genitals to define them any more than anyone else does. They especially do not want to have this experience when they are seeking help. Laverne Cox's response to Couric can remind us, as clinicians, to be mindful of our own sense of curiosity and refrain from asking questions that are inappropriate or not clinically relevant.

It is important for clinicians working with trans clients to assist those who may be seeking guidance on medical transition. Clinicians working with trans people can familiarize themselves with some common gender-affirming medical interventions that trans people seek so that when clients are ready to discuss medical treatment, there is a framework for understanding. It is important to reiterate the fact that for most trans people, medical interventions will not be accessible or affordable. Regardless of this, those who are interested in some form of medical transition will appreciate having a clinician whom they do not need to educate during their session.

## HORMONE THERAPY

Some trans people will choose to undergo hormone therapy to suppress their endogenous hormones and develop secondary sex characteristics different from those associated with sex assigned at birth. People assigned female at birth may be prescribed testosterone to move toward a more masculine or nonbinary presentation. People assigned male at birth may be prescribed both testosterone-blocking hormones and estrogen to move toward a more feminine or nonbinary presentation. In addition to the masculinizing or feminizing physical effects of hormone therapy, many people report a significant increase in emotional well-being. We will discuss hormone therapy in greater detail in chapter 12.

## GENDER-AFFIRMING SURGERIES

The term *gender-affirming surgeries* is often mistakenly applied to refer exclusively to genital reconstructive surgeries. We do not agree with this usage because it reinforces the idea that genitals are what determine identity. Rather, we use the term to refer broadly to any surgical procedure that helps someone to feel that their body is better aligned with their gender identity. There are several different gender-affirming surgeries that trans people seek for a wide variety of reasons. The benefits of these surgeries include feeling affirmed in one's body or gender, being able to wear gender-affirming clothing more comfortably, having a more fulfilling sex life, decreasing gender dysphoria, maximizing the benefits of hormone therapy (e.g., surgeries that affect hormonal balance such as hysterectomy or orchiectomy), and feeling safer when going out in public or accessing sex-segregated environments (e.g., restrooms, locker rooms). We discuss surgery in greater detail in chapter 12.

The ability to access gender-affirming surgeries varies greatly based on the client's financial means and whether they have access to medical practitioners who can provide affirming care. For example, in some states, there are insurance companies that cover gender-affirming surgeries, whereas in others, surgeries are only accessible to those who have the financial means to make out-of-pocket payments. Some clients may have the means to travel internationally to get surgery at a more affordable price; in these cases, many but not all surgeons use the WPATH criteria to determine eligibility or appropriateness for surgery. Clinicians working with clients undergoing surgical procedures will want to familiarize themselves with the options, especially regarding the financial demands of preparation and recovery from surgery.

## Legal Aspects of Transition

Some trans clients will have the desire and means to change the name they were given at birth and their gender marker, while others will not. Reasons for seeking a legal name and gender marker change may be related to feeling recognized in a way that is congruent with the affirmed or authentic gender. Laws vary state by state regarding what documents trans people can change and the processes by which they can go about doing so (Lambda Legal, 2016a). Trans people who have interest in changing their identity documents will want the most up-to-date information on laws and regulations. The National Center for Transgender Equality has an excellent resource on its website that aggregates information on how to change one's legal name and gender marker based on geographic location.

Aside from identity documents, there are other realms in which trans people will want their gender identity and transition status/history to be protected. These protections may vary widely based on geographic location. For example, a California bill (AB 1577) called the "Respect After Death Act" was passed in 2014. The law requires government officials completing a person's death certificate to accurately represent the person's gender identity according to the person's wishes (if there are written instructions), their updated gender marker on a birth certificate or driver's license, or evidence of gender-affirming medical treatment (Transgender Law Center, 2014). This law validates the notion that regardless of the gender designation on legal documents, trans people should always be referred to with their affirmed/chosen name and gender.

When working with trans people who use insurance to pay for counseling and have not had a legal name change, be mindful about the discrepancy between the legal name and chosen name. For insurance purposes, statements should include the legal name but may also include the client's chosen name, with the client's consent. In either case, you should use their chosen, affirmed name in all other communication to and with the client. It may be helpful and even necessary to have a brief conversation to clarify this practical distinction with the client.

## Educational and Vocational Aspects of Transition

Trans people going through transition may have concerns related to education, employment, career, and financial stability that can sometimes hinder or delay their transition. The concept of living "full time" in a gender role is discussed in the WPATH Standards of Care. This concept can pose tension, as sometimes these standards may push a person to socially transition at work before they are ready or before they have medically transitioned to the point where they can move more freely and safely in their workplace and other environments. Moreover, society (including medical establishments) expects that a person live "full time" prior to being eligible for genital surgery. It is not uncommon for trans people who are concerned about anti-trans bias to consciously choose to continue presenting in a gender role that is consistent with their sex assigned at birth for the purposes of financial sustainability and survival. This decision is not an indication of indecision about one's trans identity. Rather, it is a practical decision made to protect and sustain a person's life. It is essential for clinicians to respect each client's individual process and wishes for if and how they want to transition or be "out" in various parts of their lives.

## EDUCATION CONCERNS

Trans clients who are students want to be able to access their education and learn without being hindered by obstacles posed by anti-trans bias. Encourage trans clients to talk through their goals, concerns, and feelings related to their education and discuss how to communicate to teachers and administrators about needs regarding socially transitioning in the classroom setting. For some trans people, gender dysphoria may be a significant barrier to academic performance. Educational concerns related to primary education are further discussed in chapter 18 on gender expansive youth.

Clients who are interested in secondary education (i.e., attending a university) may have concerns about whether the administration will support them if the name or gender marker in their legal documents differs from how they wish to be addressed or treated. Generally speaking, a college or university registrar will make a name change in the official records if a student has completed this process through legal means. That may not be the case if a student has not completed a legal name or gender marker change. Financial aid for tuition can be yet another concern, as this may require applicants to be registered for the Selective Service or get an exemption from the Department of Defense. Navigating this may be confusing and stressful, especially because policies are subject to change and it is not always easy to get the most current, accurate information.

## WORKPLACE TRANSITION

Workplace transitions may be of significant concern for trans clients, and they may want counseling to be a place where they can safely explore whether, how, and when to transition at work. In the past, medical establishments imposed a requirement that trans people wishing to transition leave a current job and start a new job or career (Denny, 2002). Some clients may still wish to take this route, as they would rather have their employment and workplace relationships unaffected by their pre-transition identity or role. They may not have the privilege of being able to maintain their current employment due to anti-trans bias. It is important to be aware that in many states, discrimination based on employee gender identity, including termination of employment, is not protected. In other words, not all trans people have legal protections that cover employment discrimination. In the most recent U.S. Transgender Survey ($N = 27{,}715$), 16% of respondents who have been employed reported losing a job due to their gender identity or expression at some point in their life. In the year prior to the survey, 27% of respondents reported being fired, denied a promotion, or not being hired due to their gender identity or expression (James et al., 2016).

Clinicians can play a significant role in supporting trans clients as they move through workplace transitions by helping them navigate day-to-day challenges, such as dealing with coworkers who are not as supportive or understanding. For example, some trans people face the stressors of having coworkers misgender them (e.g., use the wrong name or pronouns) or create obstacles for them in accessing their workplace environments (e.g., complaining about the trans person using the restroom that is consistent with their affirmed gender). Worse yet, their coworkers may sabotage their workplace, making it physically unsafe. There may be additional stress related to well-meaning, curious coworkers who ask inappropriate or intrusive questions (e.g., questions about one's surgical status). Trans clients may benefit from training in assertiveness and boundary setting; you can assist by offering role-playing exercises that help clients ask others for what they need at work to make it possible for them to feel comfortable and successful.

Some employers have guidelines that outline policies related to a trans person's transition process. Lambda Legal (2016b) and Transgender Law Center (2016) have issued resources that assist employers in how to design and implement appropriate transition guidelines for trans employees. Your understanding of these and similar documents can help you to appreciate and understand what your clients are experiencing in the workplace. In addition, you may want to share these documents with clients who are unaware of how to go about discussing transition with their employers.

## CAREER CHOICES

Some trans clients feel that their career choices may be affected by their gender identity and/or expression. They may be in fields that are highly segregated by gender (i.e., dominated by one binary gender with little representation of the other binary gender) and therefore may seek a career change. For example, consider the following case of Joan, a trans client whose career choices and trajectory changed over the course of her life based on her gender transition.

# CASE EXAMPLE. Affirming Gender Transitions:
## *Working with Joan*

*Joan (she/her/hers), a fifty-one-year-old White trans woman, reports that having chosen a career in the military was one way she "hid" from herself and the fact that she was transgender. As a young person, Joan was encouraged to "man up" and be more masculine, especially to gain the approval of her father. Always falling short of her father's expectations, she thought that joining the U.S. Navy would be the solution to her problems. She secretly longed to work in fashion but knew this was out of the question. For many years, Joan felt grief at not being able to live as a woman. After leaving the Navy, she worked as a general contractor and continued to try to fit in with other men.*

*When she finally comes to terms with her need to transition, Joan realizes that many of the vocational skills she possesses are geared toward male-dominated professions. She feels that going back to school or changing career paths would be difficult, as well as costly, and she is not old enough to retire. During her early transition, Joan works with a clinician who is attuned to Joan's vocational concerns and refers her to a career counselor. Through career counseling, Joan is able to identify career options that utilize some of her previously acquired skills and fit her personality and interests.*

*Joan realizes that she enjoys the carpentry work she used to do in her role as a contractor and has many skills (e.g., visual-spatial skills, manual dexterity, an artistic eye) that are trans-ferrable to other careers she is interested in. She feels more confident about pursuing those careers. As a result, she starts to take classes in fashion design and merchandising. She feels excited about being able to rely on some of the skills she already had but apply them in a differ-ent way, a way that feels more consistent with her identity. Through the support of her coun-selor and career counselor, as well as making connections with other transgender women working in male-dominated professions, Joan realizes that she does not need to give up on things she enjoyed before she transitioned. She can challenge and expand her notions of gender, and this helps her to feel even more empowered as a woman. Joan feels freedom in giving herself permission to choose to express her gender role in stereotypically masculine, stereotypically feminine, and sometimes even seemingly contradictory ways.*

Helping clients understand how their skills developed over their career allows them to see how they can transfer these abilities to other types of work. Clinicians who are attuned to a range of career options and the skills that are key to success in different fields are best equipped to address work-related clinical concerns.

## Relational Aspects of Transition

It is useful to consider a trans person's transition from a systems perspective (i.e., to consider the environments, contexts, and cultures that are integral to their identities and life) and take into account the client's relationships to family members, partners, children, and communities. Trans people may differ greatly in terms of culture-based values. For example, those who have a more individualistic or independent sense of self may not express concern about their relationships and how transition will affect or be affected by them. On the other hand, people who have highly interdependent or col-lectivist views of themselves will want to discuss the ways that their interpersonal rela-tionships factor into their transition experiences. This may be especially true for people of color or those from collectivistic cultures. Relational transitions will be discussed in further detail in chapter 15.

## Safety Concerns and Transition

As is discussed throughout this book, trans people face disproportionate systemic barri-ers and violence due to anti-trans bias. Clients who are transitioning (medically or socially) may have many concerns about safety. You can help clients to explore concerns and fears, identify and strengthen sources of coping and resilience, and create safety plans. Keep in mind that transition is rarely a linear process and that the way trans clients are perceived may shift incrementally throughout different stages of transition, especially when there are external or physical changes. Early in transition is a time when trans clients may be especially vulnerable to microaggressions and anti-trans bias. Clients with nonbinary identities or those who do not wish to be perceived in a binary gender (i.e., as a man or a woman) may similarly face negative reactions from others. In discussions of safety, it is important to maintain balance and refrain from going to the extremes of fear (e.g., only highlighting possible dangers that clients face) and dismissal (e.g., reassuring clients that they will be fine, that it is all in their heads).

Assessing for client safety is important for any client and especially critical for trans clients. Given the high rates of reported suicide attempts in trans communities (40%; James et al., 2016), it is critical to assess for danger to self. We encourage you to be cautious about assuming a trans client needs to be hospitalized as a result of reporting thoughts of suicide. Unless a client is at high risk of acting on these thoughts (e.g., has a plan and means, reports hopelessness, exhibits other risk factors), it is more important to work with the client to develop a safety plan that leverages their coping skills and support system.

## CASE EXAMPLE. Assessing Trans Client Suicide Risk: *Working with Caleb*

*Caleb (he/him/his) is a twenty-seven-year-old African American trans man who has been on hormones for eight years. At the time he decided to initiate hormone therapy, he relocated and made a decision to "start life over." Caleb reports to his counselor, Dr. Simpson (a forty-eight-year-old White trans woman; she/her/hers), that his decision to relocate was related to concerns about how his family would react to his decision to transition. Caleb's family has a long history of involvement with conservative religious beliefs. Caleb recently learned from a high school friend that his mother has been diagnosed with terminal cancer, and he became very distressed about the situation. He wants to visit his mother before she dies, but he hasn't talked to any of his family members about his transition. Caleb reports that he is having difficulty sleeping due to nightmares. He also states that when he wakes in the morning he finds himself wishing he were dead.*

*Dr. Simpson begins by normalizing Caleb's experience. She feels it is important for Caleb to understand that his experience is not uncommon before she completes a suicide assessment. In speaking with Caleb, Dr. Simpson learns that Caleb does not have an intent to end his life or a plan or means to do so. Caleb states that he has a good support system, but he hasn't been sure how to talk about this with others. Dr. Simpson explores these relational challenges and works with Caleb to help him identify one or more friends with whom he can talk about his thoughts of death. In a subsequent session, Dr. Simpson gently explores Caleb's thoughts of death so as to ensure that these thoughts haven't escalated into making a plan to end his life.*

In this case example, the clinician begins by normalizing the client's reaction to a difficult family situation. After this discussion, the clinician completes a thorough risk assessment. In addition to determining that Caleb does not have a plan to end his life, Dr. Simpson also identifies protective factors present for Caleb. Most important in this example is that Dr. Simpson does not immediately assume that Caleb needs to be hospitalized.

Equally important is the need to talk with clients about the realities and subsequent fears they may have about the potential for experiencing violence and harassment. Talking with clients about ways to avoid unsafe situations may be useful to ensure their safety. Trans women of color are at high risk for experiencing violence including murder. Without unnecessarily alarming the client, having discussions about personal safety can ensure that our clients have resources to address their safety.

# Transition and Disclosure: Respecting Boundaries of Privacy

Counseling and psychotherapy modalities invite clients to share and discuss intimate details of their lives. Some clients approach counseling with little hesitation about how much to share, while others may value their privacy and choose to discuss certain topics only when necessary and relevant to the presenting concerns. Asking a person about intimate details of their life as a trans person is not an effective way to build trust in the clinical relationship. If your motivation is curiosity, your client is not the right person to provide the information you are seeking, even if that information is specific to the client. For example, trans people are commonly asked, "What was your name before transition?" The answer to this question is generally not of relevance. We encourage you to refrain from asking unless it is absolutely necessary for the purposes of legal documentation (e.g., the person has not changed their legal name, their insurance is in that name, and you need it for billing purposes). If you are concerned about how a person's name is listed in their insurance, ask, "What name is used for your insurance?" This allows the client to provide a name without having to talk about the name they were given at birth if they no longer use this name.

Gathering information about clients' experiences through their transitions may aid in developing a greater understanding, fostering empathy, or formulating an appropriate treatment plan. However, some trans clients may seek counseling for reasons unrelated to gender, and it is not always necessary to have in-depth discussions related to gender or transition. If gender is an important consideration and relevant to the clients' goals, we can trust that they will bring it up when they feel safe to do so.

# CASE EXAMPLE. Conflating Gender and Disregarding Clinical Concern: *Working with Drake*

*Drake (he/him/his), a twenty-five-year-old Latino trans man, sought counseling to overcome his phobia of dogs. Drake can easily trace this phobia back to an early childhood experience of being bitten by a dog. It is not evident to Drake's counselor, Dr. Woods (a Native American cisgender woman; she/her/hers), that he is transgender until Drake asks for a statement to submit to his insurance for reimbursement. For insurance purposes, because he cannot yet afford to change his legal name, he asks Dr. Woods to use his legal (i.e., birth-assigned) name on the statement. Upon hearing this request, Dr. Woods becomes very curious about Drake's gender history. She starts to ask questions about Drake's childhood preference of toys, gender transition, and surgical history. She suggests that perhaps his phobia might be related to his gender identity. Dr. Woods, though an expert in providing prolonged exposure for PTSD, becomes overly fixated on Drake's gender and thereby de-skilled as a clinician.*

*Drake senses Dr. Woods's curiosity and inappropriate fascination with his story and feels very uncomfortable. He has been clear that his counseling goals do not involve reviewing his gender history, and he simply wants to get help for what is affecting him in his present, everyday life. That Dr. Woods does not respect those boundaries leaves him frustrated and discouraged. He suspects that she would never have pried into a cisgender person's gender or medical history if the name they chose to go by differed from their legal name. Drake discontinues counseling and decides he needs to find a clinician who is familiar with trans people and how to respectfully interact with them. When this happens, Dr. Woods comes to perceive Drake as guarded, defensive, and avoidant. As a result, she develops an unconscious belief that trans people are difficult to work with in counseling when, in fact, she had posed a great obstacle for a motivated client.*

In this example, Dr. Woods does not understand the boundaries of privacy and misses an opportunity to provide effective treatment for Drake. Although it is not completely out of the realm of possibility that different forms of anxiety may be traced back to a gender-related experience, it is not skillful for Dr. Woods to interrupt Drake's treatment with her assumption that his gender identity is relevant to his presenting problem, or that it is a matter within her purview. Like many people from marginalized groups who experience microaggressions or a clinician's lack of cultural competence in counseling, Drake could likely have decided to give up on seeking treatment for his phobia. Drake wants to be seen as a whole person and does not want his trans identity or status (or any other cultural identity marker, such as race or ethnicity) to be the one characteristic that defines him. His choice to discontinue counseling with Dr. Woods and seek a clinician who is more skillful in working with trans clients is reasonable, as it would not be appropriate for him to spend his resources (e.g., time, money) educating Dr. Woods instead of receiving the care he needs.

As clinicians with many years of experience working with trans clients, we have heard countless reports from our clients about previous encounters with counselors that were, at best, ineffective, and at worst, harmful. Many clients have come to us after having negative experiences of inappropriate interactions with previous clinicians. We are aware that we only see or hear from those who, like Drake, continue to pursue counseling. We assume there are others who give up and do not consider that they can have a different, better, or more affirming experience. We may never hear about their experiences, but by developing competency in working with trans clients affirmatively and respectfully, you may prevent other clients from having such experiences.

# Conclusion

In this chapter, you learned about several aspects of transition, including social, medical, legal, and educational or vocational. You also learned ways of approaching conversations regarding transition with sensitivity, including asking questions related to clients' bodies or transition only when clinically relevant. We also explored concerns of client safety and addressed effective ways of conducting a risk assessment. In the following chapter we discuss your role in assessment and referral for gender-affirming medical care.

# Going Deeper:
# Questions for Clinicians and Clients

*Questions for Clinician Self-Reflection*

1.  What are the transition narratives with which I am familiar? What narratives have I witnessed in people in my life or in the media? How does this affect my concept of what it means to transition, and what assumptions might I make about my clients' transition pathways?

2.  Is my client's experience new to me? If so, how can I be sure to educate myself so as not to rely on the client for information?

3.  How comfortable do I feel talking explicitly about sex, genitals, and medical procedures?

4.  What resources in my local area can I provide so that I don't feel responsible for every aspect of the client's transition?

5.  Is a discussion of transition relevant to the presenting concerns at this moment? Am I able to understand the differences between social, medical, and legal transitions?

6.  In what ways do I need to be aware of how my opinions or feelings about transition (e.g., approval, disapproval, confusion) might come through and affect the client?

7.  (*For trans clinicians:*) How have my own choices or transition pathways shaped how I approach working with trans clients in transition?

8.  What is my comfort level with nonbinary clients who choose to medically transition?

9.  Am I familiar with gender-neutral pronoun options? Am I willing to practice to best respect the proper terms of address with nonbinary clients?

10. To what extent am I aware of the ethical and legal challenges that are common for trans people?

11. What aspects of transition am I most familiar and comfortable with? How can I further develop and maintain that familiarity and comfort?

12. What aspects of transition are newer or harder for me to understand? How can I further educate myself on these topics?

*Questions for Client Exploration*

1.  What does it mean to you to transition?

2.  How do you understand the starting and ending points of transition, if they exist?

3.  Transition can include many different components and stages. Which components are necessary for you to feel affirmed in your gender?

4.  Some trans people think of transition as a process over time rather than an event. How do you envision different stages of your transition?

5.  How do you imagine I can assist you at various times? What other resources might you need?

6.  During the transition process, the language you use that feels more affirming to you may change over time. What are the terms (e.g., name, pronouns, gender descriptors) that feel affirming to you now?

7.  *(For clients who desire medical transition:)* What have your experiences with medical professionals been like, and how does/will that inform your approach to seeking gender-affirming medical care?

8.  What concerns or thoughts do you have about how transition will affect and be affected by your work life?

9.  How do you see your transition in the context of the relationships and communities that are important to you?

10. How does transition or the changes in how you are perceived by others affect other aspects of who you are, including your cultural identities?

11. At this point, how are you feeling in relation to different aspects of your transition, and where have you been able to explore or discuss these feelings?

12. Overall, what about your transition is important for me to know and understand so that we can work effectively together? For example, are there things that have changed or stayed the same that would be most important for me to know?

# CHAPTER 12

# Assess and Refer for Gender-Affirming Medical Care

How a mental health clinician engages in the provision of assessment and writing letters of support to physicians or insurance providers regarding clients' candidacy for medical interventions can vary considerably. In this chapter, you will learn about what this role entails, including the challenges of being in a gatekeeping position, dual role concerns, what you should know about medical interventions, and what to discuss with clients so that you may provide an accurate and affirming assessment and referral.

Though many health care systems follow the WPATH SOC, there are few clear, uniform guidelines on how to conduct letter writing. Differences among providers depend on belief systems regarding trans autonomy, clinician comfort level, and adherence to the WPATH SOC or another protocol.

Many surgeons and insurance companies will ask for one or two letters from mental health providers (depending on the intervention requested), but if you work for a medical or hospital system, this assessment may take the form of clinical documentation rather than a letter. As emphasized in chapter 6, your role as a clinician is not to determine someone's gender; it is to listen to the client's concerns and help them clarify and move toward their goals.

## Belief Systems Regarding Client Autonomy

When clinicians believe that they are responsible for clients' life decisions, the result is a gatekeeping stance. In trans-affirming care (or a client-centered approach), our role is to help clients understand the choices they have. It is not our job, nor is it possible, to ensure that a client always makes good decisions or to prevent them from making bad decisions. It is important to consider each client's long-term interest in order to minimize risk and harm and to partner with clients in exploring factors that will contribute to or hinder their well-being.

Approaches or interventions that assume that clinicians know what is best and clients do not, or that it is a clinician's job to protect a client from making choices leading to outcomes that none of us can predict or control, are disempowering and replicate oppressive power dynamics. We must respect our clients' dignity and freedom to make their own choices, even if we do not agree with them. What is useful in this situation is to help the client understand the possible outcomes of their decisions, not to influence them in any particular direction.

Your comfort level in providing assessment and referral can significantly affect your trans clients. Clinicians often tell clients, "I'm comfortable writing the letter" or "I'm not yet comfortable writing a letter." We encourage you to reflect on what it means to be "comfortable" providing such a service and how much your own anxiety may inform that comfort. Being comfortable should not be equated with imagining that you would make the same decisions if you were in your client's shoes. It is important to communicate clearly to your clients if there is a legitimate concern about safety or well-being in relation to their request. Many clinicians feel anxious about professional liability and believe their licenses are on the line every time they write a letter (Campbell & Arkles, 2016). We do not encourage haphazard care that would compromise your professional role or livelihood. However, it is important to challenge instances in which your personal bias or anxiety (which is yours to manage) is a barrier for otherwise appropriate referrals. If you are able to identify your fears, anxieties, or biases, this is an opportunity to seek consultation or support in managing these feelings. We suggest seeking professional consultation as an excellent way to feel more supported in your role.

# The Clinician's Role: Gatekeeper or Advocate?

In discussing your role in assessment and referral for gender-affirming care, we would be remiss if we did not start by naming your gatekeeping power and participation in systems that are not always affirming of clients' needs for autonomy. Many of us consider ourselves trans allies and advocates, and it can be difficult for us to see ourselves as gatekeepers. At times, we have engaged in forms of gatekeeping because our clients exist in systems that require it, such as writing letters or diagnosing our clients so that they may gain access to care. We do not have the perfect answers about how to engage with these systems or manage these responsibilities; in fact, answers may not exist. However, it is important to confront these questions and keep them in the forefront of your mind as you enact this role with clients seeking gender-affirming medical interventions.

## Managing Gatekeeping Power and Dual Roles

You may be thinking, *I'm not a gatekeeper!* Regardless of how you feel about being cast in this role in relationship to trans clients, if you write letters or clients are required to meet with you for a referral to a physician who can prescribe hormones or perform surgery, then you have gatekeeping power. You can explore the anxiety you feel about gatekeeping and strategize about ways to minimize harm. It is helpful to consult with trusted colleagues and friends so that your anxieties are not unconsciously enacted in ways that can cause harm.

Great intention should be put toward establishing rapport. How you introduce your-self, your role, and the task at hand can make a difference in your ability to develop a trusting relationship with your client. Overall, you will want to create a safe environment for your clients to discuss their desires, expectations, and concerns. As much as possible, you will want to elicit an honest, collaborative conversation rather than conduct what may feel to your clients like an interrogation or test. It can be helpful to demystify the process of getting a letter as early as possible by being transparent about your approach. This may involve expressing that you are coming from an affirming stance, that you are inviting a collaboration, or that you endorse an informed consent model. We encourage you to develop your own style, but here is an example of how you might frame the conversation:

> *Before we begin, I thought it would be helpful for me to clarify my role and the purpose of our meeting today. I am not sure what you know or have been told about this process, but I think it is important for me to state what this session is and is not about. I come from an affirming stance that is informed by the evidence and belief that trans people should be supported in their identities and goals for what they want their bodies to look and feel like. Therefore, I am not here to evaluate your gender, such as whether you are truly trans. I believe you are who you say you are and no one else can decide that for you. What I am interested in discussing is your decision-making process, your understanding of risks and benefits, factors related to mental health and well-being, and any plans you have for support. I am hoping that this can be a collaborative dis-cussion and that I can ask questions and provide information that will be helpful to you in your process. In addition, I want to name that historically, the mental health provider role has not always been one that has been respectful or supportive of the autonomy of trans people, and that in my position I have gatekeeping power. I welcome any thoughts, feelings, or questions that you have about this. At the end of our con-versation, I would like to have the information I need to be able to write an accurate letter that you can provide to your doctor, surgeon, or insurance provider.*

There are times when a current counseling client will ask you to write a letter for them. For these clients, you will want to be mindful of your dual role and how that may affect the clinical relationship. It is already challenging for clients to feel that they have to convince a clinician that they are appropriate candidates for medical interventions. When this dynamic of having to perform is present, it can get in the way of being able to be candid about difficulties or mental health symptoms. It can be useful to name this dynamic with clients, such as in this example:

> *Up to this point, we have been working together to address your mental health, overall well-being, and goals for growth and healing. Now that I am going to be in the position of writing a letter for you related to medical interventions, I think it is important for us to discuss how this impacts our relationship. For example, the fact that I am holding this power to influence whether you are able to move forward with hormones/surgery can bring up a wide range of feelings. I invite you to share your feelings and concerns*

*about this letter-writing process and how it affects our work together and our relationship. You will also notice that I have some very specific questions for you, so this session and possibly more will feel different from our other sessions. Do you have any questions about this?*

We encourage you to develop your own way of framing the conversation according to your style and the clients who seek your services. It may take some trial and error, but over time you will likely find the language and communication that works best for you.

## Toward Education, Empowerment, and Advocacy

One strategy for counteracting gatekeeping is to use gatekeeping platforms (e.g., required mental health assessments) as opportunities for information sharing, collaboration, and support of clients in making decisions and providing informed consent. You can identify appropriate referrals and direct clients to resources such as websites that have accurate information about medical interventions. You can encourage conversations in which clients can ask questions or explore feelings about different aspects of these interventions, such as perceived risks, benefits, preparation, and recovery. If you are situated in a way to have power to influence a system or institution, you can educate other providers and advocate for changes that reduce or eliminate barriers to care.

# Using the WPATH Standards of Care as Flexible Guidelines

The WPATH Standards of Care (Coleman et al., 2012) are in their seventh iteration, and at the time of this publication, WPATH is working on the next version. Professional practice varies considerably regarding to what extent it utilizes, adheres to, and endorses the stances recommended by the WPATH. Medical systems that adhere to the WPATH SOC7 require that trans people seeking gender-affirming medical interventions meet with a mental health provider for a letter of support. Mental health providers often adhere to the WPATH SOC7 because it is the protocol that surgeons and insurance companies rely on, and this calls for mental health providers to play an evaluative role in a trans client's medical transition process. Some clinicians have critiqued the mental health gatekeeping role and recommended a stance of advocacy in which respect for clients and their needs are centered (Singh & Burnes, 2010).

The WPATH SOC7 state that the guidelines are flexible. We want to emphasize this in order to discourage the use of the WPATH SOC as a rigid resource to be applied in the same way for all trans clients. Experienced clinicians will understand when these guidelines are indicated and when they do not apply to clients. Some systems of care have devised their own protocols or assessment of readiness and appropriateness for gender-affirming medical care, such as informed consent models discussed in chapter 4.

Although there is a debate about the appropriateness of the WPATH SOC, as a clinician it is important for you to familiarize yourself with the standards and to stay current with the changes in the WPATH's recommendations and trans health. Many health care systems and insurance companies follow the WPATH Standards of Care, so regardless of your stance it is important to be informed about current requirements that are affecting your clients' access to care. You can access these guidelines on the WPATH website.

Although the guidelines set forth by the WPATH SOC vary based on the medical intervention(s) being requested, there are some universal components. We will discuss these themes here and elaborate on them in following sections referring to specific medical interventions. In general, the standards of care require

- a diagnosis of persistent, well-documented gender dysphoria;

- the capacity to make a fully informed decision and to consent to treatment;

- age of majority (if younger, parental consent is required, though this varies according to geographic region and health care policies); and

- if significant medical or mental health concerns are present, that they be reasonably well controlled.

In the following sections, you will learn about descriptions, risks, and benefits pertaining to different gender-affirming medical interventions. Having this knowledge can serve to aid you in assessing a client's capacity to make a fully informed decision and to thus provide informed consent.

## Gender-Affirming Medical Care: What Mental Health Clinicians Need to Know

As a mental health provider, you may be wondering what your responsibility is regarding knowing and discussing medical aspects of care with your clients. We do not advocate for practicing out of scope, as *detailed, comprehensive medical informing is not your responsibility*. However, it is important to familiarize yourself with gender-affirming medical interventions so that you can understand what your clients are talking about or dealing with and support decision making and informed consent. You will want to be aware of the benefits, risks, and side effects of hormone therapies, as these can affect mental health. You will want to know about the range of surgeries that are available and to whom, as well as information about preparing for and recovering from different surgeries, so that you can be helpful to your clients who access these surgeries. You will want to be aware of educational resources that you can provide for clients who are questioning whether interventions are right for them. Finally, you will want to ask your clients to discuss their feelings about these aspects of their health and medical care as you engage in the process of exploring emotional aspects of informed consent.

# Hormone Therapy

Some, not all, trans people desire or choose to undergo hormone therapy. Many people find that hormones help them feel more comfortable with their body and expressing their gender identity. Hormone therapy can vary depending on the client's goals and can range from brief periods of treatment to lifelong, continual use.

People also vary in terms of how they respond to hormones. Most changes from hormones will occur over two to three years, and it can take several months to notice substantial effects on appearance. There is no way to predict how fast or how much change will happen for a given individual. Regular blood tests are performed to check the body's response to hormones and ensure that safe levels of hormones are maintained.

As clinicians, it is important to be aware that hormones may influence mood. For some people, hormones help to even out fluctuations in mood. Many clients report that being on hormones has reduced or eradicated mental health symptoms. Improvements in mood may be due to decreased gender dysphoria, which may be linked with depression or anxiety symptoms, or to feeling more comfortable in their bodies or being perceived correctly by others. On the other hand, some people may have mood swings or report negative changes in mood. In our experience, this can be the case when a client is early in medical transition and their body is adjusting to hormones. Some people report that the quality of their emotions feel different. Clinicians play a helpful role in assisting clients to name, understand, and cope with the experience of their emotions. Clients may need to develop new or different coping strategies, and doing so in an intentional way with the help of a caring professional can be invaluable.

For hormone therapy, some health care systems require **one letter** from a mental health professional (consistent with the WPATH SOC7), but others may utilize an informed consent model. In other words, some trans clients seeking hormone therapy will be able to meet with a prescribing medical provider (e.g., primary care doctor, endocrinologist) to complete the informed consent process and bypass a mental health assessment. This practice has become more prevalent over time, including in large hospital systems (e.g., University of California, San Francisco [UCSF] Medical Center), community health clinics (e.g., Tom Waddell Clinic in San Francisco, Callen-Lorde in New York City), and some university health centers.

## FEMINIZING HORMONE THERAPY

Trans women and nonbinary people assigned male at birth who undergo feminizing hormone therapy will typically be prescribed two medications: an anti-androgen (sometimes referred to as a testosterone blocker or androgen blocker) and estrogen.

Androgen blockers suppress effects of testosterone in the body. Reported effects of anti-androgens include decreased sex drive, decreased frequency or quality of erections, decreased testicle size, decreased semen volume, and decreased fertility (i.e., viability of sperm). Some reported side effects include increased urine production, increased thirst, mood changes, and fatigue. If your clients are experiencing these symptoms, encourage them to discuss them with their physician.

Estrogen, which is typically prescribed as a daily pill, a weekly or biweekly injection, or a dermal patch, is what causes the development of more stereotypically, secondary "female" characteristics. Some physical changes that may occur include softer skin; breast development occurring over several years, with size varying greatly; changes in body hair, such as thinning hair or slower hair growth; redistribution of body fat (often increased fat on the thighs, buttocks, and hips); and decreased muscle mass and tone. Some reported side effects include nausea, vomiting, headaches, and mood swings.

Several things will not change as a result of feminizing hormones, and it is important to know about certain limitations that may perpetuate gender dysphoria or get in the way of being perceived correctly by others. Facial hair will not completely disappear, so many clients seek electrolysis and/or laser hair removal. The cartilage around the trachea (commonly called the "Adam's apple," a term that should be used with caution as it can trigger feelings of dysphoria) will not shrink. Vocal pitch will not rise. Bone or body structure (such as height and frame) will not change. There are times in which a client may be simultaneously happy about the positive changes resulting from hormone therapy while experiencing increased distress or safety concerns about aspects of their appearance that are not changing.

## MASCULINIZING HORMONE THERAPY

Trans men and nonbinary people assigned female at birth may seek masculinizing hormone therapy (i.e., testosterone), usually in the form of an intramuscular (IM) injection, a subcutaneous injection, a topical gel or cream, or a dermal patch. Testosterone is typically not prescribed in a pill form as the body is not able to absorb it properly and it may cause liver problems.

Testosterone dosage depends on the client's goals, how their body reacts, and the type or frequency of administration. Some clients may want to go on a low dose of hormones to have a more gradual masculinizing process or simply to support a more androgynous presentation. It is important that clients take no more than the prescribed dosage, as taking more than prescribed can be unsafe. It can also result in excess testosterone converting back into estrogen, which will be counter to the client's goals and inhibit the masculinization process.

It is not possible to predict exactly how testosterone will affect a given person. Typically, more permanent changes that result from testosterone include facial and body hair growth (though some may be reversible), increased male pattern baldness, deepening of the voice, and enlarged clitoral tissue. More reversible or temporary changes include acne (though some may be more permanent); cessation of menses (typically one to six months after starting hormones); changes in body fat distribution; decreased fat on hips, buttocks, and thighs; increased abdominal fat; increased muscle mass and strength; increased sex drive; and changes to vaginal lining or secretions (e.g., thinning of lining, increase or decrease in secretions). Some side effects of testosterone may include higher cholesterol levels, elevated hematocrit levels, higher blood pressure, increased fat around the heart and other organs, liver damage, decreased response to insulin, weight gain, headaches, and mood changes (e.g., some people report quicker, more intense emotions or increased anger). It is important to be cautious about the cultural attributions that are often applied negatively to trans masculine people who take testosterone. For example, there is a myth of "roid rage" being caused by testosterone, which can inadvertently circumvent useful discussions of situational factors (e.g., injustice) that may create reasonable anger.

In addition, be aware that cessation of menses does not indicate a lack of ability to get pregnant. Testosterone is not an adequate form of birth control. For clients who are on testosterone and have not had a hysterectomy, fertility options are still intact. Later in this chapter, you will learn more about how to address fertility concerns with your clients.

## Hormone Therapy: Considerations and Sample Questions

- Sources of information: *What resources have helped you to learn about hormone therapy?*

- Anticipated benefits: *What do you hope to get from taking hormones? What are the changes you look forward to?*

- Anticipated risks or concerns: *For you, what are the possible risks or unwanted effects of taking hormones? It can be helpful to name any fears that are present so we can take time to address them.*

- Questions: *Are there things you do not understand or would like to understand better? How can you get these questions answered?*

- Anticipated changes in self-image: *How do you imagine hormone therapy will affect how you see yourself?*

- Anticipated changes in relationships: *How do you imagine hormone therapy will affect how others perceive or treat you? How do you think this will feel for you?*

- Sex and intimacy: *How, if at all, do you think sexuality and intimacy might be affected by hormone therapy?*

- Employment/education: *How do you imagine hormone therapy will affect you in your work or school environment? Do you have any concerns about this? Do you need any resources to support you in these aspects of social transition?*

- Safety and public environments: *How do you imagine hormone therapy will affect your sense of safety and comfort in public? Do you have any specific safety concerns?*

- Body fat redistribution: *As hormone therapy generally shifts body shape and fat distribution, how might this feel for you?*

- Mood: *As hormone therapy can affect your overall mood, how do you imagine this will be for you? What resources or supports do you have available to you in navigating mood changes? Hormones can reduce or increase mental health symptoms, so what support do you have to help you in the case that you experience challenges with mood or your experience of emotions?*

- Physical energy and strength: *How do you imagine hormones might impact your physical energy or strength?*

- Goals and dosage: *There is no one set way of taking hormones, and the dosing and frequency may depend on your personal goals. For example, some people go on a more typical dose, some people prefer a low dose, and some people choose to take hormones for a period of time until they have seen certain changes and then choose to discontinue. Do you have any thoughts on what might be the best fit for you or what you may need to ask for when meeting with your doctor?*

- Limits to dosage: *Some people find that they are not seeing the wanted changes from hormones quickly enough and decide to increase their dose on their own, which can be dangerous or counterproductive. Would you be willing to talk to your prescribing medical provider if you have concerns about dosage?*

  - *For trans feminine clients: Are you aware that too much estrogen increases the risk of blood clots?*

  - *For trans masculine clients: Are you aware that too much testosterone will convert back to estrogen?*

- Changes to reproductive options: *As hormones affect reproductive options, and these changes can be temporary or longer term, what are your thoughts and feelings about how your reproductive options may be affected by hormones?*

  - *For trans feminine clients: If having genetically related children is important to you, have you considered banking sperm?*

  - *For trans masculine clients: If having genetically related children is important to you, have you considered banking eggs or embryos?*

# Gender-Affirming Surgery

Before we provide an overview of the types of gender-affirming surgical procedures, it is important to address the many important factors to explore with your clients.

## SURGICAL INTERVENTIONS: DISCUSSION TOPICS

Discussing some aspects of surgical preparation and recovery may help support your clients in feeling more informed and increase their capacity to give informed consent. While the conversation will vary based on each surgery, there are certain topics that are important to explore with clients regardless of the surgery. In this section, we name these topics along with examples of how to discuss them with your clients.

**Expectations.** It can be helpful to explore what a client knows about a particular medical procedure or surgeon. There is a great deal of information online that clients often rely on; however, this information is not always accurate or relevant to each client's circumstance. You may want to explore whether your client has been able to communicate directly with someone else who has firsthand experience undergoing the same medical procedure. If not, you can explore ways in which your client might be able to form such connections.

**Emotional preparation.** Surgery is a significant life event and often comes with a range of emotions. You can aid your clients in naming their hopes, expectations, and feelings regarding how they anticipate it will feel to undergo medical interventions. It is a normal human response to have concerns or questions prior to surgery. These questions should not be seen as ambivalence on the part of the client. Rather, as a provider, it is incumbent upon you to explore the questions and emotions in a way that normalizes the experience.

**Coping and relaxation skills.** Even though trans clients who pursue surgical interventions do so with the expectation of a positive or life-enhancing outcome, these interventions typically come with a level of physical and emotional stress. You will want to talk with your clients about coping skills, especially those that are available to them while they are in recovery. For example, if exercise is a client's main coping skill, it may be helpful to explore or teach other coping strategies the client can use while sedentary during recovery from surgery, such as relaxation skills (e.g., deep breathing, aromatherapy) that are physically passive in nature.

**Financial planning and concerns.** Some clients will receive paid time off from their employers, while others must find a way to support themselves through a time when they will not be able to work. You can help your clients think through ways to prepare so that the time they take off due to medical care does not result in financial crisis. Finances and maintaining employment can be highly stressful, so this is an area to explore with clients in case they need extra support.

**Medical stability.** Medical providers will have several concerns regarding a client's medical stability prior to surgery and how it will affect the person's capacity to undergo surgery, the surgical outcome, and recovery. Some possible concerns include cardiac health, factors that affect a person's response to anesthesia, weight and BMI, and substance use (particularly nicotine). In cases where medical stability is unclear, a number of tests may be required so that clients can receive medical clearance.

An increasing concern among trans clients is that surgeons are imposing BMI requirements for gender-affirming surgeries. There are different reasons for this, some of which have some medical basis, and others that unfairly ask trans people to live up to body ideals that are not asked of cisgender people seeking life-improving or lifesaving surgeries. If you have a client in this situation, you may have the opportunity to advocate for them, especially if surgeries are being framed as "elective" or "cosmetic" rather than medically necessary. You will want to talk to your clients about the impacts of BMI requirements and how they can manage these expectations in a way that is balanced and realistic. Some trans clients in this situation may develop eating disorder symptoms or engage in unhealthy behaviors for rapid weight loss in response to a surgeon's requirement. You will want to be aware of the ways in which messages about weight loss from physicians often contradict messages that are embedded in eating disorder treatment and recovery.

**Substance use.** It is helpful to discuss substances with clients and review what we know about physiological consequences of substance use, drug interactions with anesthesia, and considerations related to how some substances affect surgery, wound healing, recovery, and therefore eligibility for surgery. The extent to which substance use affects eligibility for surgery depends on the substance and the parameters set by the medical systems where your clients are accessing medical care. Many medical providers recommend reducing or stopping substance use two to three months before surgery to reduce stress in the body and ensure optimal health for healing and recovery. There is no true consensus regarding the cessation or reduction of most substances; in fact, this topic is quite controversial. There does, however, seem to be a clear consensus that all forms of nicotine should be avoided for one to three months prior to and following surgery. The medical rationale for this is that nicotine constricts blood vessels, slows wound healing, can result in more visible scarring, and is associated with surgical complications. Full abstinence from nicotine (including gum and patches in addition to cigarettes) must be in place before surgery. For clients who need to quit smoking, you may play a key role in supporting this process by providing smoking cessation resources or aiding your client in developing alternative coping skills.

There are several other important considerations that you may want to discuss with clients or recommend they discuss with their medical providers. Benzodiazapines and methamphetamines can increase tolerance to anesthesia and thereby increase the risk of awareness (i.e., waking up) during surgery. Some research suggests that drinking two or more alcoholic drinks a day could increase nonsurgical site infections and that cessation of alcohol use may decrease postoperative complications (Shabanzadeh & Sørensen,

2015). Although the role of cannabis in affecting the body's capacity to heal is unclear, some professionals consider it safer to switch from smoking cannabis to ingesting edibles or tinctures, as any smoke may interfere with healing.

**Recovery environment and logistics.** It can be helpful for clients to think through the logistics of their recovery and care plan, including basic life needs. This includes groceries, food preparation, laundry, cleaning, and transportation. There will be some things that clients can take care of ahead of time on their own (e.g., doing laundry, stocking up on essential groceries), but there are other things with which they will need assistance. On returning home from surgery there may be activities that the person comes to realize are difficult if not impossible (e.g., getting in and out of a bed that is elevated). Having a secure support system can help to alleviate the stress that accompanies these discoveries.

Clients undergoing surgical interventions must have a solid plan for aftercare, including physical and emotional support. Surgery should not be approached alone, and it is best to have a team of two or more people to help. You can help your clients to identify who in their lives will be reliable supports and what kind of support they need from each of those people. For example, there are certain people whom the client will only feel comfortable having visit or drop off meals, while there are others who are closer in nature and whom the client can rely on for more vulnerable needs (e.g., toileting in the initial stages after surgery, wound care). Transportation to and from presurgical visits, surgery, and follow-up visits is also important to secure ahead of time. Many people use an online platform so that friends and community members can sign up for different care shifts or tasks related to aftercare.

## SURGICAL INTERVENTIONS: OVERVIEW

Trans people who desire gender-affirming surgical interventions may choose to have some surgeries but not others (e.g., chest reconstructive surgery but not genital surgery). There are many reasons why clients desire or choose to have surgery, so it is important to refrain from making assumptions or generalizations. Some motivations for having surgery include gender affirmation, increasing physical comfort, reducing dysphoria, feeling a greater sense of ease and safety in public spaces, and increased comfort or fulfillment with intimacy or sexuality.

**Surgical interventions for trans feminine people.** People on the trans feminine spectrum, including trans women and male-assigned people who identify as nonbinary, may be interested in a number of different surgical interventions, including chest reconstructive surgery, genital reconstructive surgeries such as orchiectomy and vaginoplasty, facial feminization surgeries, and vocal cord surgery.

*Chest reconstructive surgeries for trans feminine people.* Chest reconstructive surgeries for trans feminine people are sometimes referred to as top surgeries, feminizing mammoplasties, or breast augmentation. We choose to avoid referring to these surgeries as breast augmentation surgeries because they are performed for different reasons than surgeries that cisgender women seek to augment their chest size or shape. For trans women and those on the trans feminine spectrum, these surgeries are not cosmetic; they are medically necessary in reducing gender dysphoria and, in many cases, can increase safety.

The WPATH SOC7 require **one letter** written by a mental health professional as a recommendation for feminizing chest reconstructive surgery. **A minimum of twelve months of feminizing hormone therapy is recommended** (and sometimes required, depending on the medical provider) to maximize breast growth and achieve a better aesthetic result. We acknowledge that not all people on the trans feminine spectrum desire hormone therapy, so this recommendation can become a barrier for people who want to have this surgery but do not want to be on hormone therapy.

*Genital reconstructive surgeries for trans feminine people.* Trans feminine people seeking genital surgeries will typically have two options: orchiectomy and vaginoplasty. An orchiectomy is a fairly straightforward procedure in which the testes are surgically removed. Removal of the testes means that the body no longer produces its own source of hormones sufficient to sustain bone health. An external source of hormones (for most people estrogen) will be required for life to retain healthy bone functioning. Vaginoplasty, on the other hand, is more involved in that it creates a vulva from existing body tissue.

Decision making regarding the procedure that will best align with or help meet each client's goals may involve consideration of the following factors: gender affirmation, appearance, physical comfort, increased safety, urinary function, sexual function (e.g., the ability to retain sensation or have an orgasm), and desired vaginal depth.

Preparation for vaginoplasty usually includes hair removal (electrolysis or laser hair removal depending on the quality/color of the hair) from the genital region. This requires regular visits over several months in order to ensure adequate removal, as hair follicles grow in cycles over time. Vaginoplasty is performed in one or two stages, depending on the surgical technique. The initial vaginoplasty procedure is an inpatient surgery that takes several hours. Initial recovery from vaginoplasty is typically six to eight weeks, but it may take up to six to nine months to fully heal or feel functional. Labiaplasty, a secondary surgery that aims to refine the clitoral hood and labia, is typically performed at least three months after the initial vaginoplasty procedure and requires an inpatient stay and about two to four weeks for recovery. Vaginoplasty necessitates lifelong dilation for maintenance of the vaginal opening and canal after surgery.

It is worth mentioning that there is an option of having a different kind of vaginoplasty when this better fits a person's goals or needs. This surgery is often referred to as shallow or zero-depth vaginoplasty, and it involves the removal of the penis and testicles and the creation of external genitalia only (clitoris, labia majora, and shallow vaginal canal) without the creation of a vaginal canal of more typical depth. This option is chosen by people who do not want to undergo a longer or more complicated surgery (sometimes related to medical stability), are not interested in vaginal depth for gender affirmation or penetrative sex, and do not want to perform lifelong dilation for maintenance. We encourage you to discuss this alternative with clients only when they bring it up as an available option that they are considering.

The WPATH SOC7 requires **two letters** from mental health professionals for these surgeries. Other requirements include one year of hormone therapy and a minimum of one year of living in a gender role that is congruent with the client's gender identity. There is some medical rationale for the one-year minimum requirement of hormone therapy: the client will get a sense of what it feels like to have testosterone suppressed. As mentioned previously, it is important to take into account the social and financial ramifications of having to meet the requirement of living or presenting in a certain gender expression prior to accessing surgery.

*Facial feminization surgeries.* There are a number of surgeries that would be classified as facial feminization surgeries (FFS). These surgeries aim to bring facial features into greater alignment with a person's sense of who they are and their gender identity by surgically altering bone or soft tissue in the face. FFS procedures are commonly geared toward changing the shape and appearance of the nose, forehead, cheeks, chin, jawline, and lips. Some examples are brow lift, rhinoplasty, lip augmentation, tracheal shave, and cheek implantation.

FFS procedures typically require an overnight stay (though tracheal shave is usually an outpatient procedure). Many people experience significant swelling and sometimes numbness after surgery. Although there are surgeries that are not as visible to others, having FFS can bring a great deal of attention to clients when they do not want it. It can also bring up many emotions as a person's facial appearance can be of great significance regarding one's identification.

It is important to keep in mind that access to insurance coverage for FFS, while increasing, is still very limited. Therefore, most clients will not be able to afford these surgeries unless they pay out of pocket. Advocacy efforts have been made for insurance companies to cover these surgeries, as they are medically necessary to treat gender dysphoria (as opposed to being cosmetic).

In chapter 1, we discussed body appraisal and how it affects trans clients. We highlight this concept again and urge you to be mindful and sensitive, as many discussions about facial features will reinforce narrow views of what masculinity and femininity are. Facial feminization procedures should be based on the client's interest, not on anyone else's opinion of whether their face "looks" feminine enough. In other words, when clients truly express a need and desire for these procedures, we will want to discuss and explore different options. However, the client should be the one to bring it up so that you do not inadvertently communicate to the client that they do not look appropriate or successful in their gender presentation.

*Vocal cord surgery.* This is typically sought by trans feminine clients who want a surgical intervention that will raise the pitch of their voice, which helps in having others perceive them as a woman or more feminine. To date, insurance plans typically do not provide coverage for this surgery. Many people who get this surgery travel outside of the country (commonly to Korea) for it.

**Surgical interventions for trans masculine people.** People on the trans masculine spectrum, including trans men and female-assigned people who identify as nonbinary, may be interested in a number of different surgical interventions, including chest reconstructive surgery, hysterectomy and oophorectomy, and genital reconstructive surgeries such as metoidioplasty and phalloplasty.

*Chest reconstructive surgeries for trans masculine people.* For trans men, trans masculine, and nonbinary people assigned female at birth, there are several options for chest reconstructive surgeries (also referred to as top surgeries). While in the past, it was believed that only trans men desired these surgeries, more and more gender nonconforming people who may not necessarily identify as trans but do endorse gender dysphoria are seeking these surgeries. For example, there are people who are assigned female at birth who identify as butch women who have dysphoria relative to having a chest/breasts and can benefit from these surgical interventions. Unfortunately, in many health care systems, it can still be more challenging for those who do not endorse a binary gender identity to access these surgeries (and gender-affirming medical interventions in general).

Chest reconstructive surgeries change the contour and appearance of a person's chest. Some people have the goal of attaining a masculine-appearing chest, while others pursue this type of surgery to simply have a flat or neutral chest. During these surgeries, a certain amount of chest tissue and skin are removed, and the chest is then reshaped to create a more stereotypically "masculine" aesthetic. The surgical technique involved will vary based on the surgeon; a client's age, skin elasticity, and chest size; and a client's specific goals. There are two main options for those seeking these surgeries. The most common option is referred to as a "double incision" mastectomy and is appropriate for people with a moderate to large chest size. During this procedure, two incisions are made, excess tissue and skin are removed, and the nipple is removed and then reattached/resituated with stitches. This results in scarring that remains visible, though it may fade in color over time. The other is periareolar, circumareolar, or "keyhole" surgery for people who have a small to moderate chest size, in which excess tissue is removed via liposuction around the nipple. This procedure does not leave as much scarring.

It is worth mentioning that there are some clients (especially those who are nonbinary) who may be interested in having a chest/breast reduction rather than full mastectomy with chest reconstruction. Some people may also be interested in chest surgeries with no nipple grafts. Clients may want to explore these options, the pros and cons of each, the implications for how their gender is perceived by others, and how affirmed they will feel in their bodies based on which option they choose. Many trans masculine clients will not want to consider a reduction, so we suggest that you explore this option only if the client brings it up or expresses concerns about having a full mastectomy.

Chest reconstructive surgeries are typically outpatient surgeries. Most people will need about four to six weeks away from work, school, or other regular activities, and physical activity (e.g., exercise, lifting objects, driving) should be modified or limited for at least two to six weeks after surgery.

The WPATH SOC7 require **one letter** written by a mental health professional as a recommendation for masculinizing chest reconstructive surgery. Whereas hormone therapy is required or highly recommended for trans feminine people and related to breast growth from estrogen, **there is no hormone requirement for trans masculine people seeking chest reconstructive surgeries.**

*Hysterectomy and oophorectomy for trans masculine people.* Trans masculine people seeking a hysterectomy (removal of uterus, cervix, and fallopian tubes) or an oophorectomy (removal of ovaries) may have varying reasons or motivations. These motivations may include reducing gender dysphoria, cessation of menses, eliminating the need for preventative OB/GYN care, or reducing dosage of hormone therapy (i.e., testosterone). In addition, those having genital reconstructive surgeries (e.g., metoidioplasty or phalloplasty) with urethral lengthening or a vaginectomy will typically choose or be required to have a hysterectomy. In the past, it was believed that trans masculine people taking testosterone needed to have a hysterectomy in order to prevent uterine cancer; recent studies have not validated this claim (Asscheman, Giltay, Megens, van Trotsenburg, & Gooren, 2011). Therefore, clients who are having a hysterectomy based solely on the belief that it is necessary for cancer prevention will benefit from updated information. Some clients opt not to have surgery when learning it is not absolutely necessary for cancer prevention. Still others will want this surgery or these surgeries because having organs that are associated with being assigned female brings up dysphoria or discomfort.

Having a source of sex hormones is important for bone health. Therefore, if a client is interested in having a hysterectomy, it is recommended that they be on hormones (and be aware that they will need to stay on hormones) or keep their ovaries in order to maintain a source of sex hormones. In other words, some clients opt to get a hysterectomy without getting an oophorectomy. Those who have both surgeries will need to be on hormone therapy of some kind for life; this is typically testosterone for people on the trans masculine spectrum, but there are nonbinary clients who do not desire masculinizing hormone therapy and may opt for estrogen replacement therapy instead.

There are some important fertility considerations related to having a hysterectomy or oophorectomy. If a trans masculine or nonbinary person chooses to have a hysterectomy, they will no longer be able to carry or give birth to a child. However, if they choose to keep their ovaries intact, the person maintains the reproductive option of later retrieving genetic material (i.e., eggs) for assisted reproduction with another/surrogate carrier.

As of now, the WPATH SOC7 ask for **two letters** from mental health professionals in order for a client to be recommended for a hysterectomy. In addition, twelve continuous months of hormone therapy is recommended as appropriate to the client's goals. For some clients, this will not be in line with their gender identity or goals and should be discussed with their medical provider(s).

*Genital reconstructive surgeries for trans masculine people.* Options for genital reconstructive surgeries (often referred to as "lower surgeries" or "bottom surgeries") include metoidioplasty and phalloplasty. As a note, though some medical providers, insurance companies, and WPATH SOC use terms such as "sexual reassignment surgery" or "genital/gender confirmation surgery," we do not use these terms because they reinforce genital determination (i.e., that genitals are the sole determinant of sex or gender) and suggest that those who do not have these surgeries cannot be affirmed in their gender identities. People often choose these surgeries based on their personal goals, which may include increased gender affirmation, increased ease or safety accessing public spaces such as restrooms, and increased sexual function/pleasure. Decision-making considerations for which surgery is most fitting for a particular client include appearance, function, complication rates, and emotional benefits. The number of options and choices may feel overwhelming for clients. You can encourage them to speak to their surgeons so as to understand available options and to explore the emotional components of these decisions with you. Furthermore, these surgeries are inpatient procedures and the length of hospital stays varies based on the medical system, surgeon, or specific surgery. Your clients will need to take these factors into account when coming up with their recovery plan.

Metoidioplasty (sometimes referred to as "meta") is a procedure in which existing tissue in the genital region is used to create a phallus (about four to five centimeters long) by releasing the suspensory ligament that holds the clitoris in place and cutting away surrounding tissue, thus bringing the clitoral tissue forward. This may be done with or without urethral lengthening, a procedure in which the existing urethra is lengthened and routed through the phallus with the goal of making it possible for the person to urinate while standing. Metoidioplasty can be a series of surgeries depending on client goals and the surgical technique employed.

Phalloplasty involves taking tissue from a different part of the body (the donor site is typically the radial forearm or anterior cruciate ligament of the thigh) to create a phallus, performing microsurgery to connect blood supply and sensory nerve connections, and taking a skin graft from the (other) thigh to cover the initial donor site. Phalloplasty is a series of surgeries performed in stages; therefore, your clients will have to prepare for several rounds of surgery and recovery that are spaced out over one to three years. This also means more hospital stays, more time off work, multiple co-pays (possibly greater financial strain), and more recovery periods in which assistance from others is needed. Phalloplasty can also be done with or without urethral lengthening. Typically, urethral lengthening is a factor that can increase the rates of surgical/urinary complications. For this reason, some people choose to have metoidioplasty or phalloplasty without urethral lengthening.

In addition to urethral lengthening, there are a number of other associated surgeries or procedures related to having metoidioplasty or phalloplasty. These include vaginectomy (removal of the vaginal canal or closing of the opening), scrotoplasty (creation of a scrotal sac), scrotal implants (placement of implants in the scrotal sac), penile implant (an inflatable implant or semi-rigid rod that is placed inside the phallus to allow for erectile function), mons resection (removal of excess tissue), and glansplasty (the creation of a more typical-looking glans).

The WPATH SOC7 require **two letters** from mental health professionals for these surgeries. Other requirements include one year of hormone therapy and a minimum of one year of living in a gender role that is congruent with the client's gender identity. As has been discussed previously, the one-year requirement of social transition should be viewed in the context of each individual's life and transition-related goals. Being able to be out or socially transitioned in one's life can be a privilege; for some, it can raise safety concerns or threaten one's livelihood. We, as clinicians conducting surgical assessments and referrals, are more inclined to pay attention to informed consent—in other words, whether the person is aware of the risks and benefits of surgery and how it may impact their health and lives.

## OTHER GENDER-AFFIRMING MEDICAL INTERVENTIONS

The most common procedures that trans people seek for gender affirmation are hormones and surgery; however, there are additional interventions that may help trans people in making changes to their body or physical appearance in order to reduce dysphoria or increase a sense of comfort in their bodies or gender expression.

**Hair removal or implants.** Some clients will be interested in hair removal, and this is not typically covered by insurance unless it is considered part of the preparation for a genital reconstructive surgery such as vaginoplasty or phalloplasty. Otherwise, hair removal on other parts of the body is not typically covered. However, we have witnessed more recently that some insurance companies will accept a recommendation for facial hair removal (for trans feminine clients) and may approve this request on a case-by-case basis. Some clients will inquire about hair implants to address balding or otherwise change one's hair or scalp to support affirmation of one's gender identity. These procedures are costly and typically not covered by insurance plans.

**Vocal training.** The quality and pitch of a person's voice is often associated with gender. Although some clients will express distress or concern over their voice and how it "outs" them as trans to others, there are other clients who feel very comfortable with their voice as it is. We want to underscore the importance of centering the client's goals and avoiding commenting on or suggesting that the client's voice should somehow be different (higher or lower) based on their gender identity.

Trans masculine clients on testosterone will typically experience a drop in their vocal range, but some of these clients will want vocal or speech therapy to help with this adjustment. We have found this to be especially true for people who are vocalists. Trans feminine clients, on the other hand, will not experience a higher voice as a result of hormone therapy. Therefore, more often it is trans feminine spectrum clients who seek vocal or speech therapy.

# Fertility and Family Building

Several gender-affirming medical interventions will have an impact on fertility and family-building options. Some clients will be interested in exploring these options with you, while others will make it clear that they are not interested in family building. Some people choose to bank sperm or eggs; others may choose to have children before starting hormones or to go off hormones for a period of time in order to engage in these processes. Currently, these options are not available to clients who transitioned at such a young age that they never developed reproductive capacity that is achieved during the puberty associated with their sex assigned at birth. Ideally, fertility and reproductive considerations were discussed with those clients at the age at which they began medical interventions (e.g., gonadotropin-releasing hormones [GnRH], also known as puberty blockers).

Trans feminine clients who have undergone the puberty associated with their sex assigned at birth and have not had an orchiectomy may choose to temporarily pause or discontinue hormone use in order to bank sperm or contribute genetic material to a pregnancy (via a partner or surrogate). Those who choose this option will work with their medical providers to determine whether their sperm is viable (i.e., high enough sperm count and healthy sperm).

Trans masculine clients who have completed a puberty associated with their sex assigned at birth, have not had a hysterectomy, and discontinue testosterone use may be able to get pregnant or undergo an egg retrieval (for in vitro fertilization [IVF], surrogacy, or banking eggs or embryos), but, as with cisgender people, the success of these attempts is not guaranteed. Some trans masculine people choose to stop or pause hormones in order to reinitiate menses and the ability to reproduce. They may return to taking testosterone after completing this process. Keep in mind that assisted reproduction is costly and that many insurance plans do not provide coverage for fertility preservation.

When speaking with clients about reproductive options or fertility preservation, you will want to be aware of the long history of forced sterilization among trans communities. Some of these practices still exist today in countries outside the United States. For example, in some countries people who want to medically transition must become sterile before even accessing hormone therapy.

You will also want to be aware of your own thoughts, beliefs, or feelings about family building or reproduction and maintain sensitivity about these topics, as they may increase dysphoria for some clients. It is common for clinicians to have their own biases, including those that are informed by ageism, cissexism, heterocentrism, or the gender binary. For example, some trans masculine people who are interested in becoming pregnant may be met with confusion or disbelief because providers cannot reconcile why a person who identifies as male or masculine would want to go through an experience (pregnancy) that is so strongly associated with women. For some trans masculine people, the thought of carrying a child brings up dysphoria that may or may not affect whether they choose to go forward with trying to get pregnant, while others may not have dysphoria related to the idea. There are providers who believe that becoming a parent is something that all people do or should want, and this may make them hesitant to support younger people in having surgeries (e.g., orchiectomy, hysterectomy) that affect or remove reproductive options. Another bias to keep in mind is the classist assumption that family building will be financially accessible for everyone. Assisted reproduction such as IVF or even banking eggs or sperm, as well as adoption or surrogacy, is quite costly. When speaking with clients about these options, you will want to find the balance between helping your clients to be informed of their options and being mindful of which options are truly accessible to each particular client.

## Sample Questions for Gender-Affirming Surgeries

Here are some sample questions that you may use when working with trans clients seeking gender-affirming surgical interventions. (You can download this list at http://www.newharbinger.com/40538.) Our rationale for asking specific questions is not to look for "right" answers but rather to invite a dialogue that can highlight where clients may need assistance exploring these aspects of their decision making or goals.

**Questions related to surgeries in general:**

- Where have you been able to access information about this surgery?

- What do you hope to get from having this surgery?

- How might you feel different in your body or life?

- What is your understanding about how you will need to prepare for surgery?

- What do you know about the recovery process?

- How do you expect this surgery will shift how you see yourself? How others see you or relate to you? How you will be treated in the world?

- What kinds of concerns or questions do you have about having this surgery?

- If you have had surgery in the past, how did that go?

- How might this surgery affect the aspects of your life related to dating, sex, or intimacy?

- Are you aware of the impact of substances on your healing process from surgery? (Be sure to ask about smoking/nicotine, including e-cigarettes.)

- For some surgeons, BMI (or weight) is a factor in determining readiness for surgery. Do you have any concerns about this?

- How might having this surgery affect your work, school, or finances?

- What kinds of financial preparations do you have to make in order to lessen financial or work stress through this process?

- Who is going to take care of you after surgery? How much information do they have about the surgery and recovery process? Have you discussed the specific kinds of help you will need from them?

- Who in your life may be able to help with some basic tasks or everyday responsibilities, such as laundry, shopping, or cooking?

- Who can you turn to if you are having a hard time and need emotional support after surgery?

- If you are used to being very active and it is a main coping strategy for you, what other coping strategies can you rely on?

- Are you aware that most surgeons require you to go off hormones for a period of time before certain surgeries? What information or resources do you need to prepare for this, including the possibility that dysphoria may temporarily increase while off hormones?

## Questions specific to feminizing chest surgeries:

- One year on hormones is a typical recommendation prior to having this surgery. Do you have any concerns about this?

- Is there anything that you have done to try to get a sense of what chest size would feel right for you, and how might you communicate that with your surgeon?

- What is your understanding of the scarring that will result from chest reconstructive surgery?

- What is your understanding about nipple sensation, and how do you feel about it?

## Questions specific to masculinizing chest surgeries:

- What is your understanding of the scarring that will result from chest reconstructive surgery?

- What is your understanding about nipple sensation, and how do you feel about it?

- Chest feeding: This may or may not apply to you, but if you are interested in having genetically related children, are you aware that chest/breast feeding will not be an option after top surgery?

## Questions specific to hysterectomy (and oophorectomy):

- Some people choose to have a hysterectomy but keep their ovaries intact for various reasons, such as protecting bone health or preserving reproductive options. Is this something you want to explore or consider?

- If you choose to have an oophorectomy (removal of ovaries), you will no longer have an endogenous source of sex hormones, which is important for protecting bone health. This means that you will need to commit to taking hormone therapy of some kind for life or until older adulthood. Do you have any concerns about this?

## Questions specific to orchiectomy:

- Do you think that orchiectomy is the only genital reconstructive surgery you will want? If you think you may want to have vaginoplasty in the future, have you expressed this to your doctor or surgeon?

## Questions specific to metoidioplasty:

- Are you interested in urethral lengthening? How does this fit or not fit with your goals?

- Are you interested in a vaginectomy? How does this fit or not fit with your goals? (This may or may not be a choice depending on the surgeon and technique.)

- Are you aware of the number of surgeries and recovery periods that may be involved in having metoidioplasty and the time you will need to take off from work or school? How do you think this will affect your life in the next one to three years?

## Questions specific to phalloplasty:

- Are you interested in urethral lengthening? How does this fit or not fit with your goals?

- Are you interested in a vaginectomy? How does this fit or not fit with your goals?

- Are you aware of the hair removal (typically electrolysis) that is required for your graft donor site (arm or leg)?

- Are you aware of the physical therapy that is required for you to return to full range of motion/function at your donor site (arm or leg)?

- Are you aware of the number of surgeries and recovery periods that may be involved in having phalloplasty and the time you will need to take off from work or school? How do you think this will affect your life in the next one to three years?

### Questions specific to vaginoplasty:

- What do you know about the hair removal process prior to vaginoplasty, and do you have any specific concerns about this?

- What do you know about the need to perform dilation in order to maintain results from vaginoplasty, and do you have any specific concerns about this?

- Are you aware of the different options in terms of surgical staging, timeline, and different periods of surgical preparation and recovery? How do you think this will affect your life in the next one to three years?

### Questions specific to facial feminization surgeries (FFS):

- Changes to facial appearance can vary considerably after having FFS, with some changes being subtle and others being more noticeable or significant. What are your goals, questions, or concerns related to having this/these procedure(s)?

- Changes in facial appearance may bring about strong or different reactions from people in society. How do you imagine you will navigate the changes related to how others perceive you?

## Writing the Letter: General Recommendations

The *conversation* you have with your client about informed consent is often far more important than the letter you will write, which is simply documentation of the key information gathered during the conversation. There are aspects of your conversation that you will not include in the letter, such as an exhaustive history chronicling every detail of someone's gender or mental health over their lifetime. Having a letter template (which is often requested by clinicians new to this work) is not the same as building skills in effectively discussing or assessing your client's needs or concerns.

When writing letters, it is always important to be flexible and adjust your style as appropriate to meet the needs of each client. Although there is no "right" way to write such a letter, we offer general guidelines to help you develop your own style. (You can download this list at http://www.newharbinger.com/40538.) Some of these guidelines are a review of what we have discussed thus far in the chapter, while others are related to more practical concerns or logistics.

### Writing Letters for Gender-Affirming Medical Interventions: General Guidelines

- There are very few medical procedures that require a mental health evaluation. Imagine having to get an assessment for a knee replacement surgery in order to confirm that you really experience pain when walking. It is important to keep this in mind and be sensitive as you ask clients to talk about their thoughts, feelings, and decision-making process regarding the medical intervention(s) they are seeking.

- Your role is to assess a client's understanding of the requested medical intervention. As a mental health provider, you are tasked with assessing whether your client has the capacity to make an informed decision about their medical care and whether mental health concerns are "reasonably well controlled" so as not to interfere with their medical care or capacity to care for themselves. We do not ask for early childhood likes or preferences, and the answers would not change whether or not we would provide the letter or recommendation. However, if a client chooses to share this information, we can provide an experience in which they feel heard and affirmed.

- A diagnosis of gender dysphoria is typically required to obtain insurance coverage for gender-affirming medical care. Many trans people do not agree that their gender identity is a mental health problem. Shifting the frame away from one of pathology, you might say that much of the dysphoria a client experiences is a result of a hostile and nonaccepting environment, rather than an internal state.

- We advocate drafting a letter and sharing it with the client so that they can review it before sending it to a surgeon or insurance company. This is a way to make the process more collaborative. Based on the client's feedback, you can make necessary changes or corrections and then ask where and to whom the letter should be sent and how many copies the client needs.

Your letter should include the following components:

- Identifying information: name, date of birth, gender identity, pronouns. Be sure to ask your client how they would like to be referred to in the letter (e.g., first name, Mr., Ms., Mx.).

- The name associated with the client's insurance plan (if the client is using insurance to access care). Include that name *once* at the top of the letter and thereafter use the client's name (the name they go by). For example: "Karlina Crosby (legal name: Carl Crosby), DOB 12/12/1973."

- Other client information: age, race/ethnicity, sex assigned at birth, gender identity, where the person lives, if the person is working or in school, etcetera. This can be one to two sentences.

- A statement that indicates the nature of your professional relationship with the client. If this an ongoing therapy client, how long have you been working with them? Is the client meeting with you solely for the purpose of assessment/recommendation and getting a letter?

- A brief description of who you are as a clinician, where you work, and your experience working with transgender and gender nonconforming clients.

- The name of the medical intervention(s) the client is seeking, including naming the specific surgery (e.g., phalloplasty as opposed to genital reconstructive surgery).

- The client's report of perceived risks and benefits of the requested medical intervention.

- Gender dysphoria diagnosis (include both ICD and DSM codes). It is respectful to be transparent and let the client know that you are putting this diagnosis in the letter in order to justify medical necessity. You may want to add a sentence or two that describes the dysphoria and its impacts on the client's life as related to the client's goals for medical transition or sense of self/gender. This information may not always be required.

- A *relevant/brief* statement regarding milestones related to gender or transition, such as when the client started socially transitioning (based on whatever that means to them), initiation of hormone therapy (if applicable), and other relevant medical procedures/surgeries (e.g., "had top surgery in August 2012").

- A statement about the client's mental health or relevant history, including if the person is on any medications to treat mental health concerns. If there is a significant mental health history, it is helpful to name the diagnosis and demonstrate that the concerns are reasonably well controlled and how. For example: "Karlina reports a lifelong history of mild depression, but she reports that since transition the symptoms have reduced considerably and do not interfere with her functioning. These symptoms are managed with medication and psychotherapy. All mental health concerns are reasonably well controlled."

- A statement indicating that you have evaluated substance use and determined that there are no indicators that the client's substance use is a significant problem or would interfere with medical treatment.

- A clear, strong statement about the client's capacity to give informed consent (e.g., "Karlina is aware of and able to articulate the risks and benefits of the requested surgery/procedure/service and has the capacity to give informed consent").

- A statement about the person's overall capacity to cope with stress or indications of resilience.

- You may opt to include the WPATH SOC7 criteria and how they apply to the client (though many of the above components demonstrate that the client meets the WPATH SOC7 criteria). Be sure to use the criteria corresponding to the specific procedure/service the client is requesting. Make a clear, strong statement that indicates you believe the client is an appropriate candidate for the requested service/procedure and that the surgery is medically necessary.

## CASE EXAMPLE. Trans-Affirming Letter Writing: *Working with Vivian*

*Vivian (she/her/hers) is a forty-four-year-old multiracial trans woman who is interested in having an orchiectomy. She meets with Finn, a Black nonbinary clinician, to get a letter to submit to her surgeon and insurance company. Vivian has had previous experiences meeting with mental health professionals in order to get a letter to support gender-affirming medical interventions, including hormone therapy and facial feminization surgery.*

*In discussing Vivian's history of accessing gender-affirming medical care, Finn learns that Vivian meets all the WPATH criteria for genital reconstructive surgeries. She has been on hormones for over ten years, she has the capacity to give informed consent, and her depression is well controlled through medication and exercise. She is able to articulate the risks and benefits of having an orchiectomy. She is also aware of how having an orchiectomy affects reproductive options and that it could affect sexual functioning. One of the benefits she names for having an orchiectomy is that she will no longer have to take an androgen blocker.*

*Finn explores whether the gender dysphoria diagnosis is accurate for Vivian. She reports that she has gender-related distress and discomfort that is motivating her to seek an orchiectomy. Finn documents this in the letter and includes that Vivian reports a longstanding history of gender dysphoria. Finn, who is conscious to only ask questions that are relevant or speak to the WPATH SOC7 (because the surgeon is requiring adherence to these criteria), includes the gender dysphoria diagnosis in the letter and chooses not to ask additional intrusive questions about Vivian's gender history. See the following example of the letter that Finn wrote for Vivian.*

To Whom It May Concern:

I am writing this letter at the request of Vivian Alvarez (pronouns: she/her/hers), DOB 04/22/1975, who is seeking genital reconstructive surgery (orchiectomy) under your care. It is my professional opinion that Vivian is an appropriate candidate for this procedure from a mental health perspective.

My qualifications to make such a recommendation include a PsyD in clinical psychology, specialized training and over ten years of experience in working with transgender and gender nonconforming populations, and continuing education in gender diversity. I follow the WPATH Standards of Care 7 (SOC7) as flexible guidelines in my approach to working with transgender and gender nonconforming individuals.

Vivian is a forty-four-year-old trans woman who is employed full-time as a hospice nurse. She lives with two roommates in Long Island, NY. Vivian reports a longstanding history of gender dysphoria relative to being assigned the male sex at birth and meets criteria for gender dysphoria (DSM-5 302.85; ICD-10 F64.1). Vivian hopes that having an orchiectomy will improve overall well-being, including physical, emotional, and interpersonal aspects of her life.

Vivian can clearly articulate reasons for desiring surgery, risks and benefits, and the implications of this procedure on her gender presentation and life. We discussed Vivian's aftercare plan, and she reported that her girlfriend and two roommates will be primary caregivers for both physical and emotional support. In addition, Vivian has a very supportive work environment and is planning on taking adequate time off to recover from surgery.

Vivian demonstrates adequate insight, judgment, and decision-making capacity. Vivian has a history of mild depression that is well controlled with medication and regular exercise. She has many positive coping resources, including a spiritual practice and community.

Vivian meets the following the WPATH SOC7 criteria:

1. Persistent, well-documented gender dysphoria

2. Capacity to make a fully informed decision and to consent for treatment

3. Age of majority in given country

4. Medical and mental health concerns are reasonably well controlled

Please feel free to contact me if you have further questions or would like to verify the information provided in this letter. I can be reached at (212) 555–1212 or at drfinn@email.com.

Sincerely,

Finn Triloquis, PsyD

License # PSY 020202 (NY Board of Psychology)

# Conclusion

In this chapter, you learned about gender-affirming medical interventions and key topics to discuss with clients related to providing a letter for these interventions. Although we highly encourage you to seek consultation from an experienced provider when you are new to the role of letter writing, the recommendations provided here may serve as a foundation for your learning process. In chapter 13, we address the benefits of engaging in interdisciplinary care.

---

## Going Deeper: Questions for Clinicians and Clients

### Questions for Clinician Self-Reflection

1. How do I manage the reality of being in a gatekeeping role? Am I aware of any anxiety that might influence me toward being paternalistic with clients or avoiding the responsibility of having necessary conversations with clients?

2. How do I feel about being in the role of discussing medical interventions with trans clients?

3. How do I feel about the possibility that I may have to advocate for a client if their doctor(s) or surgeon(s) disagree with my recommendation/letter indicating that the client is appropriate for the requested medical intervention(s)?

4. From whom can I seek professional consultation to have them review the letters I write while I am still new and in the process of learning?

### Questions for Client Exploration

1. Are you aware of what kinds of information or documentation your doctor or surgeon wants in order to provide the medical intervention(s) you are requesting?

2. How do you feel about the fact that I might need to include a diagnosis of gender dysphoria in the letter? How might this diagnosis fit or not fit for you?

3. *(For clients who are meeting with you just for assessment or a letter:)* How do you feel about being in a position in which you have to meet with a mental health provider to get a letter/recommendation for medical interventions?

4. *(For ongoing therapy clients who are now asking you for an assessment or a letter:)* How does the fact that I am in a position to write this letter for you affect how you feel about our relationship? How might it affect how comfortable you feel sharing with me?

---

# CHAPTER 13

# Collaborate with Interdisciplinary Providers and Trans Communities

As discussed in chapter 6, collaboration with multiple providers and community resources is often necessary to provide the most trans-affirming care. Some of you may be more accustomed to this kind of interdisciplinary work than others. No matter what your experiences are in working with providers across disciplines, there are unique facets to interdisciplinary care in trans health. In this chapter, you will learn more about how to engage in interdisciplinary work in ways that facilitate empowering experiences for trans clients and may entail advocacy on your part as a clinician.

## Interdisciplinary and Collaborative Care

As you consider the types of interdisciplinary providers with whom you will work in trans health, you may think about models of consultation. Consultation models are helpful guides, as they can be general enough to frame how you work with various types of medical providers, employers, school providers, legal providers, and even religious/spiritual leaders and community members (Ducheny, Hendricks, & Keo-Meier, 2017). Let's take a look at a potential model to guide your collaborations and consultations with providers across disciplines, and then look at these various providers more specifically.

### Trans-Affirming Consultation and Collaboration Model

Consultation models provide guidelines for how someone with specialized training and experience (the consultant) works with other collaborators (consultees) in an overall consultation (process). There are numerous consultation models that exist, which often are theoretically grounded or based in a specific setting. For instance, behavioral consultation models focus on exploring behavioral changes, and school consultation models guide providers in how to work with school systems. Consultation models are triadic, in that the consultant, consultee, and client are involved in the consultation. You may provide consultation with schools because of your work with trans adolescents. In these cases, you are the consultant, the trans adolescent is the client, and the school personnel are the consultees. No matter the consultation model you are working with, you likely will have to make some changes to make the model you use fully trans-affirming.

## General Guidelines for Trans-Affirming Consultation

- The goal of any consultation is to assess how trans-affirming or trans-informed people in the triadic roles are. When there is an identified gap in any of these, the consultant may take a role of educator and/or advocate.

- Consultees with the best of intentions may have significant gaps in their knowledge and may need supplementary resources and/ or education (e.g., trans-affirming webinars, podcasts, articles, codes of ethics).

- Be sure to consider not just your consultee (e.g., endocrinologist), but also other staff who interact with trans clients such as front desk personnel, nurses, or medical assistants who may be supporting the work of your consultee and include them in your recommendations or training efforts.

- Sometimes your clients have misinformation, internalized trans-prejudice, or difficulty advocating for themselves. Your role as a consultant is to help educate your clients on what they should expect from providers, gently challenge any misinformation, explore internalized trans-prejudice, and role-play self-advocacy scenarios.

## Interdisciplinary and Community Collaborators

As you read about the various providers you may consult or collaborate with in supporting your trans clients, consider the trans-affirming consultation model guidelines above. We suggest that you have a resource list that you update with the most current trans-affirming providers. Keep in mind that the standards of legal privacy and confidentiality apply as we work with providers across disciplines, so securing client-informed consent (e.g., signed release of information) is a necessary first step in any consultation and collaboration process.

## MEDICAL AND MENTAL HEALTH PROVIDERS

Trans clients may seek services from a variety of health care professionals, including primary care doctors, endocrinologists, surgeons, electrologists (for hair removal), and speech therapists. You also may refer to psychiatrists for medication management and assessment or other mental health clinicians.

In addition, there may be health care providers you may not typically think of as "gender specialists" working with your client on a social and/or medical transition. These providers may include proctologists, physician assistants, physical therapists, chiropractors, smoking cessation coaches, nutritionists, acupuncturists, and massage therapists. As you maintain your referral list, you may find that there are few providers who are well trained in trans-affirming practice. You may offer services to these providers, form a consultation group with interdisciplinary practitioners in order to continue learning trans-affirming approaches, or advocate affirming care when these professionals interact with your client. For instance, you may reach out to these providers to have conversations about how to best work with your trans client. Read the following case example about interdisciplinary consultation.

# CASE EXAMPLE. Providing Culturally Competent Care: *Working with Dara*

*Dara (she/her/hers) is a thirty-six-year-old Native American, two-spirit person who identifies as a "womyn." Dara doesn't like to be called a "woman" or "trans." Dara has been working with Maria (she/her/hers), an African American counselor, for three months. Dara has decided she would like to have feminizing mammoplasty. Dara shares she doesn't like the idea of "going into a plastic surgery facility where everyone's just getting a boob job." Maria explores Dara's concerns in session. Dara shares the deeply spiritual nature of this surgery and how she would like her surgeon to understand her identity as a two-spirit womyn. One of Dara's concerns is that she would like to embark on a sage ritual before the surgery and would like specific music from her tribe to be playing during the surgery. Maria validates Dara's concerns and shares that she has a list of surgeons that she thinks are trans-affirming based on her conversations with them. There is one particular surgeon (consultee) who Maria (consultant) thinks would be a good fit for Dara (client), and Maria asks Dara if she can contact this surgeon to share about the importance of Dara's gender identity and religious/spiritual identity. Dara agrees and signs a release of information for Maria to speak with this surgeon, Dr. Sinha.*

*When Maria speaks with Dr. Sinha, she talks about Dara's concerns about accessing surgery under Dr. Sinha's care. Dr. Sinha responds that she would prioritize Dara's spiritual and gender identities in the patient intake. Maria also asks about how office staff, nurses, and other medical professionals might interact with Dara. Dr. Sinha says that her staff has completed cultural competency training, but she is glad to bring Dara's concerns to the next staff meeting. Maria shares a recent article about two-spirit womyn with Dr. Sinha. Dr. Sinha tells Maria that if Dara would like to do the sage ritual, it would need to be prior to entering the building due to the inflammable medical equipment within the facility. Dr. Sinha is open to Dara's request to have her tribe-specific music playing. When Maria meets with Dara next, Maria shares about her consultation with Dr. Sinha. Dara feels more optimistic about getting her needs met and respected in surgery, and she decides she would like to meet with Dr. Sinha for an initial surgery consultation. Maria plans to be available to Dr. Sinha for any ongoing questions or concerns as Dara accesses the surgery.*

In this consultation, Maria gains a clear understanding of Dara's needs and is able to work with the surgeon to ensure that Dara feels safe in moving forward with surgery. Maria had a list of affirming providers she knew well enough to find a person who would be sensitive to Dara's needs.

## EMPLOYERS

As a clinician, you may also be working collaboratively with employers who may need help making their work environments more trans-inclusive and affirming. These situations can provide challenging ethical circumstances in that you, as a provider, are holding multiple roles—being an advocate for your client while also protecting their confidentiality. Some clients will benefit from learning about existing nondiscrimination protections and human resources supports within their work setting.

In other instances, a client's employer may request that you provide a trans or larger cultural competency training for the client's coworkers, managers, or administrators. Although there certainly may be a specific reason for you to provide the training yourself, such as a lack of trans-affirming consultants in your area or an urgent need for the training, there are times when referring to another consultant may mitigate dual role challenges. Regardless of who provides the training, it is crucial to thoroughly discuss trainings with your client, as well as the challenges and opportunities that may exist when you provide training to their employer or colleagues.

## CASE EXAMPLE. Coming Out in the Workplace and Consultation: *Working with Marques*

*Marques (he/him/his) is a forty-one-year-old Black trans man who is a college professor. Marques worked with a mental health practitioner when he began a medical transition but did not feel "safe" addressing issues concerning his career and workplace transition. Six months ago, he began seeing a different counselor named Julio (he/him/his), a Latino cisgender man and social worker, to explore issues of disclosing his trans identity to his coworkers at a large public university in the Southeast.*

*Julio explores the experiences Marques had with his previous provider, and Marques says that any time he brought up "going public" with his name and pronouns, his provider would say "it will be okay" and would ignore his fear. Marques shares that he felt minimized and invalidated. Julio validates his feelings and explores his fears of disclosing his gender identity at work.*

*Marques quickly says, "Even though I am tenured and a full professor, I am still scared I could get fired or my department chair can give me all of the bad classes to teach because my student evaluations will go down if people 'know' who I really am." Julio validates these fears and reassures Marques that he can decide the timeline he would like to proceed with in sharing with his university about his gender identity. Marques says that he "needs about a year to figure things out."*

*Julio continues working with Marques during that year, and shares that he has provided many educational consultations with this particular university on trans-affirming work environments. Julio also says he is familiar with the chief diversity officer and the director of the Equal Employment Office. During their sessions, Julio supports Marques in setting his own pace for disclosure at work, while he also continues to discuss options for either Julio or someone else to work with the university, human resources, and Marques's department and program on Marques's behalf. Marques begins to "see there are lots of options" for him and "feels like [he] is ready to disclose." After six months, Marques asks Julio to recommend a trans-affirming consultant whom he can connect with the university. Julio refers Marques to Anna (consultant), who works with the university (consultee) to ensure Marques (client) is supported in his employment and knows his rights as he shares his social and medical transition at his university. Along the way, both Julio and Anna share various legal and employment resources relevant to university settings, as well as referrals to other professionals who provide training and consultation regarding trans concerns.*

This case example demonstrates centering the counseling on the client's needs. It also addresses the use of consultation and the need to have contact with people who can assist when you have an ongoing clinical relationship with your client.

## SCHOOL PROVIDERS

You may also encounter ethical and legal issues, similar to those that arise in a work setting, when consulting with schools on behalf of your clients. An important place to begin consultations is with the relevant ethical codes and best practices statements that exist within a school discipline. For instance, school psychologists and school counselors are often members of organizations that have written statements on the ethics of creating trans-affirming spaces within schools. Similar guidelines and scholarly training may exist for school educators and administrators, but there is less ethical and legal guidance available for other school staff aside from mandatory reporting related to abuse and suicidality.

When consulting with schools, you may work with individuals (e.g., teachers) or more broadly with a campus community (e.g., faculty). There may even be an opportunity to work across a school district in providing trainings, advocacy, and guidance on how to improve policies such as bathroom access and the use of names and pronouns on class rosters. The consultant skills of conducting prior research of trans student support networks and a strong assessment of the gaps in and sources of trans-affirming practices and policies are most effective. In chapter 18, we will discuss further considerations when working with school personnel who support children and adolescents.

## LEGAL PROVIDERS

Legal issues can significantly influence a trans person's experience. You may work with legal providers if your clients need the services of trans-affirming attorneys for legal name or gender marker changes. You may also work with legal providers when providing testimony on court cases related to custody of children of trans parents or when a client you are working with experiences employment or housing discrimination.

Working with legal providers can be intimidating for your trans clients, and you may feel similarly! Reading and staying up to date on local, state, and federal laws, as well as having access to trans-affirming legal resources, can help quell some of the anxiety that can come with working with the legal system. Lambda Legal, the Transgender Law Center, the National Center for Transgender Equality, and other LGBTQ-affirming non-profit organizations have compiled resources related to local, state, and federal policies that are easy to understand in plain language.

## RELIGIOUS AND SPIRITUAL LEADERS

Although working with legal providers has a unique set of stressors, depending on your belief system and feelings about religion and spirituality, you may experience similar concerns when consulting with religious and spiritual leaders. For many clinicians, this stress may come from not being familiar with religious texts and dogma related to what religious or spiritual traditions may "say" about trans people. Depending on the client's faith system, there may or may not be a conception of sin related to gender identity. Some people are raised to value all gender identities and expressions, including their own. It will be important to check your own assumptions about various religious views about trans people. Having access to resources from religious communities that are trans-affirming means you can consult with others and do not have to be the "expert"—but rather know how to access the experts when needed.

We encourage you to lean into the religious and spiritual worlds when working with trans clients, regardless of your beliefs. For some trans people, religious and spiritual coping is an important source of resilience. In addition, across the long history of trans communities, as we talked about in chapter 3, trans people have held unique and important roles in sacred rites and rituals in numerous cultures. Knowing how to work effectively in a trans-affirming way with religious and spiritual leaders can be immensely beneficial for your clients, and in support of the legacy and lineage of trans communities and their long traditions of spirituality.

## COMMUNITY MEMBERS

As a clinician, you will also work collaboratively and in consultation with community members. This work might be as simple as knowing the best trans-affirming support groups, mentors, and leaders within the trans community. However, we encourage you to go beyond just having an updated list of resources. Knowing these leaders and community members—including their strengths and growing edges—can help you refer more effectively to resources that are a good fit for your trans clients. For example, you may not want to refer a nonbinary youth of color to a support group that traditionally is attended by older White women who identify as transsexual. It's not that there aren't overlapping issues both groups might share in common, but generational cohorts (as we will discuss in chapter 17) can have very different needs, challenges, and goals that influence how helpful a support group may be for an individual, especially when that support group has not traditionally been focused on the needs of nonbinary individuals.

Knowing and being personally familiar with the local trans leaders and community members can also help you track evolving trends, needs, and experiences that trans people are having where they live. Trans communities are often creative and develop significant resilience in response to oppression, as we discussed in chapter 9, so new support spaces and resources can evolve just as rapidly as anti-trans stigma can occur. Being connected to these community networks can also provide a space for mentoring. For instance, if you are working with a trans client who would like to remain married to their life partner but does not know anyone who has stayed in a relationship after social and medical transition, these partners can greatly benefit from a referral to people who might be willing to speak with them and share their experiences of staying in their relationship.

## CASE EXAMPLE. Facilitating Connections with the Trans Community: *Working with Timothie*

*Timothie (she/her/hers), a White, twenty-six-year-old trans feminine client, has been in counseling with Eliza (she/her/hers), a Mexican American clinician. Timothie presented with issues of depression, isolation, and feeling like an "outcast." For the past six months, Timothie had been working at a start-up company as a software developer and program coder. She had already made a social and medical transition about a year before beginning to work with Eliza, and the main counseling issues they have worked on have been related to Timothie's depression, which is unrelated to her gender identity. Timothie feels great about her gender identity, but has difficulty connecting with other people. She has a trauma history of abusive relationships, and she "just doesn't trust people"—but loves her job and the people with whom she works, who are "techy" like her. Eliza is familiar with some trans community members and leaders who not only have trauma histories, but also have found ways to thrive and talk openly about their stories. Eliza asks Timothie if she would be open to a one-on-one meeting with one of these community members who is a bit older than her but who also works as a coder in the software industry. Eliza is also aware of a local technology group called "Women Who Code," which is trans-inclusive and affirming, and she asks if she can refer Timothie to this group as well. This coding group gets together in small groups and codes together, as well as has larger gatherings with educational speakers. Eliza shares that she thinks the small group gatherings might be a good fit for Timothie to try out.*

In this example, Eliza is able to provide Timothie with referrals to community resources that have the potential to help Timothie develop healthy relationships. Eliza does not make the assumption that Timothie's depression is related to her trans identity. This is useful for ensuring that Timothie and Eliza are able to develop and maintain a trusting clinical relationship.

## Conclusion

Consultation is an important role that you may provide to other health care professionals or communities that interact with your clients. When working with providers across disciplines, utilizing a trans-affirming consultation model that helps you identify gaps and strengths in trans-affirming service provision is helpful. In addition, being prepared to connect with a wide variety of trans-affirming providers, and even provide education and advocacy for those who are just learning about being trans-affirming, is an important role. In the following section we address various aspects of counseling and psychotherapy, beginning this discussion in chapter 14 with information about individual counseling.

# Going Deeper:
# Questions for Clinicians and Clients

## Questions for Clinician Self-Reflection

1. What are the gaps in my knowledge of trans-affirming providers, and what steps can I take to address these?

2. What are the strengths in my knowledge of trans-affirming providers, and how can I share these strengths with other providers?

3. What will I do when I encounter a provider who is unaware of their limitations or is unaware that they are not being trans-affirming?

4. What are my own fears or anticipated challenges in collaborating with other providers who have a different set of skills, perspectives, or training backgrounds from my own?

5. How can I learn more about trans community members and leaders who can serve as affirming mentors and supports for trans clients?

## Questions for Client Exploration

1. How do you feel when you think about working with another provider as we continue to work together? What concerns, challenges, questions, or needs do you have?

2. What do you know about working with this [discipline-specific] provider?

3. What would be ideal for you in how your different providers communicate with each other about your care?

4. At work or school, do you feel like you are getting trans-affirming support?

5. How would you feel about talking to another trans person about this concern you are talking about? I have a list of people who might be able to help you and who have had similar experiences.

# PART 4

# COUNSELING AND PSYCHOTHERAPY

# CHAPTER 14

# Practice Affirming Individual Counseling

Like other clients, trans clients may seek support from a mental health provider for a variety of reasons that may or may not be related to gender or identity concerns (e.g., relational concerns, work stress, trauma, depression, personal growth). This chapter speaks to the concerns and dynamics that may arise when a trans client is seeking ongoing mental health services.

It is important to note that according to the WPATH SOC7 (Coleman et al., 2012), psychotherapy is **not a requirement** for those seeking gender-affirming medical services. At times it is recommended to ensure that a client's mental health symptoms are stable and do not interfere with the capacity to give informed consent or participate in one's own medical care. Before initiating counseling or psychotherapy with trans clients, you will want to consider a number of things, including goodness of fit and applying a trauma-informed lens.

## Goodness of Fit

As you may know from other clinical work, many factors affect goodness of fit. These include the client-therapist match in terms of personality and style, the therapist's proficiency with clinical skills, and logistical concerns such as location, office environment, and fees. An important issue to keep in mind is that there may not be an abundance of options for trans clients seeking providers who are affirming; in some cases, there may be only one such mental health provider who practices in their town, region, or even state. Therefore, at times, you will need to balance goodness of fit with the client's need for accessing services.

### Personality and Style

As with other clients, the personality match between a client and therapist can greatly influence the ease with which services are provided, as well as how much the client benefits from these services. You may want to reflect on the kinds of clients with whom you work best. You can consider examples of therapeutic relationships that have been successful, what you contributed to those relationships, and what qualities the clients brought. Having an awareness of these factors may help you in making conscious choices about which clients to work with or how you show up in the clinical encounters.

Some clients will want to work with a clinician who appears to be an "expert" in the field of trans health. These clients may want to see you as an authority figure, and they may be more likely to use terms of address that reflect this (e.g., "Dr. _____" instead of using your first name). In these cases, you will want to approach the work with humility while understanding that these clients may have a great need to feel a sense of trust in your expertise. While you can bring a great deal of knowledge to the interaction, you can also provide disclaimers such as "This has been my experience, but I always want to make space for the possibility that it could be different for you." You may lean toward a more formal stance or demeanor with these clients. On the other hand, there are clients who will feel more relaxed with a casual-feeling interaction. This may be the case if they are seeking a clinician who has a trans or nonbinary identity (i.e., an in-group affiliation). These clients may be turned off by an "expert" stance and will appreciate much more "realness" in the clinical interaction.

Sometimes it can be difficult to determine whether the relationship is a good match in the beginning, as trans clients may be understandably cautious in opening up to a new clinician. We recommend exhibiting warmth and a welcoming, patient stance. You will want to meet the client where they are and not try to rush the building of rapport or therapeutic alliance.

## Clinical Proficiency

Being a trans-affirming clinician does not necessarily mean having the skills to work with every client. We caution you against taking on a sense of overresponsibility for being able to treat every single concern that may arise. You will want to make sure that you identify the central concerns of the client and determine whether you are the best person to work with them.

One example of where this arises is in working with people at different ages or stages of development. A clinician who understands gender concerns but has no training in working with young children should not assume proficiency in working with trans or gender nonconforming children. There is, however, a great need for more clinicians who are skilled at working with trans youth. We encourage you to seek necessary training in childhood development and pediatric gender concerns so that you may meet this need in your communities.

Another example to consider is working with trans clients who have eating disorders. If you do not have training in treatment of eating disorders, you may want to seek training, make a referral to a trans-competent clinician with this skill set, or provide clinical consultation to a clinician who specializes in eating disorders so that they can be mindful and respectful of gender concerns. In summary, you will want to consider the whole person and whether you can provide services within your scope and clinical background.

## Location

Location concerns can become barriers for trans clients seeking mental health care. It is important to keep in mind that trans people experience a disproportionately higher rate of poverty and employment discrimination. We cannot assume it is easy for someone to take the time to travel to our offices or even afford transportation. We encourage you to consider ways in which you can be flexible in terms of the frame of counseling. This may include providing online counseling (with requisite training and licensure) for clients who live far away or have difficulty traveling to your office for any reason (e.g., cost, mobility concerns). This is especially helpful for clients who live in rural areas and do not have easy access to transportation. Most clinicians cannot provide services outside of the state in which they are licensed, so this must be a consideration.

## Office Environment

You will want to be mindful of all the cues in the environment that may signal to a trans client whether or not they are in a safe, inclusive space. If you work in an office suite with other health care providers, it is important to make sure other providers have a basic understanding of trans identities and are willing to communicate this to their clients should any problems arise in shared spaces (e.g., waiting rooms, restrooms). If you are unsure, this is an excellent place for inquiry, advocacy, and education. You may want to consider whether your office space is accessible for a wide range of people and bodies, including those with limited mobility. For example, is your space wheelchair accessible? How many steps are present? Can your chairs accommodate people with larger bodies? In this way, you can engage in active allyship to both trans people and people with disabilities (and those who live in these intersections). Chapter 19 discusses trans-affirming practice environments in more detail.

## Fee Setting

If you choose to do a significant amount of work within trans communities, it is important to be mindful about the effects of marginalization and how this may impact the ability to access services. While some trans clients have access to wealth or financial resources, others do not. You will want to be sensitive to this and challenge yourself to ask the question of what it means to profit from a group that is largely marginalized. We encourage you to think of ways to mitigate this dynamic. This may include setting aside a certain number of lower-fee or pro bono slots for those in greatest need; unfortunately, it is often trans clinicians who are expected to reduce their fees. If you are a cisgender clinician, making your services financially accessible is one way to demonstrate allyship. This may include donating a certain amount of profits to an organization that actively advocates for the needs of trans people. When we run consultation groups for therapists, we ask for an agreement that the therapists who are gaining knowledge and skills from participation in these groups (and thus increasing earning potential) set aside at least one low-fee slot for a trans client in need. Of course, we understand the need to get paid for valuable services and cover our expenses, so your ability to offer lower-fee or pro bono services will vary significantly based on who you are in the world and the kinds of power and privilege you possess.

## Applying A Trauma-Informed Lens

As described in the introduction and chapter 10, developing and applying a trauma-informed lens is crucial, even if trauma-focused work is not the presenting clinical concern or task of treatment. You will want to be sure to consider trauma broadly, including both "big T" traumas such as life-threatening incidents as well as the repeated, chronic microaggressions and slights that most trans clients experience on a daily basis (Nadal et al., 2012). It will be crucial for you to keep in mind that some trans clients will have already had prior negative interactions, ranging from hostile to dangerous, with mental health clinicians. Some of these harmful interactions happen within minutes during the first phone call or session. Even clients who have not had negative firsthand experiences may be worried about mistreatment because of what they have heard in their communities; just knowing stories of other trans people who have suffered mistreatment in clinical settings can impact a client's sense of safety and confidence in potential providers.

We use the metaphor of "walking a tightrope" to describe the double bind that trans clients face when seeking mental health services; this task involves managing their narrative so that they do not appear "too sick" or "too well" to the mental health provider. Trans clients may feel discomfort and have to perform a great deal of emotional labor in trying to figure out how they can share about their struggles and mental health concerns. On one hand, in order to gain access to gender-affirming medical services, trans clients must report having gender dysphoria and often feel that they have to be convincing in how this is affecting them in order to justify needing medical care. On the other hand, if they appear to be in too much distress, they may be deemed too unstable to receive necessary medical services. Walking a tightrope can also apply to clinicians, as you may feel that you are walking this tightrope with your client when you are dealing with restrictive systems of gatekeeping in the medical industry.

One unfortunate result of walking the tightrope is the backlash that may occur. Trans clients, having been greatly pathologized by mental health providers, may express a sentiment akin to saying, "I'm not crazy!" While we support the depathologization of trans identities and experiences, we are concerned that this kind of statement may reinforce a stigma about having mental health symptoms or mental illness, thus perpetuating ableism. This can often keep trans people who are struggling with mental health symptoms from getting the care they need. We want to find a way to communicate to our clients that there is nothing wrong with admitting they are struggling and asking for help.

# The First Interaction

The first interaction that a client has with you may set the stage for whether the relationship or treatment is successful. You will want to enter this first interaction with care and consideration. However, you also want to manage any anxiety that you might have about getting things "right." Being overly anxious or concerned about mistakes or trying to be the perfect trans ally is what may lead to the biggest errors while establishing rapport. Your clients will be able to pick up on this, and it may create greater discomfort for them. We suggest that you bring any discomfort or fear about working with trans clients to a trusted colleague, as talking through these concerns before interacting with a client may increase your awareness and reduce the likelihood of enacting harm.

The first encounter may be a client's phone call to you, but this is not always the case. It may occur before you ever talk to the client, such as when a client gathers information about you and your work when visiting your website. If you work for an agency or health care system in which you have other providers or staff completing triage, referral, or scheduling, you may not have had any interactions with the client until they are sitting face-to-face with you. It would be prudent to consider all aspects of your intake system to ensure that they are trans-inclusive, including training whoever is tasked with triage or intake.

You will have varying amounts of information about different clients, how they identify, what language is affirming to them, and what their goals are before you meet with them. Regardless of what you already know about the client (including what is provided in any paperwork that you have access to before the first encounter), we suggest that when you introduce yourself, you communicate an inclusive approach that takes into account the client's preferences and concerns.

You will want to come up with a way to open sessions that feels true to your clinical style while also making sure that you leave space for the client to lead and share what is most important to them in the moment. You may want to role-play or practice this with other clinicians so that you can become more familiar and comfortable with your initial greeting, as well as get feedback that can help you develop an introduction that fits for you and your client populations. If you meet with friends or family members of trans clients, they may be relieved to know that you have a trans-aware and affirming stance. Also, consider using greetings or introductions that reflect trans inclusivity for all your clients, not just trans clients, as gender inclusion benefits everyone and is a small intervention in a cis-centric world.

## Examples of Inclusive Introductions Between Clinicians and Clients

Example 1:

*Hi, my name is Bart Danzig, and I am a case manager here. I go by he, him, and his pronouns. From your intake paperwork, I have some sense of why you are here, but it would be helpful for me to hear directly from you what you need support with. And before we begin, I just want to make sure that I am clear on how you would like to be addressed. What name would you like me to use to refer to you? And what pronouns would you like me to use to refer to you?*

Example 2:

*Welcome to the clinic. My name is Dr. Zelda Sesame, and I'm a mental health provider who meets with clients seeking gender-affirming medical services. Before we begin, I want you to know that the general philosophy and approach of our clinic is one in which we try to support trans and gender nonconforming people in accessing whatever care they need in order to feel comfortable in their bodies and in the world. I will be asking you a number of questions today to help me determine recommendations or resources for you, the first of which is knowing the name you go by, pronouns, and what you think is important for me to know about why you are here today.*

# Assessing Presenting Concerns and Treatment Goals

Some trans clients seek care related to gender concerns, and some do not. We cannot emphasize this point enough. A common and understandable anxiety that trans clients have is the fear that no matter what they share, it will be construed as a gender concern. This is because clinicians often fixate on features of a person that stand out or are in some way different from societal norms or expectations. This may result in the therapist's creating a narrative according to the expectation that "all roads lead back to gender or trans identity" for trans clients. We recommend a balanced approach in which you listen for possibilities that a client's presenting concern may be related to gender while also refraining from manufacturing a connection between the presenting concern and gender identity that does not exist. Even if your client indicates during the first session that gender is a main topic that they would like to discuss with you, it is best to ask open-ended questions about how that concern is showing up in their life. A detailed gender history is not always necessary to understand a client's concerns. If a client states, "I am dealing with discrimination at work due to being transgender," it would be appropriate to ask about this concern and how it is affecting the client's day-to-day life. It would not be appropriate at this point to ask questions such as, "When did you know you were trans?"

As you assess your client's concerns, you may learn about other health care providers or professionals with whom they are working. Working with trans clients requires comfort and proficiency in providing interdisciplinary, collaborative care (refer to chapter 13) or concurrent therapy (refer to chapters 15 and 16 on relationship and group therapy). Obtaining a release for the exchange of information, where relevant, helps ensure continuity of care.

In listening to and centering your client's concerns, you may determine which courses of action are most appropriate for you to take and what other resources your client may benefit from. There may be a need for psychoeducation, gender-related counseling, treatment of non-gender-related concerns (some of which may be interfering with accessing gender-affirming medical interventions), building resilience and coping, and connecting to social support systems. There may be times when you find it appropriate to refer out to another mental health provider (e.g., if you do not possess skills related to treating the client's presenting concerns) or enlist the help of another provider (e.g., family therapist) as an adjunct form of treatment. Consider the case of Frannie, who is dealing with social anxiety that is interfering with her work life.

## CASE EXAMPLE. Dangers of Assuming Trans Presenting Issues: *Working with Frannie*

*Frannie (she/her/hers) is a thirty-one-year-old trans woman who identifies as HAPA, a term to describe being mixed race with Asian/Pacific Islander heritage. She is meeting with Floyd (he/him/his), a Latino gay male clinician at an LGBT community mental health clinic, for the first time. Floyd has read over the intake information provided by his colleague at the clinic, and from this he learns that Frannie is struggling with social anxiety and has had difficulty maintaining stable employment.*

*During the first session, Frannie talks about challenges with social anxiety, including assuming that others are judging her or that she is going to get fired. Floyd, in an attempt to show that he is an ally and is attuned to the concerns that trans clients face at work, makes an assumption and is too quick to respond. Before taking time to adequately listen to Frannie's concerns, he says, "This is very common for trans people, as workplaces can be stressful and you are probably feeling self-conscious about how people are responding to your gender." He then goes on to cite statistics about employment discrimination from a recent trans survey.*

*Upon hearing this, Frannie is confused. She had not shared any concerns about her gender, and she did not feel it was a significant factor at work. She feels that Floyd has the idea that all trans people are the same and that her concerns are not unique to her circumstances. She feels frustrated that Floyd did not take the time to listen to the history of her social anxiety, how it relates to familial norms of achievement and perfectionism, and the stress of being in a management role. If Floyd had taken the time to listen, he would have learned that her social anxiety and perfectionism increased more recently due to a disagreement with her father. Though we cannot say that gender has no bearing on Frannie's experiences at work, from Frannie's perspective her gender was an insignificant part of her concerns. She transitioned as a teen and navigated school and work successfully without many problems related to being trans. Frannie is now unsure as to whether she can utilize counseling, as she is worried about Floyd's being fixated on the fact that she is transgender.*

In this example, Floyd made an error by assuming that he knew why Frannie was having work-related problems. As a result, Frannie did not feel seen or heard. Instead, she felt that Floyd was only seeing her as a trans woman and not paying attention to her concerns. Floyd could have taken more time to gather background related to Frannie's presenting concerns, and he could have developed a treatment plan to address social anxiety and perfectionism. This case serves as a reminder that when working with trans clients, it is important to be aware of assumptions about the salience of gender and to center clients' needs and perspectives.

## Gender-Related Counseling

For trans clients who seek emotional support specifically related to gender concerns, having a space to talk through the complexities of gender (and societal reactions) can be powerful. Sharing one's experience with gender (and the ways in which the world has or has not been supportive) with an open-minded and empathic clinician can be a corrective experience for clients who have not felt seen or understood by others.

For clients who are in the process of gender exploration or who want to share their gender history or narrative with a clinician, we believe the best approach is to follow the client's lead and trust that they will share the most salient information when they are ready. If clients express a desire to discuss gender but have difficulty knowing where to begin, you can ask open-ended questions that demonstrate openness and attunement. You could ask, "What is coming up for you around gender?" or "What about your experience of gender is important for me to know?" This can be more respectful than approaching the client with a barrage of questions that may or may not be relevant or that the client may not be ready to discuss. A lifetime of gender-related experiences cannot be summarized in one session. It is important to refrain from communicating in subtle ways that narratives should be clear, linear, or succinct.

Keep in mind that gender can be difficult to talk about, especially for clients who have spent many years intentionally not doing so. It can be helpful to normalize nervousness or discomfort and stay attuned to how dysphoria may increase while talking about gender. Providing validation can be a powerful intervention, especially for clients whose gender has been denied or who have felt pressure to "convince" others their feelings or experiences are valid. Be careful not to privilege a person's verbal narrative, as not everyone has the same communication style or access to clearly articulate their feelings or experiences related to gender.

# Non-Gender-Specific Counseling Interventions

In this section, you will read about applications of theoretical approaches and treatment techniques to clinical work with trans clients. There is little research on empirically validated treatment approaches with trans clients. These learnings are based on clinical experience and consensus among the authors and colleagues in our professional communities. In this section, we will illustrate a few theoretical approaches to counseling with the same client.

## Relational, Psychodynamic, and Attachment-Oriented Approaches

Regardless of your theoretical orientation, the relationship between you and your clients is an essential element that influences the outcome of your clinical work. When working from a relational or psychodynamic approach, you will want to be especially attuned to the meaning of the interactions with your clients. You may want to consider present and past influences that affect your relationship with clients. The extent to which you and your client are able to form a healthy bond may be related to not only *the client's* early experiences (e.g., client's relationship to family members or early caregivers), but also *your* early experiences. These concepts are often referred to as transference and countertransference in psychodynamic theories. Consider the following example of Lyle and Pierre.

### CASE EXAMPLE: Applying a Psychodynamic, Attachment Approach: *Working with Lyle*

*Lyle (he/him/his) is a thirty-five-year-old White, gay trans man who is working with Pierre, a cisgender, Asian male clinician who utilizes a psychodynamic, attachment perspective. When asked what brought him to counseling, Lyle replied, "I feel totally neurotic. I always have, and it's going to end my marriage." Lyle reports that despite having a stable relationship with his husband of five years, Nigel, he often feels insecure about whether Nigel will stay with him. Lyle worries that Nigel, whom he describes as a "people-pleaser," will eventually be "fed up with my anxiety" and leave the relationship. Lyle's anxiety leads him to compulsively ask for reassurance, but none of the reassurance he gets from Nigel quells his fears.*

*Over the course of the next few sessions, Pierre starts to gather Lyle's attachment history and learns that Lyle never felt he was good enough for his father, who had unrealistically high standards. Lyle reports that at the age of eight, when his father left his family, he believed it was his fault. Pierre starts to notice that Lyle is expressing fears about counseling; he states, "Am I just being dramatic? You must think I'm ridiculous!" One day, when Lyle is late to session, he apologizes profusely and asks, "Are you mad at me? I'm worried you won't want to work with me anymore." Pierre sees ways in which Lyle's presenting concerns (his relationship with his husband) are being enacted in the counseling relationship (between Lyle and Pierre). He also views Lyle as having an anxious/insecure attachment style and guesses, based on Lyle's reports, that Nigel has a more avoidant style. Pierre decides to educate Lyle about attachment styles and how Lyle's attachment style may relate to his reassurance-seeking. When Pierre starts to make interpretations that connect Lyle's relationship fears to his early experiences of feeling judged and abandoned by his father, Lyle is resistant at first (reflected in his response, "Nigel is nothing like my father!") but slowly starts to see the commonalities between how he is feeling in his relationship and how he learned to cope with the loss of his father's involvement in his life. In one session, Lyle states, "I get it now. Nigel is nothing like my dad, but I'm acting as if he is going to leave because I learned that's what people do." Over time, Lyle starts to gain insight into how unprocessed grief is being projected onto his marriage. With Pierre's help, he learns skills to address these feelings when they come up for him. He is able to notice when he is feeling fearful in his counseling relationship with Pierre and talk through the fears. Pierre is able to offer unconditional regard and warmth, which provides a corrective experience that helps Lyle to relax and build trust.*

In this example, Pierre applies a psychodynamic, attachment approach in his work with Lyle. You can see some of the complexities of how early loss of an attachment may influence what occurs in a client's life and within the client-counselor relationship. What Pierre provides even in a short period of time is a corrective experience in which Lyle is able to feel more secure.

## Mindfulness-Based Techniques

Mindfulness-based techniques such as newer waves of cognitive behavioral therapy (CBT), dialectical behavior therapy (DBT), and acceptance and commitment therapy (ACT) may be useful in working with trans clients and easily combined with other theoretical approaches. These approaches are often practical and effective in teaching clients specific coping skills and ways of addressing the relationship between thoughts, feelings, and behaviors.

## CASE EXAMPLE. Applying Mindfulness-Based Approaches: *Working with Lyle*

*Pierre utilizes mindfulness-based approaches in his counseling work, and he decides that Lyle could use some support in building relaxation and coping skills. Pierre identifies a number of treatment interventions to help Lyle respond to the unhelpful thought patterns that underlie his anxiety. Lyle reports that his anxiety is most relevant to his relationship, but he acknowledges that sometimes he gets anxious at work. Despite getting positive feedback in his evaluations from peers and managers, he carries a negative belief that his employer will find out he is not "competent" and he will lose his job.*

*Pierre starts to incorporate mindfulness exercises into his sessions with Lyle. They explore breathing exercises, guided imagery, and progressive muscle relaxation. Pierre also introduces Lyle to some downloadable meditation apps he can use between sessions. Lyle starts to build meditation into his morning routine.*

*Next, Pierre incorporates CBT by introducing Lyle to the concept of cognitive distortions, which he prefers to refer to as "unhelpful thought patterns." Lyle finds great relief in the fact that there are names for the thought patterns he has come to experience as a normal part of his life. He starts to become more aware of these thought patterns. With Pierre's help, he begins to incorporate exercises to challenge these unhelpful thought patterns. Lyle starts to identify the unhelpful thought patterns, which, surprisingly, allows him to have more compassion for himself. He is even able to laugh at himself because he realizes that some of his fears are predictable. Pierre also suggests that Lyle use the double-standard method of speaking to himself as he would to a beloved friend or small child. Lyle finds this helpful in gaining compassion for himself.*

*Because Lyle can become emotionally dysregulated when caught up in a particularly challenging unhelpful thought pattern, Pierre teaches Lyle some DBT skills that help with distress tolerance and emotion regulation. Pierre helps Lyle to identify healthy distraction skills when overwhelmed with anxiety, such as taking a bath or watching videos of cute animals. Lyle finds the skill of opposite-to-emotion action, in which he chooses behaviors that are counter to his habitual responses, very helpful. At times when his anxiety is very high, he can bombard Nigel with questions and requests for reassurance (which Nigel can experience as an attack). Instead, he applies this skill by gently avoiding this behavior and instead turning inward to focus on his own feelings.*

Lyle benefits greatly from learning concrete skills that help him to manage his anxiety, build his capacity to tolerate his feelings, and increase awareness of his thought patterns. He feels a greater sense of choice in how to respond.

## Emotionally Focused Therapy (EFT)

It's not uncommon in the course of individual therapy for a counselor to make a recommendation for relationship therapy. One approach for working with couples is emotionally focused therapy (EFT), which focuses on attachment, connection, and the repetitive cycles that people in relationships can get into when there is a threat of disconnection (and thus an activation of attachment-related fears). See what happens next in the case of Lyle and his husband, Nigel.

## CASE EXAMPLE. Applying Emotionally Focused Therapy: *Working with Lyle and Nigel*

*Although Pierre witnesses great progress in Lyle's capacity to manage and soothe his anxiety, he starts to think that Lyle and Nigel would benefit from relationship counseling to address some of their habitual patterns of conflict and disconnection. He decides to refer the couple to Emma, a counselor who uses an EFT approach.*

*After meeting with Lyle and Nigel for a couple of sessions, it is clear to Emma that Lyle and Nigel get caught in a pursue-withdraw dynamic that occurs frequently when one partner is more anxious and insecure and the other is more avoidant when under stress or in conflict. Emma uses the EFT model to help Lyle and Nigel identify surface interactions and behaviors and the deeper, underlying negative beliefs and feelings that amplify conflict or disconnection. She notices that Lyle's anxiety can result in his bombarding Nigel with questions, and while Nigel tries to be patient and loving, he has his own fears of disconnection and becomes quiet or shuts down. This increases Lyle's anxiety, which then increases Nigel's withdrawal, and the two of them become even less able to come back together and connect. Emma helps Nigel to notice when he is starting to disengage, acknowledge that this is a protective mechanism because he has learned (based on his own family-of-origin experiences) to equate conflict with possible disconnection, and to engage with Lyle. Emma also helps Lyle to notice when he and Nigel are enacting their negative cycle and to pull back or soften in order to be more present and open to Nigel. Over time and through a process of trial and error, Lyle and Nigel are able to spot their habitual reactions and make different choices. They start to feel more skillful in navigating moments of tension, and they feel a greater sense of connection.*

In this example, you have read about different approaches to working with the same client. We do not advocate a one-size-fits-all approach to any kind of counseling, especially with regard to communities that experience marginalization or exist across broad cultural groups or identities.

## Conclusion

In this chapter, you learned about different factors to consider when beginning individual counseling with trans clients. We emphasized ways to begin new counseling relationships in an affirming, welcoming, and trauma-informed manner. You learned how to think about gender-related concerns (and exploration) as well as the importance of not making assumptions that a trans client's treatment goals are gender-related. Finally, you learned about utilizing different approaches with the same client in order to address the many facets of a client's concerns and experiences. This included a glimpse of an approach to relationship counseling. In chapter 15, you will learn more about relationship and family counseling with trans clients.

# Going Deeper:
# Questions for Clinicians and Clients

## *Questions for Clinician Self-Reflection*

1. What approaches that I use may be most relevant to and affirming of my trans clients?

2. What approaches that I use may be less affirming or need to be adapted to my work with trans clients?

3. Are the techniques I use the most inclusive of a broad range of gender identities and expressions, or do they rely on binary conceptions of gender and life experience?

4. In considering all the first touchpoints of interaction I have with trans clients, what am I doing well in terms of creating a welcoming, gender-affirming, and trauma-informed counseling experience? (Consider website, first phone screenings, and intake questions.)

5. What is my approach when working with clients who are using counseling to explore gender concerns? Is there anything I need to change about my approach so that trans clients feel more affirmed?

## *Questions for Client Exploration*

1. What made you decide to pursue working with me? This will help me to understand what you are most wanting and needing and how I may be able to help you meet your goals.

2. In choosing a counselor to work with, how important to you was the counselor's theoretical orientation or approach? How did that influence your choice to pursue working with me?

3. If you have been in counseling before, what approaches have or have not been helpful to you?

# CHAPTER 15

# Support Trans Clients in Relationship and Family Counseling

Relationship and family therapy can be a vitally important component of affirming counseling with trans people. We want to note that the choice of wording in describing this work is intentional; we have chosen to use the term *relationship therapy* instead of *couples therapy* in order to be inclusive of romantic and sexual relationships that involve multiple partners. We will at times refer to couples or multiple partners for the same reason.

Family systems are diverse and may include adoptions, foster relationships, divorce and remarriage, and polyamorous relationships. Family systems may or may not be supportive of the trans person, and to the extent that they are not supportive, it is important to address this dynamic in counseling. Equally important is the need to address changes in the family system when either a parent or a child has a trans identity. The approach you will take in these situations may be slightly different based on who the trans person is and the ways in which their identity is impacting the family system. In this chapter, we will talk about various aspects of relationship and family counseling and how you may approach utilizing these modalities when working with trans people and their loved ones.

## Trans Relationships in Context

Historically, gatekeeping practices required trans people to end existing relationships, including those that involved marriage, if they desired to make a medical transition. Reasons for this expectation included the belief that relationships would not succeed due to the pressures associated with one of the partners making a medical transition. Another concern was related to the fact that post-transition the couple would appear to have a "homosexual" identity. Given that "homosexuality" was a diagnosable mental health concern through 1973, health care providers wanted to ensure that a person would not be "gay" after making a transition.

Many of these assumptions are changing over time. Research has shown that trans people and their partners have loving, healthy relationships (American Psychological Association, 2015; Kins, Hoebeke, Heylens, Rubens, & De Cuypere, 2008) that, like other healthy relationships, come with their share of challenges. These challenges might include communication concerns, disagreements about money or the division of household responsibilities, and challenges with sexual intimacy. Clinicians must refrain from assuming that all relational challenges are related to a trans partner's identity.

## CASE EXAMPLE. Affirming Polyamorous Relationships: *Working with Marco*

*Marco (he/him/his), a twenty-five-year-old Latino trans man, has been in a relationship with Joe, a White cisgender man, and Elizabeth, an Asian American trans woman, for six months. Prior to Marco's becoming a part of the relationship, Joe and Elizabeth had been partners for two years. Marco, Joe, and Elizabeth have had long discussions about how to engage in their relationship in a way that meets everyone's sexual and social needs. Joe and Elizabeth, who have been supportive of Marco's transition, enjoy sexual activities that include touch that Marco does not feel comfortable with, and although they have respected his physical boundaries, they have expressed not understanding his discomfort. Marco has become increasingly uncomfortable in sexual interactions, and it is affecting his capacity to engage with his partners.*

*Marco discusses his concerns with Dr. García, a Latina cisgender clinician. She shares her concerns about having a lack of knowledge of polyamorous relationships. Marco states that because he feels comfortable in his clinical relationship with Dr. García, he would like to continue working with her and trying to discuss his relational concerns. Dr. García reaches out to a colleague who is known to be kink- and poly-friendly. Dr. García gains some basic knowledge about polyamorous relationships and the ways that Marco can negotiate to meet his needs. Marco and Dr. García talk about the challenges he is facing in the relationship, and they role-play conversations that Marco can have with his partners. Marco feels supported in working out the challenges he is facing in his relationship. Marco is able to talk with Joe and Elizabeth about his intimate desires and the ways he feels safe. Joe and Elizabeth agree to support Marco, and they are able to continue their loving and supportive relationship.*

Exploring relationship dynamics with trans people may include working with people in polyamorous relationships. Dr. García talks frankly with Marco about her lack of knowledge and then makes an effort to gain the necessary knowledge to help address Marco's needs.

# Considerations in Relationships and Family Counseling

Though many trans people in relationships will have concerns similar to those of cisgender people, several factors are important to keep in mind when providing relationship and family counseling. These factors include coming out regarding, or clue-ing in to awareness of, a trans identity; special considerations when working with more than one trans member of a relationship; grief; communication skills; and attachment concerns.

## Coming Out or Clue-ing In

The process of coming to realize and accept one's trans identity is not always linear and may wax and wane over time. We do not place value on coming out to others over the significance of "clue-ing in" to one's own identity. Before a trans person talks to a partner about their identity, it is likely that they have spent a considerable amount of time in their thought process—one that can be fraught with doubt and concern. They may also experience challenging feelings in anticipation of how one's partner may react upon learning about this identity.

Coming out can be a limiting concept, as it does not fit for all people and is too often thought to be a singular event that casts a person's life in a specific, immutable direction. This is far from the truth. Disclosing one's trans identity to others can be a lifelong process. When a person first tells another about their gender identity, they can never be sure how the other person will respond. Disclosure can be scary and emotionally exhausting, but it can also be relieving and affirming.

In some relationships in which a trans person is partnered with a cisgender person, the cisgender partner can be surprised or feel betrayed on learning their partner has a trans identity. A cisgender partner may feel as though their trans partner has been keeping secrets from them. If they have been dishonest about their gender, what else might they have been dishonest about? The sense of betrayal may also be related to concerns about the trans partner's not having been honest about their identity as the relationship was developing.

Another concern that can be very salient is related to defining and understanding the ways that the relationship may change or be perceived over time. This necessarily includes a discussion about sexual orientation and identity. It is possible that a partner has a strong identity related to their sexual orientation. Therefore, if their partner transitions, others will likely perceive their relationship and their partner's sexual orientation differently (and often they will be treated differently in society). If they were a straight couple prior to transition, they may be perceived by others as gay or lesbian and have to contend with the impacts of homophobia.

On the other hand, if a trans person's partner has a strong identity as queer, lesbian, gay, or part of the LGB community, and through transition the relationship shifts toward being perceived as straight, this can bring up a different set of feelings. For partners who have an affinity with the LGB community, as well as a history of navigating struggles related to coming out or having a marginalized identity, it can be challenging to have this lived experience become invisible.

## CASE EXAMPLE. Exploring Sexual Identity and Family Concerns: *Working with Josie*

*Josie (she/her/hers), a fifty-six-year-old African American trans woman, has been married to Andréa (she/her/hers), a forty-five-year-old Colombian cisgender woman, for nineteen years. They have three children together between the ages of twelve and eighteen. Josie came out to Andréa two years ago, and Andréa has been very supportive of Josie's transition.*

*Josie and Andréa have discussed how Josie's identity will impact their relationship and how others perceive them. They remain committed to their marriage and raising their children. Initially, the children had many questions about whether they would stay together and what would happen to their family. Their youngest child has been experiencing bullying at school related to Josie's transition and the belief that Josie and Andréa identify as lesbians.*

*As Andréa and Josie discuss their sexual identity, they come to the mutual decision that they do not identify as lesbians. They understand that this may be complicated for friends and family to understand. Josie has a strong desire to continue to engage in sexual activities that have been enjoyable in the past. For Josie, this means that although she is taking feminizing hormones, she will not have genital surgery. Josie is happy about this decision, and Andréa feels supported.*

In this example, we see that Josie and Andréa are deliberate about how they explore and come to determine their sexual orientation. This helps us to understand that some people choose ways to claim their sexual identity that may not be consistent with normative conceptions of sexual orientation. When questions related to sexual orientation, identity, and gender concerns arise in a family and are challenging to navigate, it can be useful for clients to seek relationship or family counseling for guidance and support.

## Trans People in Relationships with Other Trans People

Often people assume that trans people in relationships have cisgender partners. This is not always the case, as some trans people are partnered with other trans people. Many of the issues that can be difficult in a relationship with a cisgender person (e.g., differences in parenting style, communication issues, financial worries) are likely to also be present when trans people are in a relationship with one another.

People can have loving and healthy relationships regardless of their gender identity. Trans people may find relationships with other trans people to be easier to navigate, as they believe that the other person has a more intimate understanding of what it means to be trans. However, partners may struggle at times because even with shared affiliation and identity, no two people's experiences are ever the same. Therefore, there can still be misunderstandings or assumptions that can cause challenges or conflict.

# Grief in Relationships

Concerns regarding sexual identity in relationships can lead to feelings of grief for any partner in the relationship. Grief is a relatively common reaction to significant changes that a person experiences. Transition, be it social, medical, or legal, is one such significant change.

Grief can come about at any point in the coming out or transition process. In many cases, partners and loved ones experience what can be considered an ambiguous form of loss because there are ways in which their partner is the same person as they have always been, and, in other ways, they are different. In the following case, we explore how grief might manifest as a couple first explores a trans partner's disclosure of their gender identity.

## CASE EXAMPLE. Addressing Grief in Relationships: *Working with Denise*

*Denise (she/her/hers) is a forty-eight-year-old White trans woman who is married to Jessica (she/her/hers). Together, Denise and Jessica have three children, ages ten, fourteen, and seventeen. Denise recently told Jessica about her trans identity. Although Denise and Jessica are still living together, Denise has been sleeping on the couch in the living room because Jessica's initial response to this disclosure was negative and shaming. Jessica insisted that Denise share their bedroom and that the children not find her on the couch. Denise is willing to acquiesce to Jessica's demands as she has no other housing options at this time.*

*Over time, Jessica becomes more open to talking with Denise about her gender identity. As these conversations progress, Denise often feels like she "is taking one step forward and two steps back." Denise can see that her process of coming into awareness about her gender is far ahead of Jessica's understanding and acceptance. Jessica is still unwilling for Denise to talk with the children about her gender. As this evolves, Denise is feeling some urgency to move forward because she is interested in a social and medical transition. She also wants to honor Jessica's concerns, as they have been married for twenty-five years and love each other deeply. However, Denise has begun to feel more anxious overall and finds herself getting angry more easily with Jessica.*

*Jessica decides to seek out professional help. Her counselor, Jamie, is quick to notice signs of anxiety and depression that are exacerbated by grief over Denise's disclosure and the impacts on their relationship. Jamie works with Jessica to normalize her reactions. Jessica reports that it is immensely helpful to have her feelings validated by Jamie, and this helps her to move through them and become more accepting of Denise's gender identity.*

This case example demonstrates the complicated feelings that may arise for partners who are trying to come to terms with a loved one's gender identity or transition. Jessica benefits from getting counseling that helps her to name all the different emotions she is experiencing in response to Denise's trans identity.

In addition to grief related to the dynamics in a relationship, there can also be loss associated with changes to sexual identity and the sexual practices in which a couple engages. Feelings of grief related to sexual orientation will depend on the ways in which a person identified prior to transition and whether this shifts over the course of transition. Trans men who identified at one time as lesbians and maintain a primary attraction toward women may change the way they describe their sexual orientation after transitioning. Some may adopt a "straight" identity, while others will maintain identification as queer. Most important regarding sexual orientation is to honor and recognize the way a person self-identifies. It is not our job as clinicians to decide the correct label a person uses. It is important to be cautious so that we are not implying that a certain identity is the one that would best fit.

Sexual practices or attraction may shift over time. This shift may be related to changes in how a trans person feels about using body parts for sexual activities. In some cases, trans people have a strong aversion to sexual activity that involves genitalia. If this is the case, it is important that the couple communicate about how to be respectful of one another. Clinicians are encouraged to have frank and respectful discussions with their clients so that they might be able to understand the possible challenges that could impact their sexual experiences.

Relatedly, if a person chooses a medical transition, especially one that involves surgical interventions, the change in a person's anatomy may be challenging for one's partner(s). A partner might say, "I married a man in part because I enjoy the ways in which we have sex." The implication here is that that partner enjoys having sex with a person with a penis. If the trans partner has a plan to have vaginoplasty, it will be necessary to talk about the ways this will change their sexual interactions. As a clinician, you can help hold affirming space for partners by not making the assumption that a situation like this will be difficult or even impossible to resolve. Having frank discussions about sex and sexual behaviors can be challenging for clinicians who have had little training or experience on such topics. Without open conversations between the partners it will be hard to know if this can be negotiated in a way that allows for partners' sexual needs to be met. Working with your client(s) to explore sexuality is one way to normalize the changes they may be experiencing.

## Communication Skills

In the previous section, we addressed the need for open and honest communication in relationships with partners. Having a frank discussion can be challenging, especially when one partner feels as though they do not have power in the relationship or that they have much to lose should the conversation not be productive. You may be able to provide support for trans people and their partners in communicating more effectively with each other.

For example, you may coach partners on active listening and mirroring back what they have heard their partners say. Or, you may introduce partners to ways of communicating both appreciations and grievances. An often useful skill that you may discuss with partners is how to communicate the need for a "time-out" during conflict or heated discussions.

## Attachment Concerns

Though rarely explicitly addressed in conversations about trans people in relationships, exploring dynamics from an attachment lens can be helpful. Attachment fears, or fears related to losing connection with a loved one, can be present for all parties. Trans clients who are trying to decide whether to come out or transition often fear rejection or abandonment by partners. These fears can be significant barriers to coming out or disclosing their trans identity. Clients may fear losing relationships or families they have built over many years, or, if they lack additional social supports, they may fear losing a close relationship with someone on whom they rely significantly for support.

Because attachment-related fears are often tied to early childhood development and attachment to parents or early caregivers, trans people can experience highly distressing difficulties related to survival. When a threat of relationship loss is present, clients may experience emotional dysregulation. Although this is not just true for trans clients, it is important to highlight the risks involved with trans clients who are making decisions in their lives that can profoundly affect their relationships. These concerns are further complicated when a trans client's financial security, housing, or health may be compromised if their partnership ends. For example, a trans person who is dependent on a partner for housing, income, or health insurance may fear losing these crucial needs if they choose to transition.

There are very few resources that address specific approaches to couples or relationship counseling when one or more partners are trans. Chapman and Caldwell (2012) discuss attachment injury resolution in the context of one partner being trans-identified. The authors describe attachment injury as a moment in which a partner is unavailable at a crucial moment, leading to disconnection and disappointment in the other partner. One partner's gender transition or another partner's lack of support regarding the other's gender transition can be viewed as an attachment injury. Further, according to Chapman and Caldwell, partners of trans clients often feel a sense of abandonment, betrayal, jealousy, or resentment toward transition because it is creating more distance or disconnection.

An attachment perspective can be useful in helping your clients identify how their attachment style (e.g., secure, anxious, avoidant) may be affecting them in their relationships as they navigate gender concerns. You may be able to recognize common relationship dynamics that are playing out with regard to gender concerns and are present in other ways in the relationship. For example, you may notice how your client or their partner(s) have an avoidant tendency that is connected to their attachment style, or that a couple you are working with has a pursue-withdraw cycle enacted when they try to discuss one partner's gender transition. If you are able to recognize these common relational patterns, you may be able to offer interventions that help to increase the partners' connection, thereby lending more support to partners who are navigating transition together.

## CASE EXAMPLE. Exploring Coming Out for Gender Expansive Children in the Context of Caregivers: *Working with Ezra*

*Ezra is a biracial seven-year-old child who was assigned male at birth. Ezra's parents are separated, and Ezra lives primarily with mom (Joyce) and sees dad (Mason) on holidays and in the summer. Ezra recently began expressing to mom the feeling of being "born in the wrong body." Ezra wants mom and others to start using the name Sarah and she/her/hers pronouns to refer to her. When Sarah talks with her father about this, he becomes angry and verbally abusive.*

*Sarah talks about this experience with her mother when she returns home. Sarah's mom is not happy with Sarah's dad but also fears that his anger has the potential to hurt Sarah. Two weeks later Joyce is served with divorce papers, and among the reasons for the divorce is that Mason has accused Joyce of being an unfit parent. This accusation is due to Mason's belief that Joyce is "unable to control Ezra's bizarre behavior and is trying to make Ezra into a girl."*

*Joyce is not sure how to support Sarah and begins to work with a counselor named Susan, who has experience in working with couples and families going through divorce. Susan is sensitive to the ways that children can become a bargaining chip in contentious divorces as this one seems to be. Susan's work with Joyce focuses on how to support Sarah and how to address Joyce's concerns about parenting. Susan normalizes Joyce's concerns, and they also talk about the difficulties that can arise when both parents are not supportive of a child coming out as trans. Susan then invites Mason to attend counseling sessions, some just with the parental unit and some involving all members of the family. Through this work, Mason is able to see that his frustration about his marriage is affecting his relationship with his child. Though the parents still move forward with divorce, Sarah is removed from the parental conflict dynamic and is more supported by both parents.*

It is not uncommon for parents to be at different levels of support with regard to a gender-diverse child. This can become especially problematic and damaging for the child when one parent uses the other parent's desire to accept a child's gender to justify legal actions against that parent.

If the gender-diverse child has a trans parent, the trans parent's support for their child's gender identity and expression may also range. Exploring parents' belief systems and experiences about gender identity and gender expression, as well as how to best support their gender-diverse child, can clarify parental expectations, fears, needs, and other areas that need attention in counseling.

The implications for a family can be far reaching. The parents, children, and family system may all be impacted when a member of the family discloses their gender identity. Mental health providers are encouraged to explore the resulting dynamics and encourage family members to engage in open and affirming communication with one another.

## Conclusion

This chapter explored important considerations in relationship and family counseling with trans people. When a member of the family comes out as trans, the family system may experience stress and may not have the resources to work through these challenges. As a clinician, it is important to understand the complex issues that might impact trans people's relationships and families and ways that you can support your clients in counseling. Chapter 16 explores the use of groups and peer support for addressing client concerns.

# Going Deeper:
# Questions for Clinicians and Clients

*Questions for Clinician Self-Reflection*

1. What is my theoretical approach to working with partners and families? Is this approach an affirmative practice for work with trans clients?

2. What attitudes do I have about relational structure diversity—that is, non-monogamy and polyamory?

3. Do I have any biases about whether partners in relationships with trans people "should" behave in a certain way or demonstrate allyship? Or whether they should stay in relationships through a partner's transition?

4. When working with couples, partners, or families, how can I stay mindful of my own gender identity in order to more easily empathize with certain members of a relationship or family system?

*Questions for Client Exploration*

1. What types of interactions with other people help you to feel loved and supported?

2. What do you want your partner to know about you and the ways in which you would like to engage in sexual activities?

3. What types of support do you need from a partner to help you understand your sexual needs and to feel safe when engaging in sex?

4. What would your ideal relationship look like?

# CHAPTER 16

# Connect Clients to Group Support

Group therapy and peer support are important sources of encouragement and guidance that serve to increase resilience and strength. There are important differences between group therapy and peer support groups, yet both types of groups can be equally effective depending on the needs of your client. Finding connection in a group setting can reduce isolation and increase a sense of belonging. In this chapter, we review some of the key decision points in helping clients to access community support.

## Group Therapy

Group therapy has long been used as a clinical intervention to address the needs of clients who may be experiencing similar clinical concerns. In this section, we explore the need to be intentional about the group facilitator role, formats for clinician-led groups, screening of prospective group members, and building groups based on subgroup identities or clinical concerns.

### The Group Facilitator Role

The first thing to consider with regard to group therapy is who is appropriate to lead or be in the group-facilitation role. Many times, clinicians do not pause to consider what it means to be in this kind of position of power with trans community members. Keeping in mind that trans populations, as a whole, constitute a marginalized group in society, it is important to be aware of power dynamics that can be enacted within group settings.

Trans clinicians will want to be mindful of the dynamics that arise when being viewed as a "leader" of a demographic group to which they belong, even if their experiences are different from the experiences of group members (see chapter 21 for more on trans clinicians). Group members may display a great deal of projection and may ask personal questions of trans group facilitators or leaders; we encourage trans clinicians to be mindful of their own boundaries of privacy and to reflect on ways in which they are similar to and different from group members, as well as ways in which they hold influence and power.

The question of whether cisgender clinicians should assume group-facilitation roles for trans support groups can bring up a whole host of different opinions. Simply stated, there are some things that trans people will not feel as comfortable talking about when the group leader is not trans. Many trans people will not want to attend a group facilitated by cisgender clinicians. We do not want to discourage creating group therapy opportunities for trans community members; however, we believe that if a trans clinician is able to provide group facilitation, there are great advantages to this. On the other hand, some clients with high levels of internalized transphobia may feel less comfortable with a trans facilitator at first. We cannot emphasize enough how important it is for cisgender clinicians conducting group therapy to practice humility and to name and reflect upon their cisgender privilege (and bias) from the very start of and throughout the group therapy. If the group is co-led by two facilitators, it would be helpful for at least one of the facilitators to have a trans identity.

## Group Format

Clinician-led groups can be open or closed. In an open group, participants can join or leave the group at any time (dickey & Loewy, 2010; Heck, 2017), whereas in a closed group, people are not typically allowed to join the group after it is established and running. Open groups are better suited for support groups, while closed groups are more appropriate for process groups because of the ways that participants are encouraged to interact.

Open drop-in groups offered by mental health providers tend to be less structured than closed groups. Some models for this type of group involve having a new theme each week (e.g., coming out, workplace issues, finding a medical provider). One drawback of an open drop-in group is that it can be difficult to create a sense of community and cohesion since different people may attend each time. However, this kind of group may be more accessible for some clients whose lives do not allow for a longer-term commitment of attendance.

## Screening Members

In closed groups, members are prescreened for inclusion. It is important to screen members in a respectful manner, including use of affirming language and expression of support (Heck, Flentje, & Cochran, 2013). For providers who are just beginning to work with trans people and for those who received little to no training in work with trans people, these basic tenets are essential foundations that can prevent harm and increase the effectiveness of this treatment modality. Screening may also help to identify readiness for group participation; in some cases, individual counseling may be a better fit for a client's needs or stage of development. As a leader, you may need to make difficult decisions about who to include in the group. If possible, you should consider any preexisting relationships among members, as they may or may not pose barriers to effective group treatment. Additionally, a thorough screening process can allow you to discern the ways that people with different personality types will or will not be able to interact in a supportive manner.

## Groups Based on Subgroup Identities or Clinical Concerns

Groups are often formed based on subgroup identities (e.g., trans people of color, trans young adults) or clinical concerns (e.g., eating disorders, preparing for surgery). It is important to consider the varying needs of potential group members based on their gender identity. People who have a binary identity may have very different needs from those with a nonbinary identity. The same can be said about trans masculine and trans feminine people. Thus, when trans people with varying gender identities are present at the same group meeting, it is unlikely that everyone will get their needs met (dickey & Loewy, 2010).

Trans people with nonbinary identities may have difficulty being seen as having a trans identity by people with binary identities. There are times when it can be helpful to have a separate group for people with nonbinary identities, as there are some unique concerns that may not be adequately addressed in mixed or more binary-oriented groups.

When groups are open to trans men and trans women, there are some important considerations to make. Experiences of trans masculine and trans feminine people in society can be very different, and this is often due to patriarchy, sexism, gender-based violence, and relationships to privilege. Therefore, there are some benefits in having separate groups in which these topics may be discussed.

Racial/ethnic identity is another factor to consider with regard to groups. Groups that are geared toward providing a space for trans people of color to access support can be incredibly valuable, as there may be different concerns for people of color. For example, the concept of "coming out" in the context of familial and cultural values or concerns is nuanced and complex. Because mainstream trans narratives are based on White people, trans people of color may feel a great need to have their experiences mirrored and valued in a space that is specifically for trans people of color and led by a person of color (Chang & Singh, 2016).

Age is yet another factor that can come into play a great deal with group therapy or support. Some groups have a certain age group that predominates in the group, and people who are not part of that age group may feel alienated. For example, we have noticed a tendency for many support groups for people on the trans feminine spectrum to be well attended by older trans people; when this is the case, a younger person trying to access this group may not find all the support she needs. There are times when a young adult group can be very helpful, as generational and cohort differences can inform very different perspectives on the experience of gender in the world.

# Peer-Led Groups

Peer-led groups (in-person or online) can be a cost-effective approach for trans people to gain support. It is useful for you to know about these groups so that you may refer your clients to them. Peer-led groups differ in many aspects from groups led by mental health providers, primarily with regard to managing group dynamics and selecting topics. We explore these factors below.

## Managing Group Dynamics

Whenever a group of people comes together, differences of opinion and conflicts are possible. Because peer-led groups are open to anyone in the community, it can be difficult to manage these differences of opinion. Having established group norms can help to address problematic interactions and to ensure that members have a good understanding of the ground rules for participation. Heck (2017) provides a list of the rights and responsibilities of group members. The list covers the following topics: (a) the right to freely express one's gender, (b) the right to confidentiality, (c) the ability to receive referrals to other providers, (d) the responsibility of members and leaders to treat one another respectfully, and (e) the agreement that members not attend group under the influence of alcohol or drugs. Group agreements may vary based on group needs, and it is often respectful to invite group members to contribute to the list of agreements.

## Selecting Topics

Topics for groups may be based on what is expressed during group member check-ins. That way, the time can be dedicated in a way that responds to members' current needs and concerns. For groups that are quieter or less vocal, it can be helpful for facilitators to have a pool of possible topics, including disclosure at work or to family members, navigating physical or emotional changes related to hormones, or coping with and building resilience against stigma and anti-trans bias. In some groups, there can be a tendency to overly fixate on aspects of medical transition; group facilitators may have to be attuned to whether this conversation, which can benefit some members, is alienating in any way to members who are not engaged in this process.

People earlier in transition may have different priorities and concerns from people who are further along in transition. Some of the older members may appreciate the opportunity to support those who are early in their coming-out process. In a way, these members are paying back what others did for them when they were early in their transition. There is a tension here, as some newer group members will appreciate hearing others' experiences, while others may feel overwhelmed by the way that some people imply that the path they took is the right way to transition. Effective facilitation (whether by a peer or professional) will encourage a diversity of experiences, as there is no right way to be trans or to transition.

## Conclusion

In this chapter, we discussed the use of groups as a source of support for trans people. Whether led by a clinician or a peer, these groups can support a trans person in many ways. Groups can help people to gain basic knowledge about transition and resources in the area. They can also enable people to develop relationships with other members of the community, which can help to build resilience. Finally, groups can provide members with the opportunity to explore, in a safe environment, a range of topics commonly faced by trans people. Chapter 17 addresses issues for clients across the lifespan and the importance of understanding how one's generational or cohort experience impacts their identity and identity development.

# Going Deeper:
# Questions for Clinicians and Clients

## *Questions for Clinician Self-Reflection*

1.  How much training and experience do I have in leading groups?

2.  Do I have sufficient space in my office to accommodate a group? If not, what other options are available?

3.  How comfortable am I addressing conflicts that might arise in a group?

4.  Do I have sufficient knowledge about the needs of trans people that might best be met in a process or support group?

5.  (*For trans clinicians:*) What concerns or feelings are coming up for me in the role of group facilitator? Even when my gender identity or gender-related experiences are similar to those of the trans group members, how can I be mindful of other aspects of my identity that may be privileged (e.g., race, education, class, ability)?

6.  (*For cisgender clinicians:*) What concerns or feelings are coming up for me in the role of group facilitator? How can I be mindful of the obvious power dynamic that occurs when I am facilitating a group geared toward a demographic group to which I do not belong?

## *Questions for Client Exploration*

1.  What are your goals for joining a group? What are you most hoping to get out of this experience?

2.  Have you ever been in a group before? What did you like or dislike about the group?

3.  What are the ways you address conflict when it arises?

4.  How do you typically respond to feedback from others?

5.  What are your thoughts or needs regarding who is facilitating the group? Would you rather that person be trans or cisgender? Would you rather that person be a clinician or a peer?

6.  Given that trans communities can be small, how do you think it will be for you to run into people you know? Do you have any concerns about privacy, and what do you need to manage these concerns?

CHAPTER 17

# Affirm Trans Clients Across the Lifespan

You may be used to working with clients whose lives take a traditional developmental path—one that is expected and rewarded by dominant culture. Some trans clients will not fit this model and need you to have a more expansive view of development. For some trans people, this traditional developmental path can be disrupted as they come to understand their identity. Interruption may occur as the result of a myriad of challenges faced by gender expansive children who are targets for bullying, an adolescent's experience (or blocking) of puberty, and older trans people's struggle to find facilities that will allow them to die with dignity. In this chapter, we begin by applying a basic understanding of human development to trans people. We then discuss in more detail how the development process is uniquely experienced by trans people. We end the chapter by exploring the differences faced by trans people based on the time at which they came to understand their gender identity.

## Basic Human Development

The process of human development is a well-studied topic. Many theories have been developed to describe the various stages a person completes across the lifespan. Erikson (1980) was the first to propose a developmental process that spanned from birth to old age, ending in death. Each of these stages involve a dilemma a person might be faced with if they do not successfully negotiate the developmental stage. Below we will explore the identity stages that impact childhood and adolescence: initiative versus guilt, industry versus inferiority, and ego identity versus role confusion.

### Erikson's Stages of Psychosocial Development

The third of Erikson's eight stages is initiative versus guilt, during which a child attempts to perform tasks on their own or risk feeling guilty when needing help from others. This stage happens between the ages of three and five years old, which is also the time period where it is believed that children consolidate their sense of gender. If a gender expansive child struggles in this stage of development, they will move toward feelings of guilt rather than a sense of initiative. If the child is not affirmed in their gender identity, it is possible that they will not successfully negotiate this stage of development.

The fourth stage that Erikson proposed is industry versus inferiority, during which a child develops the capacity to engage in logical reasoning and acquiring knowledge. This stage ranges from young childhood to the cusp of the initiation of puberty and is related to the development of self-confidence. If a child is struggling with performing a logical task independently, this may be damaging to their self-esteem. They will likely also struggle in coming to understand and assert their gender diversity.

The fifth stage of development, ego identity versus role confusion, happens between the ages of twelve and eighteen and involves negotiating a sense of identity that is separate from the expectations of others. Arguably, this stage is one of the more difficult aspects of development in that it occurs while the individual is experiencing puberty. Gender expansive children who continue to express their trans identity through puberty are likely to maintain a trans identity through adulthood (Edwards-Leeper, 2017). If the child is allowed to experience an endogenous puberty, they will develop the secondary sex characteristics that are associated with the sex they were assigned at birth. Alternatively, if a child is able to access puberty blockers, they will have the time to explore their gender without experiencing a puberty that is inconsistent with their lived experience and affirmed identity.

Note that Erikson's and others' models of development are rooted in Western and White ideologies and do not represent the experiences of traditionally marginalized individuals (e.g., people of color). For many mental health providers, these are the only models of development in which they have received training. We explore racial, sexual identity, and transgender developmental models in the following sections.

## Cass's Model of Sexual Identity Development

Cass developed the first sexual identity model in 1979. This six-stage, linear model represents the process by which a person comes to understand their sexual identity development. This model emerged several years after homosexuality was removed from the *Diagnostic and Statistical Manual of Mental Disorders*. As such, the model grounded the development of one's sexual identity in a time period where some of the stigmatization regarding sexual orientation had begun to wane.

The stages of the Cass model are (a) identity confusion, (b) identity comparison, (c) identity tolerance, (d) identity acceptance, (e) identity pride, and (f) identity synthesis. Cass (1979) notes that as a person moves sequentially through these developmental stages, it is possible to foreclose at any stage; however, they can resume their identity development process at a later time. In many ways, this model is the foundation for Devor's (2004) identity model, which is defined in the next section.

# Transgender Development Models

There are three general models of transgender identity development (Bockting, 2013; Devor, 2004; Levitt & Ippolito, 2014). We describe these models below.

## Devor's Model of Transsexual Development

Devor's (2004) fourteen-stage model, named Witnessing and Mirroring, uses some of the same stages that are in sexual identity models. The model was developed in a time when the term *transsexual* was used to describe trans people, especially those who engaged in a medical transition. The model begins with a person experiencing anxiety about the sex assigned at birth. Following this, the person begins to compare their own sex and gender characteristics to those of others of the same sex. On finding differences between themselves and people who have been assigned the same sex at birth, the person will discover the concept of transsexualism (Devor, 2004). This will lead to more anxiety and confusion, partly because the person has little, if any, access to others with a trans identity. This begins another period of confusion, which is eventually resolved as the person begins to tolerate a trans identity, yet there is a delay in fully accepting one's trans identity. After a person makes a transition, they move to a place of acceptance, integration, and finally pride.

Devor's (2004) model was one of the first to explain the developmental process for a trans identity. The model is deeply rooted in the assumption that a trans person will complete a medical transition. Although this certainly still happens, it is far from a ubiquitous experience in trans communities. Another concern with this model is that the challenges involved in some of these stages are likely rooted in the assumption of certain kinds of discrimination that prevent trans people from being open and proud about their identities. For example, when Devor developed this model, there were few, if any, legal protections for trans people. Even though discrimination is still widespread, increased protections and awareness of trans people in society can reduce anxiety and doubt for some trans people. A final shortcoming is that, like traditional development models, Devor's model was developed to represent the experiences of White transsexual individuals and may be limited in its applicability to varied subgroups within trans communities.

## Bockting's Model of Transgender Identity Development

Bockting (2013) offers a developmental model based on the changes that occur across the lifespan with regard to one's gender identity. Beginning in childhood, according to this model, the challenges involve knowing the difference between gender identity, gender expression, and one's gender roles. While it is unclear how many children will retain their gender identity through puberty and beyond, it is generally accepted that if a person maintains their identity through childhood, they will continue to identify as trans (Bockting, 2013).

Some children begin to express their gender identity being different from the sex they were assigned at birth as young as three to five years old. Imagine a four-year-old boy (as assigned at birth) who insists to his parents that he is really a girl. This can be confusing and challenging not only for the child but also for the parents, as they are unlikely to have considered this as an option for their child. However, their support is crucial, as the more a child is supported by their parents and other people in their life, the more likely they are to have successful mental health outcomes (Edwards-Leeper, Leibowitz, & Sangganjanavanich, 2016; Ehrensaft, 2012; Olson et al., 2016).

The second developmental period is adolescence (Bockting, 2013). Like childhood, this can be a challenging period. In addition to understanding their gender identity, the adolescent is also dealing with the challenges associated with puberty. Adolescents who begin to go through an endogenous puberty may experience significant emotional distress as their bodies begin to develop in ways that are inconsistent with their affirmed gender.

For a trans male-identified teenager, beginning a menstrual cycle can be quite disruptive, and the adolescent may express the feeling that their body has betrayed them. If the child does not have access to puberty-blocking treatment, either due to cost or lack of parental support, it is important for a mental health provider to work with the adolescent to develop coping skills to deal with the emotional reactions to these bodily changes.

Also important during childhood and adolescence are the challenges youth face in the school setting. Gender expansive youth experience bullying, discrimination, and violence in schools (Kosciw, Greytak, Giga, Villenas, & Danischewski, 2016). Depending on the school system, there may be little done to address this mistreatment. The goal would be to ensure that the highest-level administrator is supportive of a "hate-free" educational environment. This must include sanctions for school children, faculty, and staff.

Bockting (2013) then focuses on adulthood. Adults may transition at any point in their lives. Even though many people do not transition until adulthood, they often report having understood that their gender was different from a young age. Of those adults who choose to medically transition, few (less than 1%) report regret for having made a transition (Kuiper & Cohen-Kettenis, 1998).

People who transition during adulthood face important developmental concerns. For young adults who transition, it is important for providers to have a discussion about the desire to be a parent. Hormones and surgical interventions may affect fertility and create a situation in which it is impossible for a trans person to provide genetic material to assist in the process of pregnancy and childbirth (American Psychological Association, 2015).

Adults who are already established in a relationship, with or without children, may need support regarding disclosure of their gender identity to their spouse and children. It is generally thought that the best time to disclose one's gender identity to children is before or after they are in puberty (White & Ettner, 2007), in part because adolescents are experiencing their own difficulties with puberty and the resultant hormonal surges.

Another area of consideration relates to employment. Some trans people will leave their employer because they do not feel safe in the workplace. Others may decide to return to school for retraining. Others still will stay in the workplace and work with their management to ensure that they have safety protections in the event a coworker discriminates or engages in harassment. Many companies have enacted nondiscrimination policies in recent years that include protections for trans people.

The final area of development noted by Bockting (2013) is older adulthood. There are challenges for trans people who come out in this time of life, just as there are challenges for those who came out earlier in life and are now facing older adulthood. There are many valid reasons why a person may decide to wait to come out, including family or workplace concerns. Historically, some health care providers assumed that a person who waits that long to claim their gender identity must not really be trans; otherwise this would have happened earlier in their life.

People who transitioned at a younger age and are now facing adulthood may have health concerns that are difficult to address, in part because it can be challenging to find culturally competent health providers. Further, older adults have reported mistreatment in long-term care facilities, including staff's deliberate use of the wrong name or pronoun for the patient (National Senior Citizens Law Center, 2011).

Another challenge in older adulthood is the lack of knowledge about the long-term effects of "cross-sex" hormone treatment. Little to no research has been conducted to understand the implications and risks of being on exogenous hormones. Given that people are starting this treatment as young as sixteen years old, it is important to focus research on the potential risks associated with this treatment.

## Levitt & Ippolito's Model of Transgender Identity Development

Levitt and Ippolito (2014) developed a theory that was based on the completion of interviews with trans people with varying identities across the gender spectrum. The model is rooted in the experiences of White trans people in the United States and, as such, does not represent trans people of color or people from other parts of the world. Furthermore, although Levitt and Ippolito explore a variety of identities, the participants in the study primarily lived in the southern region of the United States. It is possible that a person's identity is negatively impacted by an unwelcoming climate in the South, and that a person may have a very different experience in another part of the country.

The main finding of this research was related to the inability of trans people to find a way to explain and understand their gender in a world where they continually fought to be seen and understood while also fighting for basic safety needs. This core finding is represented by three clusters: (a) the experience of being perceived as "damaged goods" since childhood, (b) the ways in which another's story helps a person to understand their own life, and (c) the process of coming into one's identity, which is evolving and includes attention to safety and authenticity needs. Levitt and Ippolito (2014) further describe categories within these clusters. For example, the first cluster includes having to hide or ignore one's identity, which can lead to isolation amid the mistreatment from peers and others. To address this, they point out the ways that community support and resilience help bolster one's personal image and provide the necessary drive for a person to claim their gender.

Bockting's and Levitt and Ippolito's models both explore the process of coming to terms with a gender that is different from the sex a person was assigned at birth. In addition to the emotional process of claiming this identity, several physical challenges arise through transition, which may be different from one person to the next. Regardless of how a person makes a transition, these experiences may be a part of their journey.

All three of these developmental models take some version of a stage approach to understanding a trans person's identity. Further, they all assume that the transition trajectory is from female to male or vice versa, ignoring the identity development of people with nonbinary identities. Although this is an emerging part of the trans community, the truth is that nonbinary people have existed throughout history in indigenous cultures. There is a need to develop a model of identity that addresses the unique challenges faced by people with nonbinary identities. The following case example explores one of the challenges faced by adolescents.

## CASE EXAMPLE. Understanding a Trans Adolescent's Experience of Puberty: *Working with Jackson*

*Jackson (he/him/his) is a fourteen-year-old African American trans masculine adolescent. Jackson began his menstrual cycle at age eleven. Menstruation was very difficult for him, and he experienced a significant bout of depression during this time. Jackson's parents are divorced, and after much disagreement and a number of child custody battles, Jackson's mother finally has sole custody of her son. His mother has been very supportive of Jackson, but as long as his father was in the picture, there was no option for affirmative care.*

*Jackson's mother takes him to see a counselor once a week. Jackson was initially reluctant to speak openly to the counselor, Jana (she/her/hers), who is a White cisgender woman. Although she was very supportive of him, Jackson wasn't sure he could trust a White woman. Over the course of six months, Jackson eventually begins to trust Jana because she models humility and creates a space in which Jackson feels heard.*

*Jana works with Jackson to help him develop coping skills and introduces him to mindfulness activities. Initially Jackson wasn't very confident in his ability to engage in these activities, but over time he learns how helpful these are as he practices them during his counseling sessions. Although Jackson still struggles with emotional difficulty every time his menstrual cycle occurs, he has yet to find a provider who will prescribe medication to halt his menses. He feels better equipped to regulate his emotions and tolerate the distress related to menses, and he feels some comfort knowing that Jana is actively advocating on his behalf and trying to locate a trans-friendly physician who can treat Jackson and help him reach his goals.*

This example addresses the type of emotional distress an adolescent might face when they experience an endogenous puberty. This can be just as distressing for a person assigned female at birth as it can be for someone assigned male at birth. Jana works with Jackson to help him develop coping skills and to advocate for his access to medical care.

# Lifespan Considerations

Being aware of issues commonly faced by trans people at various life stages will enable you to better support clients of all ages in counseling. Some factors to consider include puberty, menopause, parenting, aging, and end-of-life considerations.

## Interruption of Puberty

Puberty fits within Erikson's ego identity versus role confusion stage. Erikson (1980) posits that this stage of life is critical in the development of one's identity. The difficulty associated with this time period is about gaining a clear understanding of yourself at a challenging time in life.

For trans people, there are generally two concerns regarding puberty. The first revolves around the difficult emotional process that is brought on by this normal life stage. For a person with a trans identity, beginning to develop secondary sex characteristics associated with the sex they were assigned at birth can be, at best, bothersome, and at worst, a constant reminder of the ways they have been betrayed by their body. It is understandable that adolescents will turn to various coping methods to alleviate the constant stress or dysphoria brought on by these changes. Even if an adolescent was allowed to live as an androgynous person in childhood, they may receive strong and unrelenting messages from parents, teachers, and peers about what it means to be male or female and the social consequences for not conforming with these expectations.

Having to live as an androgynous person (or having a gender that is not legible within the gender binary) can easily be alleviated, when desired, using hormone or puberty blockers. Although this process is expensive and not always covered by insurance, it provides a simple and effective means of delaying the process of puberty. By delaying puberty, a person is given the opportunity to explore their gender identity without the constant onslaught of bodily changes and social repercussions. The positive side of this relates to not forcing a child or adolescent to experience a puberty that is inconsistent with their affirmed gender. One drawback is the fact that puberty blockers will delay development in such a way that the person will be unable to provide the genetic material necessary to create a family. There are many different ways to create a family, as explored later in this chapter; however, many people find it important to have a genetic connection to their children. It may or may not be developmentally appropriate to have a discussion with a twelve-year-old about their plans for parenting later in life. Even if one deems the topic of discussion to be relevant, it is possible that the twelve-year-old is not ready to make this decision. If they decide they want to be a biological parent, then it will be important for the adolescent to allow enough of the maturation process to happen so that they have viable eggs or sperm that can be cryopreserved for later use. Questions about being a parent may not readily come to mind for those working with adolescents; however, these may be important conversations that you, as a clinician, can facilitate with sensitivity.

## Early Menopause

Trans masculine individuals who desire to masculinize their body through the use of hormones (e.g., testosterone) have the added challenge of initiating an artificial menopause if they have not reached the age at which this would have occurred naturally. It is not uncommon for medical providers to advise trans masculine patients that they will cease to have vaginal secretions that are often a part of one's sexual experiences. There is little to no research on the changes in vaginal secretion; however, anecdotal experience indicates that there can be a significant change in the amount of secretion. Hot flashes and other hallmark experiences of menopause are also likely to occur.

Should a trans masculine person later decide they would like to give birth to a child or contribute gametes (i.e., eggs) to the process of assisted reproduction with another gestational carrier (e.g., a partner or surrogate), it is possible to stop taking testosterone, which will, depending on a person's age, lead to the resumption of a menstrual cycle.

Some people believe that taking testosterone is a safe form of birth control. This is not the case, as trans masculine people should be clearly informed. In fact, trans masculine people who take testosterone and have a cessation of menses can still in some instances get pregnant. This is something that a client's medical doctor should include as part of obtaining informed consent for hormones; however, this is not always discussed. Mental health providers, therefore, can provide this helpful information to assist clients in making informed and safe decisions.

## Parenting

As addressed earlier in this chapter, some trans people would like to be parents of a child to whom they are genetically related. Readers are encouraged to explore writings that have covered this topic in detail (Chang, Cohen, & Singh, 2017; dickey, Ducheny, & Ehrbar, 2016). There are many ways to become a parent. These include childbirth, adoption, fostering, and blending families. Each of these methods includes various risks and rewards. The cost of adoption makes this method of creating a family difficult for many people. There are also parts of the country in which adoption by a trans person is illegal. Becoming a foster parent is a long process that includes numerous invasive inquiries. This process includes a home visit to determine the suitability of the home for a foster child.

Blending families is a relatively common but often challenging practice. There are no guarantees that bringing children from one marriage or partnership into another will be the best choice for the child or the family system. These challenges can be complicated when one (or both) of the parents has a trans identity. It is not uncommon for children to experience bullying and other mistreatment based on their family formation. As a clinician working with such families, it will be important to attend to these challenges and provide your clients with the resources (e.g., Our Family Coalition, http://www.ourfamily.org) to address any concerns.

## Older Adulthood

The concerns of adults that were addressed earlier in this chapter may become amplified in older adulthood. Given the era that an older trans person grew up in, it is likely that they are especially sensitive to experiences of transphobia and discrimination (Porter et al., 2016). Even though the climate has improved considerably in the past fifty years, the damage regarding this type of discrimination has likely already made a significant impact on older trans adults.

When thinking about transphobia and discrimination, it is important for mental health providers to consider the ways that these experiences impact a person on a psychosocial level (Porter et al., 2016) by considering both protective factors and risks. One key psychosocial protective factor is social support from family, friends, and coworkers that enables an older trans adult to feel safe to explore their gender and talk to others about their identity. Another protective factor for older adults is the resilience they have developed over their lifetime (Porter et al., 2016). The fact that a trans person has lived to older adulthood is an indication that they have developed strengths and coping mechanisms that will assist in managing the reactions they have to negative experiences.

Psychosocial risk factors for older trans people include depression, suicide, and substance abuse (Fredriksen-Goldsen et al., 2014). Another risk is a lack of social support such that they cannot attend to activities of daily living or other basic care needs. This can put the trans older adult at risk for developing opportunistic health infections or becoming vulnerable in other ways. Where cisgender people may be able to rely on family members for support with their activities and basic needs, this may not be possible for the trans older adult, who may have lost contact with family members as a result of disclosing their affirmed gender.

## End-of-Life Decisions

Like everyone else, trans people are faced with end-of-life decisions, such as where they would like to reside in later stages of life and where they would like to receive medical care for health problems. Some trans people with greater economic access may also have to engage in estate planning, including establishing wills and trusts. However, there are fewer clearly laid out or affirming options for people who do not fit dominant culture norms for gender and sexuality. This is due, in part, to a lack of trans awareness in many medical systems, institutional expectations in end-of-life facilities, and a lack of understanding or support from family and friends. It can be hard enough to negotiate the end of life without these complicating factors. These considerations can be extremely anxiety-provoking for trans people, and you may be able to play a supportive role in helping clients to identify needs, feelings, and concerns related to planning for later stages in life as well as death.

Nursing homes have a long history of housing patients based on their perceived sex. This is especially challenging for people who have not made a medical transition and those with a nonbinary identity (dickey & Bower, 2016). It is important for mental health providers to advocate for their clients to ensure that they are provided a living space that is affirming and will enable the person to experience death with dignity.

Another consideration that relates to death is the ways in which a trans person's life is remembered. If you are working with a trans person at this stage of life, it is important to know what a person's final wishes are and to be certain that these are communicated to organizations that are responsible for carrying out funerals, memorial services, and burial (Porter et al., 2016). Does a person who served in the U.S. military prior to transition to a female identity want that history divulged at her funeral? Some trans people may choose to celebrate their history even at the risk of outing themselves to others for the first time. As with most recommendations in this book, we as mental health providers are charged with ensuring that the wishes of the trans person are known to officials and are carried out.

## CASE EXAMPLE. Transitioning in Older Adulthood: *Working with Veronica*

*Veronica (she/her/hers) is a sixty-six-year-old Latina trans woman whose wife of forty years, Elizabeth, recently died. Veronica experienced significant grief related to this loss. Up until Elizabeth's death, Veronica was still using he/him/his pronouns. Veronica had spoken once with Elizabeth about her trans identity, but this conversation had been difficult and had resulted in a six-month separation. Veronica and Elizabeth went to counseling for six months, which helped them to reconcile. One of the challenges that Veronica had during this process was that she didn't feel supported by either the counselor or her wife in realizing her affirmed gender. Although they were back together, Veronica continued to struggle with her trans identity as she knew that Elizabeth would not support her.*

*About two months after Elizabeth's death, Veronica finally feels as though she has the freedom to express herself as a woman. She and Elizabeth did not have any children, and as a result, Veronica now feels as though a social transition might be possible. This is what prompted her to start feeling more comfortable going by she/her/hers pronouns and initiating other aspects of social transition. She has not made a decision about whether she would like to make a medical transition. For now, she is content to make a social transition.*

Veronica prioritized her relationship with Elizabeth until Elizabeth's death. It isn't uncommon for trans people to wait until their partner dies to begin to openly explore their trans identity.

## Conclusion

In this chapter, we explored the developmental concerns that exist for trans people and the ways that a person's gender development might be interrupted based on their identity. Trans people are faced with many challenges, some of which they have in common with their trans peers, and others that are unique to their personal experience of having a trans identity. Even if you do not typically work with clients from a development perspective, it is important to explore these developmental challenges to be certain that your clients have the necessary coping skills that will build resilience. Chapter 18 is devoted to the lives of gender expansive youth.

# Going Deeper:
# Questions for Clinicians and Clients

*Questions for Clinician Self-Reflection*

1.  What type of training have I received in models of a person's developmental process?

2.  What assumptions do I hold about "normal" gender identity development or the development of other identities?

3.  What are my beliefs about the time in which a person comes to understand their gender identity?

4.  In what ways do I explore a client's identity development during the intake process and ongoing care?

5.  What types of information do I need from my client that will help me understand the challenges they have faced with regard to interruptions in their identity development?

*Questions for Client Exploration*

1.  What are the ways that you have come to understand your gender identity?

2.  How would you describe the process in which you came to identify as a trans person?

3.  What types of experiences did you have as you entered and completed puberty (if applicable)?

4.  What is your plan for becoming a parent?

5.  As you age, what resources do you have to ensure competent support for your health needs and other end-of-life decisions?

# CHAPTER 18

# Support Gender Expansive Youth

As you learned about in previous chapters exploring trans-affirmative terms, language, and identities, gender expansive youth have gender identities and gender expressions that can rapidly evolve. Therefore, the knowledge you will need to most effectively and affirmatively work with gender expansive children and adolescents will evolve as well. Furthermore, the foundational knowledge of early lifespan development we will provide in this chapter can help you contextualize presenting issues in counseling trans people later in life and in any stage of life. You will also explore some of your own experiences and feelings about working with gender expansive youth in order to be most effective in this role.

## Gender Diversity in Childhood and Adolescence

Counseling children and adolescents typically involves applying foundational knowledge of developmental milestones and often follows an Eriksonian perspective (Erikson, 1980), which we discussed in chapter 17. In this regard, clinicians working with children and adolescents share context about these milestones with families and caregivers in order to further understand how best to work with youth. Families and caregivers of gender-diverse children, however, may not have current and affirmative information about gender diversity, particularly in youth, so there can be many stereotypes, myths, and trans-negative attitudes that clinicians must address.

Then there are the fears that are, to some extent, embedded within myths and stereotypes that parents and caregivers will express directly to their children and adolescents and/or to you as the clinician:

- I'm worried my child will get bullied because "he" is too "feminine."

- If I don't "fix" my child's gender now, what will happen to "her" in the future?

- My teenager is going to get hurt when they start to date.

- I'm worried about what my family is going to think about me "letting" my teenager "do this" (referring to gender identity and/or gender expression).

- I do not know what I did wrong to cause this to happen.

## Common Myths, Stereotypes, and Attitudes

- My child is acting too much "like a boy."

- My child is acting too "feminine."

- There is no way I am letting my "boy" paint "his" fingernails.

- There is no way I am letting my "girl" not wear a shirt at the playground.

- My teenager is just doing "this" (referring to gender identity and/or gender expression) to rebel against me.

- My teenager will grow out of this stage—it's just a "phase."

- My child's friends are influencing my child—she can't really be transgender.

- My child is too young to make these kinds of decisions.

You can see, whether it is the stereotypes and myths or the more explicit fears, there tends to be a lack of information families and caregivers have about gender in general—much less about how gender expansive youth may identify and express their gender, or how they can help their children navigate the discovery and expression of their gender.

However, you grew up with a lot of gender stereotypes and myths, too. Therefore, as in so many aspects of trans-affirming and trans-centered care, a first step in developing a trans-affirmative approach to the treatment of gender diversity in youth is to explore what you think about and experienced around gender growing up. In doing so, you will revisit some of the themes explored in previous chapters.

Once you have examined your own experiences, it is helpful to know about gender development in childhood and adolescence. The families and clients with whom you work will most likely view you as the all-knowing expert of everything that has to do with gender and will ask you a good deal about what the research shows. Even families, parents, or caregivers you work with who are absolutely unsupportive will quiz you on everything that has to do with gender. Along with having solid knowledge about gender identity and development, it is important to have some ways of explaining very complex ideas about gender to people who may be struggling with their own gender identity or are in pain, disbelief, or denial about their child's gender identity. Helping family members who need this information will allow them to be the best advocates they can be for their child. Below is a quick reference list of knowledge that can help you when working with gender expansive youth and their parents and caregivers:

- Gender is a social construct that is "mapped" onto sex assigned at birth, meaning society defines what being a "boy" or "girl" is based on birth-assigned sex.

- Gender identity and expression are two different but overlapping constructs. Gender identity is a person's internal sense of identifying as a boy, girl, in between, or neither. Gender expression, on the other hand, refers to a person's external appearance or behavior.

- There are different cultural conceptions of what gender "should" and "could" be, and there tend to be negative consequences for those children and adolescents who step out of those boxes.

- Gender expression and identity tends to start between two and four years old for many people; however, there are some people who come into awareness about gender expression and identity much later in life.

- Gender can be fluid and evolving for cisgender young people.

- Gender can be fluid and evolving for trans young people.

- All-gender play (i.e., playing with peers who are both similarly and differently gendered) is healthy for children and adolescents.

How did you feel reading this list? Did it make sense, or were there areas you want to learn more about related to gender expression, identity, and fluidity as an affirming clinician?

## Questions to Consider About My Early Gender Experiences

- How did I express my gender as a child? As an adolescent?

- What did I hear about my gender that was empowering and affirming?

- What did I hear about my gender that was disempowering and not affirming?

- How do the experiences above influence how I view and understand gender diversity in childhood and adolescence?

- What are the areas related to gender diversity in childhood and adolescence I need to gain further knowledge about based on my own experiences and knowledge?

- How might I react to parents who have beliefs about gender that are similar to those that I was raised with?

- How might I react to parents who have beliefs about gender that are different from those that I was raised with?

These questions are critical, whether you are a gender therapist or not, in order to identify ways to become a more affirmative clinician with gender expansive young people.

# Understanding and Addressing Adultism in Work with Gender Expansive Youth

Adultism refers to the power and control that adults have in the lives of children and adolescents. For gender expansive youth, adultism is an issue that can appear in terms of families and caregivers trying to "control" gender identity and gender expression in a way that is in conflict with the child's wishes. This restriction of expression can be emotionally damaging to gender expansive youth. Regardless of whether you are working with gender expansive children or adolescents, it is important that you have skills in understanding and addressing adultism with families and caregivers. It is critical to be able to challenge adultist notions regarding gender diversity with accurate information about affirmative approaches. Therefore, you may have to educate the family about the importance of family acceptance and support as well as the deleterious effects of restriction and repression of gender diversity. For instance, family acceptance has been shown to reduce rates of suicidality, depression, and anxiety with gender expansive youth (Ryan, Russell, Huebner, Diaz, & Sanchez, 2010).

As a clinician, you can guide families and caregivers in how to communicate acceptance in validating ways, thereby challenging adultism that gender expansive children and adolescents experience. For instance, parents may describe forcing their child to adhere to a cisgender identity and gender expression because they are afraid of what their child may experience as a gender expansive young person. You can guide parents to consider the mental health impacts on their child of having to hide who they are from their parents, as well as to understand the power of family acceptance in a successful transition and overall well-being. Adultism can show up in unexpected ways within families. Because gender is so fluid in childhood and adolescence, some families may struggle when their child or adolescent begins to identify with a cisgender identity and expression after exploring a gender expansive identity and expression. You can support families in this regard by helping them explore the related feelings they are having about this shift in self-definition.

In doing so, it is helpful to have a list of affirming resources for families and caregivers, ideally including other parents of gender expansive children and adolescents that they can connect with and learn from in the process of supporting their children. It is also important to refer these families and caregivers to books and online media that provide psychoeducation that is affirming of gender expansive youth, such as Gender Spectrum (https://www.genderspectrum.org) and Trans Youth and Family Allies (http://www.imatyfa.org). Many of these families and caregivers may be starting from a knowledge base of no information about gender diversity across the lifespan. Knowledge can provide relief and affirmation for the families as well as their children.

# The Journey from Grief to Acceptance

As you support families and caregivers, uproot adultism, and help family members and caregivers find ways to be affirming of their gender expansive youth, keep in mind that they are on a journey that cannot happen overnight. Families and caregivers often believe their children are "perfect as they are," and as their gender expansive child goes through the process of exploring and affirming their gender identity, they experience fear and grief. They not only fear how their child may be treated in the world based on their gender identity and gender expression, but they also experience grief related to "losing" who they believed was their "son" or "daughter."

This grief is real and is important to explore and validate. Simultaneously, as a clinician you must work to ensure that this grief is not played out in the family in a way that harms the gender expansive youth. It can be helpful for families and caregivers to have their own spaces to process their grief so it does not take over the needs of the gender expansive youth. You might see family members and caregivers in individual sessions, or refer them to another clinician for individual, family, or group counseling where they can further explore their own reactions, needs, fears, and other emotions they are experiencing as they learn more about their child's gender identity. You can also validate that, just as gender expansive youth have a journey from recognizing their gender identities and expressions to exploring and accepting them, they, as families and caregivers, are moving through a similar process of recognizing, exploring, and accepting *their* identities as caregivers of a gender expansive child. Supporting them by providing information about the "typical" stages they may move from, such as denial, bargaining, sadness, anger, and ultimately acceptance, can help them understand that acceptance is a process that may take some time. Continuously coming back to affirming the best intentions for the gender expansive youth is your guideline for all interactions with families, caregivers, and school personnel and other advocacy that may be needed to develop safer and more positive environments for the young person. You can also refer families and caregivers to support groups and other resources (including online) to support them in taking the next steps on their journey.

We take a closer look at gender diversity in childhood and common presenting issues in the next section.

# Gender Expansive Children

If you work with gender expansive children, you will likely be working with families who experience a lot of confusion and fear related to their child's gender; they may hear the word "trans," in particular, and have binary notions of what trans means—such as that their child is a completely different gender than they thought they were. This may be the case, but because gender is so fluid, it is tough to know until a child grows more and more into their gender. It is helpful, therefore, to be aware that terms such as *gender expansive* and *gender creative* can be more helpful than using *trans* to describe children who are still exploring their gender expression and gender identity. These terms are not only less "binary" but can also normalize gender fluidity for parents and caregivers who are struggling with how to "do the right thing" regarding their children. That said, if children use terms such as *trans* or *transgender* to describe themselves, then you should also use those terms.

There has been immense debate on what affirming approaches "mean" when working with gender expansive children. We encourage you to follow the affirmative approach outlined by Ehrensaft (2016), in which clinicians help family members and caregivers follow and support the child's expression of gender and gender identity as opposed to controlling or guiding their gender play. This approach entails both individual and family counseling to support the child, as well as meetings with school personnel and other community members who may interact with the gender creative child in order to advocate for best treatment and the least restrictive environments for this child.

It is important to understand that treatment efforts geared toward guiding children to wear clothes and play with toys traditionally associated with their sex assigned at birth (typically via behavioral modification) are considered to be "conversion" or "reparative" therapy by leading scholars in the field (SAMHSA, 2015). This clinical approach is damaging to the child and may have adverse implications throughout their lifetime. WPATH has also stated that these treatment approaches are ineffective and unethical (Coleman et al., 2012). We encourage clinicians to avoid engaging in such efforts, even if it's as a well-meaning attempt to help a child be better accepted by peers, and to correct family members or caretakers who try such strategies with a gender-diverse child.

As you begin to work with families and caregivers of gender expansive children, it is important to guide them in decisions about when, where, and how to support children in their gender identity and expression. For instance, sometimes a stepwise approach—where children express their gender only at home, school, or in public—is best, to gain a sense of how the child does and to advocate safer environments as the child explores their gender. If the child would like to express their gender at school, but if school personnel are not affirming, you can help facilitate gender exploration in other settings that are affirming (e.g., community setting, family outings, holiday gatherings, religious/spiritual setting) so the child and parents can have a positive experience. However, if the child is experiencing intense dysphoria, you may have to work rapidly with the family to facilitate the child's gender expression within a school environment that is less than affirming. This entails much work with school personnel. Regardless of timing and setting for children's gender exploration, the guiding principle should be *What is in the best interest of the child at this time?* in terms of their overall psychosocial well-being and comfort.

In the next section, we discuss some of the common approaches to working with gender expansive adolescents.

## Gender Expansive Adolescents

Just like gender expansive children, gender expansive adolescents can claim or create language to describe their own gender expressions and gender identities best. Adolescence in general is a time of immense self-exploration of many parts of one's self, and gender is one of those aspects of self-expression. This can be confusing for families and caregivers, as they may be more familiar with language such as *trans* or *transgender*, whereas gender expansive youth may feel they are more aptly described as *genderqueer, gender nonbinary, gender blender, genderfluid*, or a host of other identities. Therefore, the guiding affirmative principle in counseling is to seek to understand the language that is important to the gender expansive adolescents, and to work with families and caregivers in affirming this language.

Adolescence and puberty raise challenges for many young people, but these developmental periods can be especially intense and challenging for those with a gender expansive identity. Not all gender expansive youth identify their genders in childhood, and many are just coming to understand their gender expression and gender identity. During this time, they are learning new language and terms that may resonate with how they experience their internal sense of gender and how they want to share their gender with the outer world. Some gender expansive adolescents may feel open to exploring their gender in a nonbinary manner. Others may experience their gender in a binary way, stating that they are a "girl" or a "boy" (in contrast to what is expected based on sex assigned at birth), and may experience dysphoria related to their changing bodies as puberty begins. In these latter instances, families and caregivers may select medical interventions to enable their adolescent to "pause" puberty so they may further explore their gender without the occurrence of physical changes associated with their sex assigned at birth (e.g., breast growth, lowering of the voice, body hair).

Regardless of the intensity of feelings related to gender identity and gender expression, especially in adolescence it is important to monitor client mood related to anxiety, depression, suicidality, nonsuicidal self-injury, and substance abuse. Because of the immense stigma gender expansive adolescents experience in society, there are numerous mental health issues that clinicians should assess for in an ongoing manner. When working with gender expansive adolescents, you should also be prepared to explore the topics of dating, sex, and family planning, including issues related to intimate partner violence and staying safer in their sexual practices. For gender expansive youth, depending on the culture, adolescence can also be a time of finding their own voice and way in life as they develop independent thoughts and feelings about the world. Often this growth in independence and self-expression can clash with the expectations of parents and caregivers, so family counseling may be helpful in supporting the family unit. Read the following case example of Trish to see how these multiple considerations may play out in working with a young client and their family.

## CASE EXAMPLE. Supporting Transition in Adolescence: *Working with Trish*

*Trish (she/her/hers) is a fifteen-year-old who identifies as a "trans girl." She is from a Croatian immigrant family who is supportive of her gender identity and gender expression. Trish and her family contact you, as she has been feeling depressed and worthless, sleeping all day, and having some suicidal thoughts (though she does not endorse any intent, plan, or means to act on these thoughts). Her parents, who have been her biggest allies in her gender identity, are starting to doubt if they "made the right decision" to support Trish as a trans girl. The more depressed Trish becomes, the more her parents doubt their decisions and begin to quiz Trish about whether she is "really trans." You work with Trish in individual sessions, and in your assessment Trish meets the criteria for major depressive disorder, but she is experiencing no distress about her gender identity. Trish feels "really scared of losing her parents' support" when it comes to her gender identity. You meet with the family and Trish in a family counseling session and provide psychoeducation on major depressive disorder, explore the family history of mental health, and facilitate communication on how Trish and her parents can address her depression. You also address the parents' apparent confusion between Trish's depression and her gender identity. In this collaborative discussion, you refer Trish to a psychiatrist for a medication assessment and to a trans-affirming support group for young women with depression.*

As is common for parents of trans youth, Trish's parents are worried about whether they are making the "right" decision in supporting Trish's identity. They have confusion about the overlap between gender dysphoria and depression. This is an opportunity to provide education and help parents understand that mental health symptoms are often overlapping yet distinct from gender concerns.

# Medical Interventions for Gender Expansive Youth

We want to acknowledge that there is a great deal of fear and misinformation surrounding medical interventions for trans and gender expansive youth, and this is sometimes perpetuated through the media or by those who are not familiar with the pathways that are available for young people who transition. The most basic facts to know are that gender-affirming medical interventions are typically not available to youth until puberty. The focus for children who are prepubertal is on gender exploration and social aspects of transition, and potentially on planning for medical interventions at a later time. Beyond that, access to gender-affirming medical interventions and the policies that dictate who is involved in decision making, consent, and the provision of care vary widely based on geographic region and medical establishments. In this section, we offer a brief overview of medical interventions available at the time that this book was written (2018). The field of pediatric trans health is continually changing, and those of you who work with children and adolescents are strongly encouraged to attend conferences and get involved with organizations that are geared toward gender expansive youth and their families, in part to get the most up-to-date information on what is possible in this realm. There are also a number of excellent books and resources that are specifically geared toward supporting therapeutic work with families with gender expansive youth (Brill, 2008; Brill & Kenney, 2016; Ehrensaft, 2016; Krieger, 2017).

Gender expansive youth who reach puberty may, at that time, start taking medications (often referred to as puberty or hormone blockers) that inhibit the development of secondary sex characteristics and other changes that usually occur during puberty. These medications are not prescribed (and are not effective) until the individual reaches the stage of puberty when secondary sex characteristics are beginning to develop, which is commonly referred to as Tanner stage 2 (Hembree, 2011). Some young people stay on these medications until the age of majority and then choose to start hormone therapy to feminize or masculinize. Some adolescents start hormone therapy at younger ages, such as fourteen to sixteen years old; this requires parental consent in most U.S. states. Some youth have access to surgeries as well, most commonly "top" or chest reconstructive surgeries. At this time, access to genital reconstructive surgeries is limited and therefore less common for adolescents, but this may change in coming years.

As mentioned in chapter 17, if gender expansive adolescents you work with take steps to suppress puberty or begin hormones, it is important to initiate discussions about how this might affect their reproductive options. This is an early developmental exploration about whether your client would like to build a family using their own genetic material (e.g., eggs or sperm). Of course, when it comes to actual medical services related to fertility preservation, it is best to refer your client to a medical professional who can answer questions about the medical aspects of this process. As a mental health provider, however, you can play an important role in helping someone explore how they feel about having children or making sometimes life-changing, irreversible decisions at an age much younger than most. In these instances, it is also helpful to connect gender expansive youth with other gender expansive people across the lifespan who have made a variety of family-building decisions, or to read about such stories online.

# Advocacy on Behalf of Gender Expansive Clients

When working with gender expansive youth, you are likely to work more regularly with professionals across disciplines to support the client's gender identity and gender expression than you would when working with older trans people. For instance, you may be in regular contact with the school principal, counselor, psychologist, or teachers regarding your client; or, if your client is prescribed hormone treatment designed to pause puberty, with this medical professional.

Advocacy with gender expansive youth may include helping them to develop their own self-advocacy skills or conducting a basic "Trans 101" training for school educators. You will need to draw upon your professional ethics code and that of the professionals you are working with—in addition to legal guidelines—in order to set expectations for affirmative treatment. It is our hope and expectation that schools and other institutions will work affirmatively with gender expansive youth, but commonly this does not happen due to a lack of information or outright discrimination. Consider the following case example.

## CASE EXAMPLE. Bullying in School: *Working with Zoey*

*Zoey (she/her/hers) is a thirteen-year-old seventh grader at a local middle school where you work as a school counselor. She identifies as a trans feminine teen and is an Alaska Native. You became aware of the challenges that Zoey faces in some of her classes and in the school cafeteria when Zoey's father called to express concern about Zoey's safety. He reported that Zoey's school performance is deteriorating and that she has been saying that she doesn't want to go to school. Zoey was reluctant to tell her father that there is a group of students who have been calling her names and following her into the bathroom and threatening her, and they have broken into her locker on more than one occasion and stolen her homework. Zoey is worried that the situation will only get worse if her father talks about this with the school. One of the people who has been bullying her has threatened that he will "make her pay" if she talks about this with others.*

*You are aware that your school has talked about instituting policies that forbid bullying, but no action has been taken to this point. It is clear to you that Zoey, and possibly other students, experience bullying and other types of harassment and discrimination. You assure Zoey's father that you will check in with Zoey once or twice during the school week in a way that respects Zoey's privacy. You reach out to a colleague at the other middle school in your district to discuss ways to develop and enact antibullying policies in your school district.*

This case portrays a common school experience for trans adolescents. Bullying happens in schools regardless of the presence of antibullying policies. When policies are present, school staff have a mechanism for addressing the bullying, such as providing emotional support and a safety plan for those who have been victimized and providing education and discipline for those who are displaying bullying behaviors.

# Teaching Self-Advocacy Skills to Gender Expansive Youth

As you are working with gender expansive youth to affirm their gender expression and gender identity, you will also help them set expectations for interacting with others. This is a challenging area, as there is still immense discrimination against trans people in schools, places of worship, and other public settings. Therefore, teaching gender expansive youth how to advocate for themselves can be a practical way to increase their resilience and well-being.

Here are some questions that we have used with gender expansive youth to help them develop self-advocacy skills:

- What do you like about your gender?

- Are there other parts of your identity (e.g., race/ethnicity) that you like as well? If so, what do you like about that identity?

- What are the pronouns and names you expect people to use to describe you and to refer to you?

- How do you know you are being treated unfairly related to your gender?

- How can people treat you to show they support you as a gender expansive youth?

There are numerous ways to teach clients self-advocacy skills, several of which are shown below.

## Strategies for Teaching Self-Advocacy Skills

- Using role-plays to explore how to talk to a teacher, parent, or other adult in their life about their gender

- Exploring the client's boundaries about what questions they are or are not comfortable answering related to their gender

- Educating the client about the difference between secrecy and privacy; supporting them in making choices regarding disclosure that are most appropriate for them in different settings

- Identifying the pronouns and names that they feel best fit their gender identity and gender expression

- Helping the client understand how to ask for what they need related to bathrooms and other gender-segregated facilities

- Coaching the client on how to report an incident of bullying from peers or adults

- Journaling, drawing, or play activities exploring how they experience and describe their gender

- Exploring communication issues related to dating and sex

- Examining how to communicate with family members about their needs and wants related to their gender

Read the following case example to see how to work with self-advocacy in a session.

## CASE EXAMPLE. Using Role-Plays with Nonbinary Students: *Working with Jimmy*

*Jimmy (he/him/his), a twelve-year-old, White, nonbinary adolescent, presents for counseling with his parents. He was assigned female at birth, but at age six, he shared with his parents that he was a boy. Now that he has entered puberty, Jimmy has asserted his identity as nonbinary, and he does not like gender-neutral pronouns. He wants his family and school peers to use the pronouns he/him/his. Jimmy shares with you that he has been bullied at school recently, and this bullying usually happens in the boy's bathroom. He doesn't want to stop using the boy's bathroom, but he also has a hard time imagining telling his parents or school teachers what is happening.*

*You ask Jimmy if you can role-play a few different scenarios related to what he has been experiencing. The goal of this role-play is to support Jimmy in exploring his fears. He agrees. You first have him consider what he might tell a teacher about what he is experiencing. You ask him to imagine speaking with a teacher he feels might be supportive. Jimmy shares that he wants to tell one of his teachers whom he feels most comfortable with because this teacher supports him and "gets" that he is nonbinary; he doesn't have to explain his identity to the teacher. You conduct the role-play, with you in the role of the teacher and Jimmy opening up to you. Next you explore in a role-play what he would feel comfortable sharing with his parents, and it emerges that he is scared his parents will "make him be cisgender again." Finally, you explore what he might say if bullying were to happen in the bathroom, and Jimmy says he "doesn't know" and feels "stuck with what to say." You ask Jimmy to role-play a person with bullying behavior and you role-play Jimmy so he can hear some options he has to stand up for himself—such as saying he has the right to use the bathroom and sharing what happened with a teacher.*

Your work with Jimmy helps him understand the ways these bullying experiences are impacting him. By engaging in role-play scenarios, you help Jimmy to develop some skills to address what he is experiencing in school.

# Conclusion

Gender expansive youth are inspiring and creative in their gender identities and expressions. They can also challenge everything that families and caregivers (including you) think about gender. You as a clinician, therefore, are often serving as a bridge of sorts—a bridge of education, understanding, affirmation, and validation—as families and caregivers go on a journey they may have never expected to be on. Because gender expansive youth often have little power over their lives, addressing adultism, working collaboratively with necessary stakeholders in children's lives, and teaching self-advocacy skills become critical components of affirming counseling. The next and final section covers special topics and concerns. We begin by addressing the ways we can create a trans-affirming practice environment.

# Going Deeper:
# Questions for Clinicians and Clients

## Questions for Clinician Self-Reflection

1. What would I find most challenging about working with a gender expansive child?

2. Would I prefer to work with a gender expansive child or adolescent? Why?

3. What are the professional ethics and legal resources I have to support advocacy with gender expansive youth and their families or caregivers?

4. What therapeutic interventions might I use to explore self-advocacy skills and support the journey from grief to acceptance of families and caregivers for their gender expansive youth?

## Questions for Client Exploration

1. Can you tell me in your own words how you describe your gender?

2. Can you share with me an experience when you felt supported in your gender within your family or with your caregivers?

3. Can you share with me an experience when you did not feel supported in your gender within your family or with your caregivers?

4. Can you tell me about a time you stood up for yourself when someone treated you unfairly?

5. Can you tell me about your friends who are supportive of your gender?

**PART 5**

# SPECIAL TOPICS AND CONCERNS

CHAPTER 19

# Create Trans-Affirming Practice Environments

As you read about your role in working with trans clients in part 4, you may have begun to think about whether your work environment supports this role, is inclusive, or is affirming of trans clients. It is a natural consideration as you intentionally become trans-affirming. This chapter explores how the context of the environment where you practice can send a message to trans clients that your office is a space where they can take risks, share who they really are, and discuss their needs and the challenges they face in the world. You may work in one setting or in many places as a clinician, so keep these work spaces in mind as you read this chapter.

## Safe Space, Safer Space, or Empowering Space?

As you reflect on the place where you practice with clients, there may be things you can control, like how you decorate the space, as well as things you can't control, such as what clients will see as they enter your building. You may have concerns about the office climate as you think about the message your practice space sends to clients regarding how and if they are welcome.

The dilemma trans clients face regarding your office space can parallel what they experience in the world outside of counseling. When trans people access services from others—from hair stylists to health care providers—there are often several questions on their mind:

- How will people here treat me as a trans person?

- Will I be asked invasive or annoying questions about my gender?

- Will providers or other people accessing services here stare at me while I am here?

- How fast can I get away from this office if I find myself feeling unsafe?

- Am I going to have to educate this provider on being trans (even if it has nothing to do with why I am here)?

- What should I tell this person—or leave out of my story—in order to get the services I need?

This is just a sample list, and you can imagine how exhausting it can be to have these questions as you do something as simple as going to the grocery store or as significant as accessing your first counseling session as a trans person embarking on a social or medical transition. The internal dialogue that these questions can create can also heighten gender dysphoria or make it difficult for a person to feel comfortable accessing public spaces or going to social events.

Many of these questions can shift depending on where a trans person is in their own gender identity development. For instance, you may work with clients who change their clothes in their car from the ones they wore to school or work to clothes that fit their affirmed gender identity. For some clients, this is just something they do and feel good about. For others, they may sit frozen in their cars afraid of who might see them. Consider offering a plan ahead of time to walk the client from their car or bathroom, where they change clothes, into your office. This is not the most common way to begin a session with a client, but for some trans clients this is a life-affirming way to support them in their gender identity and gender expression.

There are many considerations to reflect on when thinking about making your practice space affirming for trans clients. As we addressed in chapter 6, your role as a clinician is to develop safer spaces for trans clients. You cannot always control the transphobic person a trans client may encounter in a bathroom, even if they are single-stall bathrooms! However, you can use the safer spaces framework to continuously identify ways to make your environment safer. Taking this one step further, you can think about the environment in which you practice not as a space that has to empower trans clients, but rather as a space in which you support them in empowering themselves. Shifting your thinking in this direction can be a huge relief in helping you to hold appropriate boundaries between what is and is not your responsibility and viewing clients with greater respect and autonomy.

Let's take a closer look at your practice space and marketing materials; bathroom access; intake forms, paperwork, and electronic medical record systems; and your first contact with clients. As you read through these sections, keep in mind there are things you can control and influence, as well as things you cannot. However, some things you think you cannot control you can actually have a long-term influence on, making your practice more affirming to trans clients.

## Your Practice Space and Marketing Materials

When people think of going to counseling, they often imagine the all-knowing doctor and the Freudian couch. Or, if a client has a better idea of what counseling actually feels like, they may have the image of a touchy-feely space with soft meditation music in the office waiting room and a couch with big, comfy pillows. Then there is the image you had in mind when you created your practice space. You probably thought intentionally about how to convey a welcoming space, how to situate everything from furniture to art, and whether personal photographs from your own life did or did not fit in the space.

Intentional reflection is the type of approach needed as you assess how trans-affirming your practice space is for trans clients. Remember the questions you read above that might be in a trans client's mind; it is important to consider what they see, experience, and feel as they enter your space. You might consider displaying images or icons that are trans-affirming. Having books about and written by trans people, books on multicultural and social justice competence in counseling, and images and symbols of diverse cultures gives clients visual cues that their gender identity and other intersecting identities are valued. We want our clients to know that all of their identities are welcome in our practice space.

Although it is tempting to just have the identities you value in your space (why not, we all have our own identity), it is important to strive to include identities with which you do not identify. Regardless of the beliefs and values you hold and the cultural traditions you engage in, you can place images of diversity strategically.

Creating safer spaces for trans people begins before they enter your office, with your marketing materials, including paper brochures and business cards, as well as your online presence. Here are some things to consider in this regard.

## Creating Trans-Affirming Marketing Materials

- List your pronouns below your email signature line and on your business cards and other marketing materials. Stay away from the term *preferred pronouns*, as pronoun use is not a preference like whether you like cream in your coffee or not. You might also include a link to an educational resource about pronouns. This is an intervention that increases awareness for other colleagues and destigmatizes the use of pronouns that are different from those associated with a person's sex assigned at birth.

- Talk about the training and education you have completed regarding trans clients, and other identities such as people of color or immigrants, in your marketing materials. Many of our clients have let us know that these communications and clues signaling awareness of cultural concerns are what first made them decide to contact us.

> • Include whether you have access to all-gender, single-stall, or other trans-affirming bathrooms. If you don't, consider mentioning how trans people can feel safe in the bathrooms within your building, such as with a single-key access to bathrooms rather than public bathrooms. You may be able to advocate for an all-gender restroom with your landlord if you are interested in working with trans clients.
>
> • Include a trans-affirming symbol, which you can easily access from the Internet or have printed in a sticker form.

In addition to your marketing materials, consider the conversation you have with trans clients before they ever get to your office. This can be an ideal opportunity to give information about your theoretical conceptualization in working with clients, style of counseling, pricing structure, and specific ways you have endeavored to make your office a safer space for trans clients.

## Bathroom Access

Although we discussed bathroom access above, it is an important topic to address further. Depending on where a trans client is in their own gender identity development, they may or may not think much about bathrooms. Clients who identify with the gender binary of "man" and "woman"—or who choose no/low disclosure—may be more comfortable with binary gendered bathrooms, especially if they feel they are typically perceived correctly by others as their affirmed gender.

Other trans clients who want to socially and medically transition but are early in their transition may worry a lot about bathrooms and their safety. (Contrary to some trans-discriminatory state and federal policies across the United States that are trying to get people to think that trans people are going to hurt cisgender people in bathrooms, it is important to know that this situation is exactly the opposite. Trans people can be and are hurt in bathrooms by cisgender people. This can range from being stared at, resulting in emotional pain, to being physically and sexually harassed and even murdered). Your reflection on bathroom use centers not only on whether you have a single-stall or all-gender bathroom, but also on the conversations you have with your clients about the bathroom experiences and considerations they have in the world and your own building.

For genderqueer and nonbinary clients, bathrooms may continually serve as an annoyance or barrier. Your role as a clinician is to support them in finding bathroom access that feels safe and processing the emotions they have living in a world that does not understand affirming bathroom access for people with gender fluidity. Several apps have been designed to track trans-affirming bathrooms and single-stall bathrooms (e.g., Refuge Restroom) that allow you to locate all-gender restrooms. Some of these apps focus specifically on the existing all-gender bathrooms within a university campus or work setting. Ultimately, we believe processing bathroom experiences with trans clients can be empowering. As a clinician, this means you need to support trans clients through the natural anxiety, concern, pain, or indifference that comes up regarding bathrooms. We cannot wait until there is a time when we do not have to talk about bathrooms, and are able to just think about things like whether or not the restrooms are clean. For now, bathrooms are a crucial part of making sure trans clients stay healthy and do not have to avoid bathroom use, which can result in health concerns.

## Intake Forms, Paperwork, and Electronic Medical Records

You may update your intake forms, paperwork, and electronic medical records each year, which is a great practice and a good way to think about ensuring that these materials are trans-affirming. Because trans-affirming care is rapidly evolving as people realize that health care should be accessible to trans people in a culturally responsive way, you may want to make a regular practice of making adjustments to your forms and paperwork to ensure they are relevant for trans clients. One way to do this is to use open-ended questions about gender identity, racial/ethnic identity, and so forth, which would look like this on your forms:

Write the word(s) that describe your gender identity here: _____

Write the word(s) that describe your racial/ethnic identity here: _____

You may use a client-tracking software program that has checkboxes for sex and gender and doesn't allow these fill-in-the-blank options. In these cases, you can write to the software developers and request trans-affirming options. It may seem overwhelming to do this, but we have found it takes a simple email request, and often software companies want to stay up to date with their practices because they value your business! We advise using a two-step approach (Lambda Legal, 2016a; Tate, Ledbetter, & Youssef, 2013) for electronic data gathering.

### Using a Two-Step Question to Assess Gender

1. What is your current gender identity?

   ☐ Male

   ☐ Female

   ☐ Transgender Male/Trans Man

☐ Transgender Female/Trans Woman

☐ Genderqueer, neither exclusively male nor female

☐ Additional Gender Category (please specify):

_____

☐ Decline to answer

2. What sex were you assigned at birth on your original birth certificate (check one)?

☐ Male

☐ Female

☐ Decline to answer

This option is not perfect—too many checkboxes, and the word *other* can be overwhelming and non-affirming. However, we also understand that some larger health care and government institutions are slow to change the above options. If you happen to work in a practice setting where you are limited to large electronic medical record systems, it is important to engage in good advocacy (which we talk more about later in this chapter). For example, you may work for a large health care system where you can contribute to the development and use of a tool that captures more useful gender-related information than the forced binary of "male" or "female." This tool might include sex assigned at birth, gender identity, pronouns, and an organ inventory. The organ inventory is helpful in identifying the kinds of preventative care that a trans client may need. For example, knowing that a client has a uterus may prompt OB/GYN preventative care, even if the person has changed their gender marker to "M" on the medical record. These choices are progressive and vitally important to tracking trans care. You can create a safer space for trans clients by exploring their experiences of completing the paperwork and ensuring you gather the most important terms, pronouns, and language that are trans-empowering for them.

## Your First Contact with Clients in Session

Each of the above considerations in trans counseling leads to your first in-session contact with clients. As you meet with a client for the first time, there are numerous opportunities to continue being trans-affirmative (especially if you are working in a practice setting that has limited electronic medical record options). It is a good time to reintroduce yourself to the client, even if you have spoken on the phone, reminding them of your name and pronouns and asking about theirs. In this initial phase, you can begin to integrate the trans resilience perspective discussed in chapter 9 as you assess mental health diagnoses, trauma history, family history, sexual history, and other aspects of your client's life to ensure you are taking a strengths-based approach.

In addition, as we talked about in chapter 2, many trans clients do not trust providers because they have heard bad stories or myths or have had personal experiences of poor treatment in health care. It can be useful to have a short introduction—or elevator speech—about being trans-affirming that you can use when first talking with clients, and it is important to listen to and notice their reaction. If a client comes in thinking they have to "say the right things" to get a letter of referral for hormones from you, nothing you say will sink in right away. The client instead will have to ease into an experience of trans-affirming counseling with you, and you can provide gentle reminders of this along the way by saying the following:

- *Some people naturally have concerns about "saying the right thing" to get medical treatment they need, and that is because counseling used to be that way. I do not practice that way, so feel free to ask any and all questions you have about the process.*

- *My goal is to help you get the trans-affirming resources you need, and if you encounter any stumbling blocks, I am here to help you move through them and around them.*

The following case example pulls together the information you just read about to illustrate what each of these ways to create safer and more trans-affirming practice settings might look like:

## CASE EXAMPLE. Establishing Initial Rapport: *Working with Mikel*

*You receive a call from a person named Mikel (she/her/hers), a seventy-one-year-old transsexual-identified woman who uses a wheelchair. Mikel found your counseling brochure in her health care provider's office, and she noticed the trans-affirming symbol included in your brochure. Mikel is just starting to explore her gender identity. You share your pronouns with her and ask the name and pronouns she wants you to use. Mikel says she likes transsexual, because that is the word she grew up with, and you share that it is an important part of your role as her counselor to use the words that feel good to her. You share information about parking and your fee structure, and you also share that your role is to be an advocate for her to make sure she receives the best and most affirming treatment. You let Mikel know that your office space is accessible to people with a range of abilities, and she shares that she uses a wheelchair. You also share that the bathrooms in your office are single-stall and therefore accessible to people with a range of identities and needs. When Mikel comes into your office, she immediately sees images of diverse people, even people with a range of abilities, and the paperwork she completes has spaces where she can write in her gender identity.*

This example shows the ways that you can begin to engage with your clients in an affirmative manner. It is important that the messages about your affirmative approach are consistent, from your marketing materials and language with clients to the space where you practice.

# Your Role of Advocacy in Creating Safer Practice Spaces

You have already learned about the role advocacy has in counseling trans clients, and this role extends to your practice environment(s) as well. Advocacy can happen on two levels. You can advocate *on behalf* of trans clients, or you can advocate *with* trans clients. If you are working in a private practice where you control much of your office setting, you likely are working on behalf of trans clients as you endeavor to make your office more trans-affirming and a safer space. You are thinking of the trans-affirming images clients see and the experience they have of you as a clinician. However, you may be working in a larger corporate, nonprofit, or government setting where you have less control over the environment. In these cases you may be advocating on behalf of trans clients wherever you can, but there may also be opportunities to advocate with trans clients. For example, if you work for a medical system, you can help create advisory boards consisting of trans members so that their voices may be centered in the design or implementation of trans health care services.

In your advocacy role, you may work with personnel in military hospitals and Veterans Administration (VA) settings in developing safer office settings, medical data reporting procedures, and clinical care practices to improve the experience of trans military service members and veterans. However, there can be stumbling blocks. Holding focus groups with trans consumers who receive clinical services can provide important data for your advocacy work in improving service provision. Additionally, you may be able to work with trans veterans who are leaders in local and national trans communities to provide firsthand stories of trans client experiences, needs, challenges, and expectations. These stories will provide the "heart" of advocacy and may have a significant impact in terms of systemic change on larger levels.

As a clinician engaging in advocacy, do not underestimate the impact of a small act of advocacy on behalf of or with trans clients; it's actually these small acts of advocacy in collaboration with others that can have huge impacts. An example of advocacy is when group providers come together and ask for an additional men's bathroom to be changed into a single-stall bathroom. You can also ask to change a "Unisex" sign on a single-stall bathroom to a more affirming sign that reads "All Gender," or advocate for a bathroom that has a baby changing station, nursing station, and single-stall access for people with disabilities and trans people who want to use the bathroom in privacy. Something that seems out of reach in your practice environment might be closer to reality than you think. Gather with other trans-affirming clinicians and providers and have ongoing discussions about how to continuously advocate changes in your environments.

## Conclusion

In this chapter you learned about your role as a clinician in developing safer spaces for trans clients with whom you work. From your office decorations and overall environment to forms, paperwork, electronic data, and bathrooms, there are numerous opportunities for you to improve your practice setting(s) for trans clients. The best news is that when you do these things and advocate on behalf of and with trans clients, you often make the practice setting safer for all people because they notice that efforts are being made to support some of the most marginalized people in society. In the following chapter we explore the ways that you can engage in advocacy.

# Going Deeper:
# Questions for Clinicians and Clients

*Questions for Clinician Self-Reflection*

1.  What messages does my practice space communicate to trans clients across a range of identities—such as no/low disclosure (a.k.a. "stealth"), nonbinary, and trans people—and across a range of cultural identities and belief systems?

2.  What improvements can I make in my office space, paperwork, forms, electronic records, or marketing materials to make these more trans-affirming?

3.  What is the privilege—or lack of privilege—I have when it comes to accessing bathrooms? How does this influence how much action I take in making sure there are accessible bathrooms within my practice space(s)?

4.  What opportunities do I have to work with others in my practice space(s) or building in making the overall environment more trans-affirming?

5.  How can I advocate *on behalf of* or *with* trans clients in developing safer practice spaces for trans clients?

*Questions for Client Exploration*

1.  My goal is to make my office environment as trans-affirming as possible. Is it okay to ask you from time to time about any concerns you may have related to this?

2.  Typically, paperwork or questionnaires can be gendered. How did it feel to complete my intake paperwork, and were there any concerns that came up for you? I also invite you to share any other experiences of navigating paperwork with other providers or systems.

3.  Bathrooms can be a huge stressor or an awesome experience, once you are using the right bathroom for you, or something in between. What do you want me to know about your experiences of using bathrooms as a trans person here and elsewhere?

4.  Are there any aspects of your life that you wish were more inclusive? How would you want them to be different?

# CHAPTER 20

# Be a Strong Trans Advocate

Advocacy is an integral part of clinical practice with trans clients (dickey, Singh, Chang, & Rehrig, 2017). Whether you work as an academician, researcher, or clinical practitioner, advocacy with and on behalf of trans clients can be easily incorporated into your work. In this chapter we will expand upon some key aspects of advocacy that you will want to consider in your role.

## What Is Advocacy?

The idea that advocacy is part of a clinician's role may not have been a part of the training you received in or following graduate school. Advocacy can be defined as engaging in activities that are designed to remove or diminish barriers faced by others. Advocacy can have different meanings based on the setting in which it takes place. From an organizational perspective, it can be defined as engaging with decision makers to develop policies and rules that prioritize the safety of trans people (Lating, Barnett, & Horowitz, 2009). A group may work together to provide information about a human service need such as affordable housing for trans people. This might involve educating elected officials or making statements at public meetings that elucidate the ways in which trans people are discriminated against or experience differences from their cisgender peers in access to housing.

Thinking back to our discussion in chapter 8 regarding various systems of influence in a person's life, advocacy can be applied at individual, micro-, exo-, and macrosystemic levels. On an *individual* level, advocacy efforts would be targeted at addressing concerns that primarily impact the individual. We consider writing letters of referral for hormones or surgery to be a part of one's clinical practice; however, it can also be seen as an act of advocacy. You are effectively lending your voice to ensure that your client has access to the care they need.

When advocating on the *microsystem* level, the efforts you make on your client's behalf will also have an impact on other people's lives. For example, you may be working with an adolescent who has been experiencing mixed support at their middle school. Work that you do to help ensure that the school is enforcing its antibullying policies will help not only your client but also anyone else at the school who is experiencing bullying.

The exosystem includes environmental elements that have a profound influence on a person's development even though that person is not directly involved with them. One example would be a parent's workplace. The parent may be having difficulty in their workplace after their coworkers learned about their child's identity. In your work with the family, the parent may ask for your support in addressing the workplace issues. Although this does not directly affect the adolescent in the same way that it does the parent, if the parent feels safe in the workplace, they are also likely to have more energy to be present for their family.

The *macrosystem* is the level where advocacy work can have the largest and most lasting impact. The macrolevel includes local, state, and national policy development. As engaged citizens, we have the ability to interact with our elected officials and make our position known. Another way to engage in change at a macrolevel is to work within our respective professional organizations to ensure that training resources, policies, and conference programming is inclusive of trans topics.

Advocacy has different applications based on the context of the interaction and the client(s) you are advocating for. With all types of advocacy, it is important to ensure that you do not inadvertently breach your client's confidentiality. If you are working on an exo- or macrolevel, you could inadvertently describe the need for change in a way that identifies your client. In this type of situation, prior to the conversation, make sure that you are able to talk about the needs in a general way that does not allow others to identify your client(s).

# Advocacy and Clinical Practice

There are a number of ways that clinicians can engage in advocacy on behalf of their clients, including letter writing, political engagement, and social media engagement.

## Letter Writing

Letter writing has been a part of work with trans clients since the medicalization of trans people's identities and the development of the WPATH SOC, which you have read about throughout this book. As we explored in chapter 12, you will write letters of referral when a physician or insurance company requires a referral from a mental health clinician prior to initiating medical care (e.g., hormones and/or surgery). Although clinicians provide an advocacy role that calls for the release of protected client information such as diagnosis and treatment recommendations, use caution when divulging information about your client. Letters should include only that information which is truly necessary (Budge, 2015; Budge & dickey, 2017). This means that unless there is a reason to do so, you should not include a diagnosis of gender dysphoria. It may be simplest to start from a boilerplate or sample letter and use this as a format for all of your letters. However, in doing so, you may neglect to address the nuanced concerns that a specific client has. Furthermore, simply changing the name and the pronouns to fit the current client has the potential for communicating inaccurate information.

## CASE EXAMPLE. Advocacy Through Letter Writing and Diagnosis: *Working with Heather*

*Heather (she/her/hers) is a thirty-two-year-old Alaska Native who identifies as a woman. Heather has been working with Dr. Simmons (she/her/hers), who also has a Native American identity, for about a year. Heather originally sought care for depressive symptoms and recently developed awareness of her gender identity. Heather's health insurance will cover a number of gender-affirming medical interventions and mental health care. Heather has decided that she would like to initiate hormone therapy. Dr. Simmons works with Heather to help her understand the requirements of her health insurance, which include letters—that must state a diagnosis of gender dysphoria—for any medical interventions.*

*Dr. Simmons opens a conversation with Heather about these requirements. Heather is distressed that she would need to have a diagnosis. Her cultural background is not aligned with Western medicine, and she is beginning to question her desire to make a medical transition. Dr. Simmons works closely with Heather to understand the cultural challenges and how her desires for a medical transition are in conflict. Heather talks about the conversations she had engaged in with elders from her tribal community, who have been supportive of her identity exploration. They have been cautious about endorsing her interest in hormones but have not given a clear signal that she should not begin this treatment.*

*Although Dr. Simmons also has a Native American identity, she realizes that Heather's experience as an Alaska Native is very different from her own. Dr. Simmons often finds herself thinking about the ways her tribe would respond. Dr. Simmons realizes that she needs to be cautious in how she works with Heather so that she does not unduly influence Heather in a direction that is based on her own cultural norms, values, or worldviews. At the same time, Dr. Simmons reaches out to a colleague who has experience in work with Alaska Natives to gain more knowledge about the ways that trans people are understood. Dr. Simmons is careful to not assume that all Alaska Natives hold the same beliefs, and she double checks with Heather to be sure she has a good understanding.*

In this case, Dr. Simmons approaches working with Heather with humility and refrains from making assumptions based on some aspects of shared identity. She speaks openly with Heather about diagnosis and provides a space in which Heather can explore diagnosis, how it relates to distress, and the meaning it has for her in her culture and community.

Your clients may also ask you to write letters to simply state that they have a diagnosis of gender dysphoria and are being treated by you, or to state the client's affirmed gender. Your client may use these letters to support changing their gender marker on identity documents, or they may carry this letter while traveling in the case that a professional's endorsement provides them protection. Though these letters do not have legal binding, they can have an influence on legal concerns (e.g., changing a passport gender marker) and often provide a sense of safety for clients (Keo-Meier, Ducheny, & Hendricks, 2018).

## Engagement in Political Issues

The notion of the personal being political, which arose from the feminist movement, is applicable here. Gender, which is deeply personal, is not without political significance. Like other marginalized groups that have experienced challenges in changing the political landscape, trans people have seen significant progress that has been short-lived in some cases. In 2017, it was hard to keep up with the changes that influenced hard-fought rights for trans people. Some of these rights were completely stripped away, and others were tenuously upheld.

As providers, we need to engage with political efforts for the purpose of ensuring that our clients are able to live, love, and work in safety. This work does not necessarily entail running for an elected office, though that might be an option. Becoming involved in political efforts can include donating money to political causes or not-for-profit organizations that address the needs of trans people. You can also make calls or send messages to your elected officials. A final way you might consider getting involved is to volunteer your time for an organization in your community that serves trans people. This might involve completing basic office duties, providing rides to medical appointments, serving on the board of directors, or assisting with fund-raising efforts. There are many ways to get involved, and a simple call to an agency can help you to find a position that is commensurate with your experience and that works in your schedule.

## Engagement with Social Media

In this day and age, information sharing happens rapidly via social media sites (e.g., Facebook, Twitter). Clinicians have gained a more visible online presence and have platforms from which they can share information and professional opinions. This is different from providing direct clinical services; instead, clinicians share their perspectives with a broader, more public audience. When using social media, there are many opportunities in which clinicians can advocate for trans equality, health care, and rights.

For example, many clinicians have Facebook profiles and join different affinity groups, which may include groups geared toward professionals working with trans clients. One way you might get involved in advocacy is by providing affirming, accurate information about trans people in these groups. Another example of advocacy that you might choose is to challenge practices that are exploitative or not adhering to current best practices. Yet another way to advocate is to post information about how to support organizations that are trans-led and trans-centered. We have participated in crowdsourcing campaigns to support organizations that provide healing justice funds and mental health scholarships for queer and trans people of color, and in posting about this online we have been able to encourage our professional communities to do the same. While you may not consider these ways of engaging with social media as advocacy, it is important to understand the power or influence you may have as a health professional. Your support in these forums can go a long way in shifting attitudes or increasing awareness.

## Staying Current as a Knowledgeable Trans-Affirming Provider

Regardless of the work you engage in, it is important to stay current with developments in the field of trans health, respectful language, resources, and the ways in which changing political landscapes affect trans people. One of the simplest ways to stay current is to read articles in popular media outlets, peer-reviewed literature, and writings that center trans voices.

Another way is to seek continuing education programs or conferences, but keep in mind that some people who conduct this type of training do so from a pathologizing or outdated perspective. People attending these conferences include medical doctors, nurses, physician's assistants, counselors, psychologists, and other health care providers.

### List of Trans Conferences with Provider Training

- Gender Odyssey (Seattle, WA, and Los Angeles, CA)
- Philadelphia Trans Wellness Conference (Philadelphia, PA)
- Gender Spectrum (Hayward, CA)
- Gender Infinity (Houston, TX)
- UCSF National Trans Health Summit (Oakland, CA)
- WPATH Biennial Symposium (location varies)

Staying current brings its own challenges. The costs associated with obtaining affirming training, including certification programs, can be prohibitive, which can result in a form of "gatekeeping for gatekeepers." This is one of the reasons that trans providers and providers who are people of color are not adequately represented in trans health.

If you are unable to find or afford a training program in your area, it might be useful to find colleagues near you with whom you can consult. Participation in ongoing consultation groups can be an enriching way to stay connected to current approaches to trans- or gender-related care while also building connections with other clinicians who do similar work. We have found it invaluable to have spaces in which we can consult about cases with colleagues who are also invested in approaching care in an affirming and culturally informed way. Groups may involve peer consultation or be led by a more advanced gender therapist. We can share one example of how this might look in practice. Coauthor Sand runs consultation groups from their private practice. The groups are structured with two main components: a didactic topic or focus (usually involving one or two readings per month) and time for case consultation. In this group, the focus is on an affirming and social justice–oriented approach to care, which sometimes is focused on ongoing counseling or healing work, sometimes on referral for medical interventions (i.e., letter writing), and sometimes both. The groups run in time-limited cycles and occur both in person and online. There are a number of gender therapists who provide a similar service in person and online; we encourage you to find such a group if you would like to have a space to continually build upon your skills and forge stronger connections with other gender therapists.

# Conclusion

In this chapter, we explored the ways that providers can engage in advocacy efforts and stay current in their knowledge of trans people's lives and experiences. Becoming involved in advocacy does not have to take a significant amount of time or money—you can engage in advocacy with just five minutes a day! Staying current is critical as it will help to ensure that the trans people you are working with are offered the most relevant care based on up-to-date knowledge and practices.

# Going Deeper:
# Questions for Clinicians and Clients

## *Questions for Clinician Self-Reflection*

1. What are the ways that I can engage with local, state, or federal political efforts?

2. What organizations in my community are serving the needs of trans people?

3. What community events are happening in support of trans people? Can I volunteer my time or other resources in support of the event?

4. What knowledge do I need to ensure that I am up to date?

5. How can I connect with other professionals who are doing work in this field so that I may stay up to date with current practices and build professional connections?

6. What changes are happening in regard to trans health care that I need to know more about?

## *Questions for Client Exploration*

1. On a scale of 1–10, how comfortable do you feel advocating for yourself with _____ (health care providers, pharmacists, employers, attorneys, police, first responders)?

2. Is it okay if we do a role-play to explore how you might advocate for your rights with your _____ (health care providers, pharmacists, employers, attorneys, police, first responders)?

3. How do you experience me, as a clinician, in my role with regard to advocacy? Are there ways in which you would like me to advocate for you, and what does that mean for our work together?

4. I want to be sure that the work I have been doing with your [school, place of work] has helped. Have things changed for the better? What other changes might be necessary?

5. As you think about your needs, how can you be certain those are met, whether by yourself or by others?

# CHAPTER 21

# Empower Trans Counselors

Although this book is for clinicians of all gender identities, this chapter focuses specifically on those who are trans, nonbinary, or gender nonconforming. We have written this chapter based on the special concerns that have come up for us as clinicians who identify under the trans, nonbinary, and gender nonconforming umbrella. We hope that this may support you as you navigate serving trans clients who may be similar to or different from you. For cisgender clinicians, this chapter may also be helpful in increasing your understanding of some of the dynamics that trans clients and clinicians often navigate. We think this will allow you to be more skillful clinicians and stronger allies.

Much of this chapter was informed by years of personal and professional experience working as trans clinicians, as well as conversations held over many years with peers. Some of these conversations have occurred online, within consultation groups, and at trans provider workshops and panels at professional and community conferences. For this reason, we want to acknowledge and express appreciation for the collective wisdom that has informed the content of this chapter. As most training in mental health assumes and centers cisgender clinician identity, relying on community for shared knowledge and experience for how to be trans-affirming clinicians in our roles has been both necessary and empowering.

## Working Within Our Communities

There are many reasons why you may or may not choose to work within trans communities. We do not assume that working with trans clients is of interest to all trans clinicians. In fact, doing so would be pigeonholing and placing an unfair burden or responsibility on us. If you are reading this book, however, we assume that you have some interest in working with trans clients or are already doing so.

Some of you, having recognized a real gap in the competency of mental health providers working with trans clients, may feel called to serve your communities. This recognition may stem from having received subpar or harmful mental health care yourself from unskilled providers. Most of us know that at this time, most clinicians have never received formal clinical training on working with trans clients. Many of us feel called to fill this gap so that we may help reduce disparities and contribute to the health and well-being of our communities. Though trans clinicians have become more visible in existing leadership and administrative roles within trans health over time, power structures must also shift so that we can not only have a "seat at the table," but also center our needs and voices to ensure that these structures belong to us.

Although some of us have actively pursued a specialization in working with trans people, some of us have fallen into this kind of work based on others referring trans clients to us on the assumption that this is a clinical specialty. We may be the only option or one among a few options for trans clients seeking trans clinicians. For this reason, many of us have unintentionally developed a specialization.

## Clinician Self-Disclosure

Self-disclosure, simply defined as what you decide to reveal about yourself to clients, is a common concern for trans clinicians. Clinician self-disclosure has been a "hot topic" across various theoretical approaches, although many feminist-centered clinicians view self-disclosure as a vital component of building rapport with clients and debunking myths about the clinician being "all-knowing." We strive for an egalitarian client-clinician relationship and acknowledge that issues of social justice affect clients and clinicians. From this perspective, self-disclosure makes you "real" to the client and can facilitate client healing.

Deciding whether, what, and how much to disclose can be challenging for many reasons. If you are a trans clinician, you will likely feel this tension about self-disclosure related to your gender identity in addition to all of the other issues related to clinician self-disclosure. To help you make these decisions, begin by considering that clinician self-disclosures typically fall into three different categories: (a) information about your professional background or stance, (b) feelings, reactions, and responses you have to the client or counseling interaction, and (c) information about your personal life.

Professional self-disclosure may include sharing details about your clinical training or background, such as your theoretical orientation. Many of us have to make decisions about how much to disclose on online marketing platforms (e.g., clinician pages on websites or search engines) about the kinds of clients we work with or our clinical areas of practice. We believe that stating that one practices from an affirming stance with trans clients is generally helpful, as unfortunately, clients cannot always make this assumption when seeking a mental health provider.

Self-disclosure of feelings, reactions, or responses to your client or the clinical interaction is related to sharing what is coming up for you internally (i.e., thoughts, sensations, emotions). This may include expressing your feelings about what a client has shared or deciding to show a visible facial expression that communicates an empathic response. For example, the clinician's expression of anger about a way that a client has been mistreated may allow that client to identify or access their own anger. Ideally, this kind of self-disclosure is done with the aim of benefiting the client and is done at clinically appropriate times.

Personal self-disclosure may include sharing details about your life, such as where you grew up, whether you are married, if you have pets or children, where you will be when you are out of the office, or aspects of your cultural identity. It could involve disclosing that you also have a trans identity or sharing some aspects of your own transition. There are likely some aspects of who you are that you have a choice about disclosing and others that you do not. In other words, some aspects of who we are tend to be more visible, while others are only known when we choose to communicate them. For example, some queer therapists of color may feel like they have power over whether to disclose being part of the queer community but do not have the power over whether to disclose their racial identity because it is more visible. The power of choice in self-disclosing about a physical disability may be less than the power of choice you have in self-disclosing about having a disability that is not always visible to others.

The choice of whether, how, and how much to share about your own gender identity or experience of being trans or nonbinary is, of course, a highly personal one. In addition, we recognize that the choice to disclose this information varies among clinicians; that is, there may be some who feel that based on appearance, your gender identity or trans identity may be more or less apparent to others. Samuel Lurie (2014) conducted focus groups for trans clinicians with a focus on self-disclosure. One theme was an erroneous assumption that trans therapists always have the choice of self-disclosure when, in reality, intentionality and planned self-disclosure is not always accessible due to physical appearance, online presence, personal or professional writing, or general community knowledge.

There is no right or wrong answer in terms of whether or how much to self-disclose, but we recommend being intentional about the risks and benefits for both you and your clients. For example, some trans clinicians choose not to disclose being trans on a public level (e.g., website) but opt to disclose that information to clients on a case-by-case basis. This way, the information is more controlled or private. This may be especially important for clinicians who live or work in areas in which they are concerned about their own safety. There are other clinicians who feel that being trans is so integral to their work that they want to share this with all prospective clients. You may need to do some trial and error to find a style or approach that works well for you. You may find that some clients, if they are aware that you are trans or nonbinary, will be very interested in your gender history and will ask very specific questions about aspects of transition (e.g., coming out, having surgery). You will need to be prepared for these types of questions and how you choose to respond to them.

The extent to which you engage in self-disclosure may be related to your theoretical orientation, your personality, your developmental stage as a clinician, the client's presenting concerns, the stage of treatment, or other power or cultural dynamics. Above all, any kind of disclosure (that you have choice about) should be clinically relevant and useful. When used appropriately, self-disclosure can be a powerful therapeutic tool, especially for clients who have never felt connected to other trans people. On the other hand, when misused, self-disclosure has the potential to cause harm to the client or the therapeutic relationship. Reckless self-disclosure without a solid clinical rationale or foundation may take away from the client's agency or sense that they can take up space in the therapeutic encounter or relationship. There are certain forms of clinician personal reactions (often referred to as countertransference in psychodynamic or relational schools of thought) that could prompt inappropriate self-disclosure that is motivated more by the clinician's unexamined needs than clinical rationale. These motivations include wanting to gain the client's trust, wanting to be liked or admired, difficulty tolerating being in a position of power or authority and wanting to be more like a peer to the client, feeling overidentified with the client and making or expressing assumptions about similarities, feeling isolated as a trans clinician (perhaps being the only local trans clinician), and the ways in which internalized transphobia is operating for the client or clinician.

## Questions for Reflecting on Self-Disclosure

- Is my self-disclosure in the client's best interest?

- How much is appropriate for me to disclose? How much is too much for me to disclose? How will I know when I have said enough?

- Is there a clinical rationale for my self-disclosure?

- What are possible clinical benefits that could result from my self-disclosure?

- What are possible harms or disadvantages that could result from my self-disclosure?

- Are there any benefits or harms that could result from *not* choosing to self-disclose?

- Is my self-disclosure something that must be shared urgently or in this moment? If so, what is the reason? Is this reason clinically valid?

- Am I initiating this disclosure, or is this disclosure on my part something that I feel my client is initiating?

- How might my self-disclosure affect the therapeutic relationship?

As we shared before, decisions about self-disclosure with trans clients are not unique, so you can ask some of the same questions when working with cisgender clients. However, when working with cisgender clients there is often the additional understandable fear of anti-trans bias or rejection. You may wonder about certain clients' attitudes toward and feelings about trans people in general. Of course, cisgender clients who know you are trans often self-select your practice or clinical context, so you may assume that they are trans-friendly. However, there may be instances in which you have a client who is unaware of your identity or experience as a trans person. This can certainly bring up uncertainty about whether and how to disclose one's own trans identity.

## CASE EXAMPLE. Navigating Self-Disclosure: *Working with Pablo*

*Pablo (they/them/their) is a thirty-eight-year-old Mexican American trans man who is seeking counseling with Luke (he/him/his), a forty-seven-year-old White trans man and clinician. Pablo is seeking support for gender-related concerns (e.g., navigating shifts in their relationship and sexuality, needing a letter for surgery) and non-gender-related concerns (e.g., getting support in dealing with an autoimmune disorder). Luke is the only trans therapist in the suburb where Pablo lives. Although it is not important to Pablo that their therapist be trans, Pablo has had several negative experiences with therapists in the community who claim to be trans-friendly but have enacted both gender-based and racial microaggressions toward them. Pablo is wondering whether they might have a different experience if they try working with Luke. Pablo has some reservations. First, they are concerned that Luke may not understand their experiences as a man of color. Second, Pablo is aware that Luke is close friends with one of their close friends. Finally, Pablo has heard good things about Luke being affirming and supportive but is still nervous about asking for a letter of support for top surgery. They feel awkward about this and are not sure if they should say something to Luke about these concerns.*

*Luke is an experienced clinician. Over the years, being the only trans clinician in the local area, he has worked with a wide range of clients. He has made and learned from plenty of mistakes. At one point he realized he felt isolated and needed support. When attending a trans health conference, Luke made connections with other trans clinicians who wanted to build support and a professional community. He started a trans clinicians' consultation group that meets online every month. Luke has also done a great deal of work on himself regarding understanding his White skin privilege and ways in which, though he has struggled financially, he has had much greater access to financial resources than many of his clients.*

*During the first session, Luke asks Pablo a number of questions that help Pablo to name their concerns. Luke acknowledges that although the two of them may have some similarities (e.g., both being on the trans masculine spectrum), they also have obvious differences (e.g., Pablo being a person of color, Luke being a White person; Pablo being in the position of the client, Luke being in the role of clinician and having gatekeeping power). Pablo appreciates that Luke names that they exist within a small community and that they may discuss this if this brings up any concerns. These preliminary conversations take a small portion of the first session, but they go a long way in helping Pablo to feel that the clinical relationship is off to a good start.*

In this example, Pablo seeks a trans clinician in the hopes that they will not encounter some of the challenges they have experienced in previous counseling experiences.

They are still concerned, however, because of small-community issues and not knowing whether Luke will be skilled in working with trans men of color. Because Luke has gotten support that has allowed him to better learn to navigate dual roles as well as examine his White privilege, he is able to provide a safer space for Pablo in counseling. Luke is able to skillfully address Pablo's concerns, and his transparency in the process sets a foundation for effective, collaborative work.

# Relational Dynamics: Transference and Countertransference

Being a trans clinician working with trans clients can bring up myriad concerns. Here we summarize some common dynamics that can arise and possible ways of addressing them. When we refer to *transference*, we are referring broadly to the client's feelings and thoughts toward the clinician and the therapeutic relationship, whether they are informed by the present-day interaction with the clinician, the client's social conditioning, or both. When we refer to *countertransference*, we are referring broadly to the clinician's feelings and thoughts toward the client and the therapeutic relationship. This can also be informed by the present-day interaction with the client, the clinician's social conditioning, or both. In many schools of thought, the concepts of transference and countertransference—described in other terms by different theoretical orientations—are seen as useful tools when recognized and examined. Regardless of your training or approach, there are useful takeaway messages as these issues concern the relationship between clinician and therapist. We think that the information here is particularly useful for our practice with people whose experiences may be very similar to our own.

One initial question to consider is, what is motivating a trans client to seek a trans clinician? Some clients will have the assumption that they will not have to educate trans clinicians with regard to gender concerns. Griffin Hansbury (2011) writes about clients seeking him out in order to obtain an experience of "twinship and mirroring" (p. 212), or in simpler terms, to feel a sense of kinship, identification, and validation from someone who may have a similar (trans) identity or experience. As with all clients, you may gain a great deal of useful or diagnostic information by asking the client to name what made them contact or pursue working with you.

Although every client is different, we think it is useful to name a few transference themes to be aware of in trans-trans clinical relationships. The client may:

- look at the clinician as a role model;

- feel pulled to make choices about transition that the clinician will approve of;

- have fears or judgments based on the clinician's gender identity or choices regarding transition;

- feel a strong pull to establish being autonomous or different from the therapist;

- have or express a desire to be friends with the clinician;

- have curiosity about the clinician's gender or transition experience and ask (or not ask) about this or seek this information elsewhere (e.g., doing an online search to gain information);

- have fears about privacy and confidentiality given small-community dynamics (e.g., the client knows that you are also seeing one of their acquaintances), which may bring up hesitance to share openly;

- experience isolation, loneliness, and rejection as a result of living in an area where they do not know any trans people; and

- be experiencing significant microaggressions and macroaggressions and may not have a "mentor" to help them navigate these experiences.

Additionally, although every trans clinician is different, we think it is useful to name a few countertransference themes to be aware of in trans-trans clinical relationships. The clinician may:

- feel pressure to agree with the client, which may lead to avoidance when the client may benefit from being challenged;

- feel more anxiety about self-disclosure or navigating small communities;

- assume similarities that do not exist, thereby circumventing important conversations about other differences (especially those that relate to other aspects of culture and power, such as race and class);

- feel an inflated sense of responsibility to ensure that the client's life or transition is going well, sometimes leaving less space for when a client is not doing well or for the client's need to build a sense of agency and empowerment;

- feel a need to prove oneself as a "good" clinician, especially if the gatekeeping role is uncomfortable;

- feel a sense of hopelessness or powerlessness regarding systems that are transphobic or cis-centric;

- feel overwhelmed if they are suffering from anti-trans bias themselves and then hear about a client's experiences with anti-trans bias, which could potentially lead to burnout;

- feel envious of the client for having access to resources that they did/do not (e.g., insurance coverage for gender-affirming medical interventions, support groups);

- put undue pressure on themself to have the answers to all concerns related to gender;

- have their own need for mirroring and belonging and want to be seen by the client as a community member even though there are many differences;

- feel pressure to take all trans clients, especially if there are no other trans therapists or no/few good options for trans-affirming therapists in the community;

- feel guilty about having the gatekeeping power to diagnose trans people with gender dysphoria while simultaneously helping clients to gain access to care;

- feel an obligation to be "out" or visible so that clients can find them, whether or not this fits with one's personal needs or values; and

- feel a need to offer the client a better experience than they had when seeking therapy or trying to access medical interventions through mental health gatekeeping.

It is important to note that we do not have a value judgment on transference and countertransference; rather, we think it is useful to raise awareness about these dynamics and reactions in order to provide more effective care and reduce any potential harm. When you and your client can name and work through these reactions (whether briefly or in great depth), the working alliance in the trans-trans relationship may be strengthened.

# Trans Clinicians Working with Children and Families

If you work with younger trans clients, you will be negotiating relationships with both your young client and their primary caregivers. You may have a significant role in being the first or only openly trans adult the child or their family has met. Being in this role may mean that you are navigating the projections of multiple family members based on how they are dealing with their child or loved one's stage of gender identity development or transition.

When working with parents or family members who are not affirming or supportive of your client's trans identity, you may experience difficult feelings. It is not uncommon to fear that the family will be resistant to you as a trans therapist, even if they consciously seek you out to help their child. They may fear that you will influence their child toward a certain direction or decision (e.g., assume that you will push the young person toward a medical transition), when in fact you are simply doing your job in guiding the client through their own process of exploration or inquiry. In these situations, your personal experience may be a useful tool in understanding and having empathy for your client. However, family members' reactions may bring up your own familial experiences of being supported, judged, or rejected for being trans. These dynamics can be difficult to hold in your role, and we encourage you to seek support or consultation when needed.

Conversely, some family members may look to you as if you have a "crystal ball"; they may expect that since you are trans, you will know everything about trans identity, medical interventions, or exactly what their child's future will look like through transition. They may also feel cautious about offending you, which may hinder them from being able to easily express their emotions or concerns. You may need to emphasize to these clients that though you have experience and knowledge that may be useful, your job is to center your trans client's voice, experience, and needs.

# Finding Our Own Support and Valuing Ourselves

We all need support at times, yet there are some ways in which being a trans clinician can create challenges in seeking adequate support for ourselves. Whether you need support in the form of counseling to work on your own personal growth or healing or seek consultation to discuss clinical issues, you are likely to have some significant concerns about how to go about getting this support.

If you are in need of your own therapy, you may or may not feel that there are many options to choose from. In communities in which there are few trans or trans-affirming clinicians to begin with (e.g., you are the only one you know about), finding a clinician who is trans-affirming for yourself (whether or not your concerns are related to gender) can be challenging. If there are others, they may be colleagues or friends and you may have reservations about the dual or multiple role implications of working with them. If there is not someone local who seems like an appropriate option, you may want to consider someone with whom you can engage in online or distance therapy. You may experience a challenge if you are in need of support regarding your own gender or transition experience yet do not feel you can access available resources. For example, if there is a trans support group, you may have clients who attend the group or you may even be the facilitator of the group. Another challenge you may face is that if you are in an addiction recovery program, you may have concerns about sharing that kind of support space with clients or having your anonymity compromised. We want to strongly encourage you to consider your needs, as it is hard to be an effective clinician when you are not well resourced.

Professional education and consultation may also be something you identify as necessary for your professional development. You are not expected to have all the answers when it comes to gender or trans identities (even when your clients believe this to be the case). Though you may have special insights into the experiences of your trans clients, there are times when taking courses or seeking consultation with other clinicians can be extremely useful. Some of the benefits of ongoing consultation and education include increased knowledge, a greater set of skills, burnout prevention, and a sense of community. An online search may yield information about consultation groups run by clinicians with advanced experience or specialization in gender-related work.

What you have to offer as a trans clinician is significant, but this may not always be reflected to you in your interactions with other providers or in professional communities. In our experience, trans clinicians are often asked to provide services or education for little or no cost. This can be especially exhausting and insulting when the organization or person expresses entitlement in demanding your time or services. For example, you may receive a telephone or email request from other clinicians asking something to the effect of, "Do you have ten minutes to teach me how to work with transgender clients?" Requests such as these devalue our work as clinicians and minimize the kind of time, intention, and effort that a clinician needs to invest to gain training and skills to properly care for trans clients. We have witnessed many of our trans clinician colleagues, out of a true desire to increase awareness and thus reduce harm by other clinicians, reach a state of burnout by giving their services away. We encourage you to be thoughtful about when to offer pro bono or low-fee services and when to honor your work and what it is worth by asking for fair compensation.

There is also the issue of overt and subtle transphobia and cis-centrism within the field of trans health. It can be very stressful to be the only trans person or clinician in a room or community of cisgender providers or to notice the conspicuous absence of trans leadership within the field. There are inevitable microaggressions from even the most well-intentioned colleagues or self-proclaimed allies. You may have had the experience of being cast as an "advocate" or "activist" rather than seen as a provider, as this is a common occurrence for trans providers. At times you may even feel pressure to perform gatekeeping or decline a trans client's request for a letter to prove that you are professional, discerning, and unbiased. Cisgender clinicians do not typically have to confront these concerns in their work. We believe these dynamics are part of a system that must be changed to center and value trans voices, participation, and leadership. In the meantime, we want to validate these experiences as common rather than unique or characterized as one individual's problem. We acknowledge the great deal of emotional labor that it takes to be in the clinician's role and take care of yourself with regard to some of the same concerns (e.g., anti-trans bias) that your clients are facing. In our experience, connecting with other trans clinicians and supportive friends and colleagues has helped us to build the resilience we need so that we can continue to advocate positive change.

## Conclusion

In this chapter, geared toward trans and nonbinary clinicians, we have covered some of the common themes gathered from the collective experience and wisdom of our trans personal and professional communities. You have learned about a number of topics, including whether to choose specialization in working with trans clients, self-disclosure, transference and countertransference, and seeking your own personal or professional support. We encourage you to reflect on and develop your own personal style in navigating your role, one that is honoring of your own needs, values, and limits as well as what is in your clients' best interest.

# Going Deeper:
# Questions for Clinicians and Clients

## *Questions for Trans/Nonbinary Clinician Self-Reflection*

1.  How much do I want to specialize in working with other trans people?

2.  What does it feel like for me to be in the clinician role with other trans people as clients?

3.  What kinds of trans clients are drawn toward working with me, and why might that be?

4.  What is my style in managing dual or multiple role dynamics as a trans client in trans communities?

5.  What is my style in managing self-disclosure (online, on the phone, during a clinical encounter)? How much of a choice do I have? Are there certain things that I feel very comfortable disclosing, and why? Are there certain things that I feel very uncomfortable disclosing, and why?

6.  In what ways are internalized transphobia or cis-centrism present in my work, whether they are coming from my client or me?

7.  What, if any, patterns or themes do I recognize in my clients' transference or reactions toward me as a trans clinician?

8.  What, if any, patterns or themes do I recognize in my own reactions or countertransference toward trans clients? If it differs depending on the client, what factors contribute to these differences?

9.  What challenges come up for me as a trans clinician working with parents and family members of trans people, and how do I manage them?

10. In what ways do I seek support for myself as a trans clinician? Do I have adequate support or community?

11. In what ways do I limit myself or refrain from allowing myself to receive support as a trans clinician? Are there supports or resources I need to seek out or create?

12. How much do I value my own work as a trans clinician? Do I ask to be fairly compensated? Or do I give away my time and expertise?

*Questions for Client Exploration in a Trans Counselor–Trans Client Relationship*

1.  What motivated you to choose to work with me?

2.  (*If a client indicates that your trans identity was a motivating factor in choosing to work together:*) What is it about working with a trans clinician that is important to you?

3.  What expectations or hopes might you have of me as a trans clinician?

4.  There may be ways in which we are similar and others in which we are different. For example, we may both identify as trans in some way, but our specific identities or ways that we see or talk about ourselves may be very different. I invite both of us to make room for these differences and discuss them when they come up. Is this something we can agree on?

5.  As you may know, I do a great deal of work within trans communities. We may have overlaps in terms of people we know. How would you like to navigate this when it comes up?

# Final Remarks

To our readers, we invite you to continue to use this book as a reference and resource in your work with people of all genders and to consider the skills and interventions provided as a means of empowering yourself and your clients, thereby challenging and dismantling systems of injustice.

As trans health is a continually evolving field and one that is greatly influenced by cultural norms and political climates, we strongly encourage keeping current. We acknowledge that the information we have set forth may change greatly over time, and we aim to update these teachings as needed to keep up with these changes.

We thank you for joining us in the continual process of learning and challenging ourselves to become better clinicians and allies to trans clients and communities. We hope you have enjoyed building a stronger foundation for providing affirming care and engaging in the self-reflection we view as so crucial in this process. Thank you for dedicating yourself to this learning process.

# Acknowledgments

We would like to acknowledge the many people who helped us bring this book to fruition. At New Harbinger, we thank Elizabeth Hollis Hansen, who kept us on track and expressed excitement about this book project at each step, and Vicraj Gill and Rona Bernstein, whose feedback continually challenged us to be more intentional and skillful in clarifying our message. Sand would like to thank trans colleagues and community members whose resistance, resilience, and invaluable wisdom have supported their life-long learning process and will to fight. Special thanks to Conrad Wenzel and Dr. Avy Skolnik for countless hours of critical conversations, strategizing, empathy, and laughter. lore would like to thank Drs. Stephanie Budge, Robin Buhrke, Michael Hendricks, Dan Walinsky, Donna Thomas, Barry Chung, Colt Keo-Meier, and Cindy Juntunen. Personally, he is grateful for those who have held his hand through challenging times including Adrianne, Kevin, Rafe, Duane, Robin, Connie, Michelle, Jane, Heather, and Kali. Their support, humor, and love are his buoy in rough seas. Anneliese would like to thank the trans community of color in Atlanta, New Orleans, the deep South, and India for reminding her so many years ago that trans people were not here to be helped or saved—but to have their ancient, sacred, and valued roots restored, respected, remembered, and enacted. Anneliese is grateful for the many community and scholar activists she has worked alongside for trans justice, including her chosen brothers, Dr. Theo Burnes and Mr. Jesse McNulty, Sr., as well as Ms. DeeDee Chamblee, Ms. Courtney Evans, Tracee McDaniel, Jamie Roberts, B. T., Amney Harper, Mick Rehrig, Dr. Faughn Adams, and all of the trans clients, students, and co-conspirators with whom she has had the honor to work.

# APPENDICES

# Trans-Affirming Glossary— A Quick Reference Guide

Language, words, terms, and descriptions evolve rapidly in trans communities. Being trans-affirming means staying up to date with those evolutions, honoring how language becomes more personal and reflective of people's experience, and cultivating curiosity about differing usages of language by different people. We combined and slightly modified the glossaries of several trans-affirming organizations listed at the end of this appendix (American Psychological Association, Fenway Health, Lambda Legal, PFLAG) and added terms from a few other glossaries. We have also included organizations that update their glossaries regularly.

## List of Terms

**Ally:** A cisgender person who supports and advocates for trans people and/or communities. People with a justice orientation may not use the term *ally*, which they feel can distance themselves from a group (such as trans people) that is historically marginalized, but instead use *co-conspirator* or *accomplice* to denote that they are willing to make sacrifices to support trans rights and access to important resources.

**Asexual:** A person who may not experience sexual attraction or has little interest in sexual activity; asexuality exists along a spectrum.

**Cisgender:** A person whose sex assigned at birth or body corresponds with their gender identity; generally preferred over terms such as *non-trans* or *natal/bio man/woman*.

**Cisgenderism:** A systemic bias based on the ideology that gender expression and gender identities are determined by sex assigned at birth rather than self-identified gender identity. Cisgenderism may lead to prejudicial attitudes and discriminatory behaviors toward trans people or to forms of behavior or gender expression that lie outside of the traditional gender binary (American Psychological Association [APA], 2015, p. 860).

**Coming out:** A process of disclosing or actualizing a (typically marginalized) identity that is not apparent to others; coming out as trans can include sharing information about one's gender identity or history that is in contrast with one's sex assigned at birth or current gender expression.

**Cross-dressing:** Changing one's gender expression in a way that is different from expectations related to sex assigned at birth through clothing, hairstyle, accessories, or makeup. Cross-dressers typically do not consider themselves trans, but some trans people formerly identified as cross-dressers prior to coming into a trans identity.

**Female-to-male (FTM):** Individuals who are assigned a female sex at birth and wish to change, are changing, or have changed their body and/or gender role to a more masculine body or gender role. FTM persons are also often referred to as transgender men or trans men (APA, 2015, p. 861). Some do not find this term affirming, as it prioritizes sex assigned at birth and reinforces binary gender.

**Gender-affirming surgery:** Surgery to change primary and/or secondary sex characteristics to better align a person's physical appearance with their gender identity. Gender-affirming surgery can be an important part of medically necessary treatment to alleviate gender dysphoria and may include mastectomy, hysterectomy, metoidioplasty, phalloplasty, breast augmentation, orchiectomy, vaginoplasty, facial feminization surgery, and/or other surgical procedures (APA, 2015, p. 861).

**Gender binary:** A system in which gender is characterized as two mutually exclusive categories of male/boy/man and female/girl/woman.

**Gender dysphoria:** "Discomfort or distress related to incongruence between a person's gender identity, sex assigned at birth, gender identity, and/or primary and secondary sex characteristics" (Knudson, De Cuypere, & Bockting, 2010). In 2013, the fifth edition of the *Diagnostic and Statistical Manual of Mental Disorders* (DSM–5; American Psychiatric Association, 2013) adopted the term *gender dysphoria* as a diagnosis characterized by "a marked incongruence between" a person's gender assigned at birth and gender identity (American Psychiatric Association, 2013, p. 453).

**Gender expansive:** A term describing individuals who stretch their culture's conceptions of gender identity, expression, roles, and/or norms. May be used as an umbrella term that includes trans and nonbinary people.

**Gender expression:** An individual's presentation, including physical appearance, clothing choice and accessories, and behavior that communicates aspects of gender or gender role. Gender expression may or may not conform to a person's gender identity (Fenway Health, 2010, p. 1).

**Genderfluid:** People who experience their gender as changing, dynamic, or evolving over time.

**Gender identity:** A person's internal sense of having a gender, whether it is as a man, woman, or another gender; gender identity is not always visible to others and may not correspond with sex assigned at birth.

**Gender nonconforming:** A term to describe individuals whose gender expression, gender identity, or gender role differs from expectations based on sex assigned at birth.

**Gender role:** The way that gender is expressed through appearance, behavior, personality, or role and is perceived by others, whether these factors are associated with being a boy/man, girl/woman, or another gender. Gender roles and norms are culture- and context-dependent.

**Gender variant:** A term describing a person who expresses their gender in a way that does not conform with gender norms associated with sex assigned at birth. Many people avoid this term because it suggests abnormality rather than difference or diversity.

**Genderqueer:** A person who does not identify with binary gender and may consider themself both, neither, or moving fluidly between categories of male/man or female/woman.

**Hormone therapy (hormone replacement therapy, HRT):** A medical intervention involving the use of hormones to feminize or masculinize one's body or appearance, typically to better align one's appearance with one's gender identity.

**Intersex:** A term describing people who have physical sex characteristics (i.e., chromosomes, genitals, and/or gonads) that are not considered typical within the binary framework of male/female. Some examples of these conditions include ambiguous external genitalia, lack of typical responsivity to sex-related hormones, and inconsistency between external genitalia and reproductive organs (Fenway Health, 2010, p. 2).

**Male-to-female (MTF):** Individuals whose assigned sex at birth was male and who have changed, are changing, or wish to change their body and/or gender role to a more feminized body or gender role. MTF persons are also often referred to as transgender women or trans women (APA, 2015, p. 862). Some do not find this term affirming as it prioritizes sex assigned at birth and reinforces binary gender.

**Passing:** The concept of blending with cisgender people or not being perceived as trans based on one's appearance. This idea is a goal for some trans people and is offensive to others.

**Queer:** An umbrella term that can describe sexual orientation or gender identity that does not conform to societal expectations of being heterosexual or cisgender. Some LGBT people may find this term pejorative; therefore, it should be used only when a person self-identifies using this label.

**Sex (sex assigned at birth):** Sex marker (M or F) given at birth based on external genitalia.

**Sexual orientation:** A term that refers to an aspect of identity or experience related to sexual attraction (physical or emotional), behavior, or identity, often in relation to others' gender identity and/or expression. Examples of sexual orientation identities include lesbian, gay, bisexual, queer, heterosexual, asexual, or pansexual. Some people experience their sexual orientation as fixed, while others experience it as fluid or dynamic. An important distinction is that sexual orientation is different from gender identity.

**Stealth:** A phrase used by some trans people typically to indicate the choice to keep one's trans identity private. This term may be considered offensive and reinforcing of a stereotype of trans people as deceptive; some trans people prefer the terms *no-disclosure* or *low-disclosure*.

**TGNC:** An acronym for people or communities that are trans and/or gender nonconforming.

**Trans:** A common umbrella term and shorthand for the term *transgender*.

**Trans feminine:** An umbrella term that describes a person/people assigned male at birth whose gender identities exist along a feminine spectrum of gender. This may include trans women or people who identify as nonbinary.

**Trans masculine:** An umbrella term that describes a person/people assigned female at birth whose gender identities exist along a masculine spectrum of gender. This may include trans men or people who identify as nonbinary.

**Transgender:** An adjective and umbrella term that describes a person/people whose sex assigned at birth differs (in varying degrees) from their gender identity.

**Transgender man, trans man:** A person whose sex assigned at birth is female but who identifies as a man.

**Transgender woman, trans woman:** A person whose sex assigned at birth is male but who identifies as a woman.

**Transition:** A process of shifting one's gender expression or body to better match one's gender identity (typically moving away from gender expression or body that is associated with sex assigned at birth). May include social, legal, and medical components. Not all trans people choose to transition, and transition pathways are highly individual.

**Transsexual:** A term historically used to refer to trans people who changed their bodies through medical interventions. This term is no longer in popular usage and may be considered offensive, though some people (often of older generations) still use it to refer to themselves (APA, 2015, p. 863). Transsexualism is currently classified as a medical diagnosis in the World Health Organization's (2016) *International Classification of Diseases, 10th revision.*

**Two-spirit:** An identity in some Native American cultures referring to people who identify as both male and female. This term has been used to describe both gender identity and sexual orientation.

## Organizations with Trans Glossaries

American Psychological Association. (2015). Guidelines for psychological practice with transgender and gender nonconforming people. *American Psychologist, 70,* 832–864. doi:10.1037/a0039906

Fenway Health. (2010). Glossary of gender and transgender terms. Retrieved from http://fenwayhealth.org/documents/the-fenway-institute/handouts/Handout_7-C_Glossary_of_Gender_and_Transgender_Terms__fi.pdf

PFLAG. (n.d.). National glossary of terms. Retrieved from https://www.pflag.org/glossary

Lambda Legal. (n.d.). Glossary of LGBTQ terms. Retrieved from https://www.lambdalegal.org/know-your-rights/article/youth-glossary-lgbtq-terms

# Trans-Affirming Counseling Resources

## Competencies, Guidelines, and Standards

American Counseling Association. (2010). American Counseling Association competencies for counseling with transgender clients. *Journal of LGBT Issues in Counseling, 4*, 135–159. http://dx.doi.org/10.1080/15538605.2010.524839

American Psychological Association. (2015). Guidelines for psychological practice with transgender and gender nonconforming people. *American Psychologist, 70*, 832–864. doi:10.1037/a0039906

Coleman, E., Bockting, W., Botzer, M., Cohen-Kettenis, P., DeCuypere, G., Feldman, J., … Zucker, K. (2012). Standards of care for the health of transsexual, transgender, and gender nonconforming people, 7th version. *International Journal of Transgenderism, 13*, 165–232. http://dx.doi.org/10.1080/15532739.2011.700873

## Trans-Affirming Organizations

Gender Spectrum: http://www.genderspectrum.org

Lambda Legal: http://www.lambdalegal.org

National Center for Transgender Equality (NCTE): http://www.transequality.org

Sylvia Rivera Law Project (SRLP): http://www.srlp.org

Trans Youth and Family Allies: http://www.imatyfa.org

Transgender Law Center (TLC): http://www.transgenderlawcenter.org

# Further Reading

Brown Boi Project. (2011). *Freeing ourselves: A guide to health and self-love for brown bois.* Retrieved from https://brownboiproject.nationbuilder.com/health_guide

Erickson-Schroth, L. (2014). *Trans bodies, trans selves: A resource for the transgender community.* New York, NY: Oxford University Press.

Feinberg, L. (1997). *Transgender warriors: Making history from Joan of Arc to Dennis Rodman.* Boston, MA: Beacon Press.

Mock, J. (2014). *Redefining realness: My path to womanhood, identity, love, and so much else.* New York, NY: Simon & Schuster.

Singh, A. A. (2018). *Queer and trans resilience workbook: Skills for navigating gender identity and sexual orientation.* Oakland, CA: New Harbinger.

Stryker, S. (2008). *Transgender history.* Berkeley, CA: Seal Press.

Stryker, S., & Aizura, A. (Eds.). (2013). *The transgender studies reader 2.* New York, NY: Routledge.

Stryker, S., & Whittle, S. (Eds.). (2006). *The transgender studies reader.* New York, NY: Taylor & Francis.

Testa, R. J., Coolhart, D., & Peta, J. (2015). *The gender quest workbook: A guide for teens and young adults exploring gender identity.* Oakland, CA: New Harbinger.

Veaux, F., Hardy, J., & Gill, T. (2014). *More than two: A practical guide to ethical polyamory.* Portland, OR: Thorntree Press, LLC.

Wiseman, J. (1996). *SM 101: A realistic introduction.* San Francisco, CA: Greenery Press.

# References

American Counseling Association. (2010). American Counseling Association competencies for counseling with transgender clients. *Journal of LGBT Issues in Counseling, 4*, 135–159. doi:10.1080/15538605.2010.524839

American Psychiatric Association. (1980). *Diagnostic and statistical manual of mental disorders* (III). Washington, DC: Author.

American Psychiatric Association. (2000). *Diagnostic and statistical manual of mental disorders* (IV-TR). Washington, DC: Author.

American Psychiatric Association. (2013). *Diagnostic and statistical manual of mental disorders* (5th ed.). Washington, DC: Author.

American Psychological Association. (2009). Report of the task force on gender identity and gender variance. Washington, DC: Author. Retrieved from http://www.apa.org/pi/lgbt/resources/policy/gender-identity-report.pdf

American Psychological Association. (2015). Guidelines for psychological practice with transgender and gender nonconforming people. *American Psychologist, 70*, 832–864. doi:10.1037/a0039906

American Psychological Association. (2017). Ethical principles of psychologists and code of conduct (2002, amended June 1, 2010, and January 1, 2017). Retrieved from http://www.apa.org/ethics/code/principles.pdf

Anderson, L. (2013). Punishing the innocent: How the classification of male-to-female transgender individuals in immigration detention constitutes illegal punishment under the fifth amendment. *Berkeley Journal of Gender, Law & Justice, 25*(1), 1–31. doi:10.15779/Z38WM13S8T

Arkles, G. (2009). Safety and solidarity across gender lines: Rethinking segregation of transgender people in detention. *Temple Political & Civil Rights Law Review, 18*, 515–560.

Asscheman, H., Giltay, E. J., Megens, J. A., van Trotsenburg, M. A., & Gooren, L. J. (2011). A long-term follow-up study of mortality in transsexuals receiving treatment with cross-sex hormones. *European Journal of Endocrinology, 164*(4), 635–642. doi:10.1530/EJE-10-1038

Austin, A., & Craig, S. L. (2015). Transgender affirmative cognitive behavioral therapy: Clinical considerations and applications. *Professional Psychology: Research and Practice, 46*(1), 21. doi:10.1037/a0038642

Bacon, L. (2010). *Health at every size: The surprising truth about your weight.* Dallas, TX: BenBella Books.

Beck, A. T., Steer, R. A., Brown, G. K. (1996). Manual for the Beck Depression Inventory-II. San Antonio, TX: Psychological Corporation.

Benjamin, H. (1966). *The transsexual phenomenon: A scientific report on transsexualism and sex conversion in the human male and female.* New York, NY: Julian.

Bockting, W. O. (2013). Transgender identity development. In D. L. Tolman & L. M. Diamond (Eds.), *APA handbook of sexuality and psychology: Vol. 1. Person-based approaches* (pp. 739–758). Washington, DC: American Psychological Association.

Brill, S. (2008). *The transgender child: A handbook for families and professionals.* New York, NY: Simon and Schuster.

Brill, S., & Kenney, L. (2016). *The transgender teen.* New York, NY: Simon and Schuster.

Brown, L. S. (2010). *Feminist therapy.* Washington, DC: American Psychological Association.

Budge, S. L. (2015). Psychotherapists as gatekeepers: An evidence-based case study highlighting the role and process of letter writing for transgender clients. *Psychotherapy, 52,* 287–297. doi:10.1037/pst0000034

Budge, S. L., & dickey, l. m. (2017). Barriers, challenges, and decision making in the letter writing process for gender transition. *Psychiatric Clinics, 40,* 65–78. doi:10.1016/j.psc.2016.10.001

Burnes, T. R., Long, S. L., & Schept, R. A. (2012). A resilience-based lens of sex work: Implications for professional psychologists. *Professional Psychology: Research and Practice, 43,* 137–144.

Butcher, J. N., Graham, J. R., Ben-Porath, Y. S., Tellegen, A., & Dahlstrom, W. G. (2003). *MMPI-2: Minnesota Multiphasic Personality Inventory-2.* Minneapolis: University of Minnesota Press.

Campbell, L. F., & Arkles, G. (2016). Ethical and legal concerns for mental health professionals. In A. A. Singh & l. m. dickey (Eds.), *Affirmative counseling and psychological practice with transgender and gender nonconforming clients* (pp. 95–118). Washington, DC: American Psychological Association.

Carmel, T. C., & Erickson-Schroth, L. (2016). Mental health and the transgender population. *Psychiatric Annals, 46*(6), 346–349.

Cass, V. C. (1979). Homosexual identity development: A theoretical model. *Journal of Homosexuality, 4,* 219–235.

Cauldwell, D. O. (1949). Psychopathia transexualis. *Sexology, 16,* 274–280.

Chandra, A., Copen, C. E., & Mosher, W. D. (2011). Sexual behavior, sexual attraction, and sexual identity in the United States: Data from the 2006–2008 National Survey of Family Growth. *National Health Statistics Report, 36,* 1–36. Retrieved from https://ncfy.acf.hhs.gov/sites/default/files/docs/19877-Sexual_Behavior_Sexual_Attraction.pdf

Chang, S. C. (2016). EMDR therapy as transgender-affirmative care. In M. Nickerson (Ed.), *Cultural competence and healing culturally based trauma with EMDR therapy: Innovative strategies and protocols* (pp. 177–194). New York, NY: Springer Publishing.

Chang, S. C., Cohen, J. R., & Singh, A. A. (2017). Family concerns across the lifespan. In A. A. Singh & l. m. dickey (Eds.), *Affirmative counseling and psychological practice with transgender and gender nonconforming clients* (pp. 143–159). Washington, DC: American Psychological Association.

Chang, S. C., & Singh, A. A. (2016). Affirming psychological practice with transgender and gender nonconforming people of color. *Psychology of Sexual Orientation and Gender Diversity, 3*(2), 140.

Chang, S. C., Singh, A. A., & Rossman, K. (2017). Gender and sexual orientation diversity. In Singh, A. A. & dickey, l. m. (Eds.), *Affirmative counseling and psychological practice with transgender and gender nonconforming clients* (pp. 19–40). Washington, DC: American Psychological Association.

Chapman, D. M., & Caldwell, B. E. (2012). Attachment injury resolution in couples when one partner is trans-identified. *Journal of Systemic Therapies, 31*(2), 36–53.

Clements-Nolle, K., Marx, R., & Katz, M. (2006). Attempted suicide among transgender persons: The influence of gender-based discrimination and victimization. *Journal of Homosexuality, 51*(3), 53–69.

Cloud, D. H., Drucker, E., Browne, A., & Parsons, J. (2015). Public health and solitary confinement in the United States. *American Journal of Public Health, 105,* 18–26.

Coleman, E., Bockting, W., Botzer, M., Cohen-Kettenis, P., DeCuypere, G., Feldman, J., ... Zucker, K. (2012). Standards of care for the health of transsexual, transgender, and gender nonconforming people, 7th version. *International Journal of Transgenderism, 13,* 165–232. doi:10.1080/15532739.2011.700873

Crenshaw, K. (1991). Mapping the margins: Intersectionality, identity politics, and violence against women of color. *Stanford Law Review, 43,* 1241–1299. doi:10.2307/1229039

Davis, A., & Martinez, E. (1994). Coalition building among people of color. *Inscriptions, 7,* 42–53.

Denny, D. (2002). The politics of diagnosis and a diagnosis of politics: How the university-affiliated gender clinics failed to meet the needs of transsexual people. *Transgender Tapestry, 98,* 17–27.

Department of Justice. (2012). National standards to prevent, detect, and respond to prison rape. Retrieved from https://www.ojp.gov/programs/pdfs/prea_final_rule.pdf

Deutsch, M. B., Green, J., Keatley, J., Mayer, G., Hastings, J., Hall, A. M., ... Fennie, K. (2013). Electronic medical records and the transgender patient: Recommendations from the World Professional Association for Transgender Health EMR Working Group. *Journal of the American Medical Informatics Association, 20*(4), 700–703. doi:10.1136/amiajnl-2012-001472

Devor, A. H. (2004). Witnessing and mirroring: A fourteen-stage model of transsexual identity formation. *Journal of Gay and Lesbian Psychotherapy, 8,* 41–67.

de Vries, K. M. (2012). Intersectional identities and conceptions of the self: The experience of transgender people. *Symbolic Interaction, 35*(1), 49–67. doi:10.1002/symb.2

Diamond, L. M. (2009). *Sexual fluidity: Understanding women's love and desire.* Cambridge, MA: Harvard University.

dickey, l. m. (2014). Privilege: I seem to have it, now what? In Z. Keig & M. Kellaway (Eds.), *Manning up: Transsexual men on finding brotherhood, family & themselves* (pp. 195–201). Oakland, CA: Transgress Press.

dickey, l. m., & Bower, K. L. (2017). Aging and TGNC identities: Working with older adults. In A. A. Singh & l. m. dickey (Eds.), *Affirmative counseling and psychological practice with transgender and gender nonconforming clients* (pp. 161–174). Washington, DC: American Psychological Association.

dickey, l. m., Budge, S. L., Katz-Wise, S. L. & Garza, M. V. (2016). Health disparities in the transgender community: Exploring differences in insurance coverage. *Psychology of Sexual Orientation and Gender Diversity, 3,* 275–282. doi:10.1037/sgd0000169

dickey, l. m., Ducheny, K. M., & Ehrbar, R. D. (2016). Family creation options for transgender and gender nonconforming people. *Psychology of Sexual Orientation and Gender Diversity, 3,* 173–179. doi:10.1037/sgd0000178

dickey, l. m., & Loewy, M. (2010). Group work with transgender clients: A call for action. *Journal for Specialists in Group Work, 35,* 236–245. doi:10.1080/01933922.2010.492904

dickey, l. m., Reisner, S. L., & Juntunen, C. L. (2015). Non-suicidal self-injury in a large online sample of transgender adults. *Professional Psychology: Research & Practice, 46,* 3–11. doi:10.1037/a0038803

dickey, l. m., Singh, A. A., Chang, S. C., & Rehrig, M. (2017). Advocacy and social justice: The next generation of counseling and psychological practice with transgender and gender nonconforming clients. In A. A. Singh & l. m. dickey (Eds.), *Affirmative counseling and psychological practice with transgender and gender nonconforming clients* (pp. 247–262). Washington, DC: American Psychological Association.

Diemer, E. W., Grant, J. D., Munn-Chernoff, M. A., Patterson, D. A., & Duncan, A. E. (2015). Gender identity, sexual orientation, and eating-related pathology in a national sample of college students. *Journal of Adolescent Health, 57*(2), 144–149.

Ducheny, K., Hendricks, M. L., & Keo-Meier, C. L. (2017). TGNC-affirmative interdisciplinary collaborative care. In A. A. Singh & l. m. dickey (Eds.), *Affirmative counseling and psychological practice with transgender and gender nonconforming clients* (pp. 69–93). Washington, DC: American Psychological Association.

Edwards-Leeper, L. (2017). Affirmative care of TGNC children and adolescents. In A. A. Singh & l. m. dickey (Eds.), *Affirmative counseling and psychological practice with transgender and gender nonconforming clients* (pp. 119–141). Washington, DC: American Psychological Association.

Edwards-Leeper, L., Leibowitz, S., & Sangganjanavanich, V. F. (2016). Affirmative practice with transgender and gender nonconforming youth: Expanding the model. *Psychology of Sexual Orientation and Gender Diversity, 3*, 165–172. doi:10.1037/sgd0000167

Ehrensaft, D. (2012). From gender identity disorder to gender identity creativity: True gender self child therapy. *Journal of Homosexuality, 51*, 111–128. doi:10.1080/00918369.2012.653303

Ehrensaft, D. (2016). *Gender creative child: Pathways for nurturing and supporting children who live outside gender boxes.* New York, NY: The Experiment.

Erikson, E. H. (1980). *Identity and the life cycle.* New York, NY: Norton.

Fenway Health. (2010). Glossary of gender and transgender terms. Retrieved from http://www.fenway health.org/documents/the-fenway-institute/handouts/Handout_7-C_Glossary_of_Gender_and _Transgender_Terms__fi.pdf

Fredriksen-Goldsen, K. I., Cook-Daniels, L., Kim, H. J., Erosheva, E. A., Emlet, C. A., Hoy-Ellis, C. P., … Muraco, A. (2014). Physical and mental health of transgender older adults: An at-risk and underserved population. *The Gerontologist, 54*(3), 488. doi:10.1093/geront/gnt021

Goodman, W. K., Price, L. H., Rasmussen, S. A., Mazure, C., Fleischmann, R. L., Hill, C. L. … Charney, D. S. (1989). Yale-Brown Obsessive Compulsive Scale (Y-BOCS). *Archives of General Psychiatry, 46*, 1006–1011.

Goodmark, L. (2013). Transgender people, intimate partner abuse, and the legal system. *Harvard Civil Rights-Civil Liberties Law Review, 48*, 51–104.

Grant, J. M., Mottet, L. A., Tanis, J., Harrison, J., Herman, J. L., & Keisling, M. (2011). Injustice at every turn: A report of the national transgender discrimination survey. Retrieved from http://www.endtransdiscrimination.org/PDFs/NTDS_Report.pdf

Gray, J. (1992). *Men are from Mars, women are from Venus: A practical guide for improving communication and getting what you want in your relationships.* New York, NY: Harper Collins.

Hansbury, G. (2011). King Kong & Goldilocks: Imagining transmasculinities through the trans–trans dyad. *Psychoanalytic Dialogues, 21*(2), 210–220.

Hartling, L. (2005). Fostering resilience throughout our lives: New relational possibilities. In D. Comstock (Ed.), *Diversity and development: Critical contexts that shape our lives and relationships,* (pp. 337–354). Belmont, CA: Thomson Brooks/Cole.

Hayes, S. C., Strosahl, K. D., & Wilson, K. G. (2012). *Acceptance and commitment therapy.* New York, NY: Guilford Press.

Heck, N. C. (2017). Group psychotherapy with transgender and gender nonconforming adults: Evidence-based practice applications. *Psychiatric Clinics, 40*, 157–175. doi:10.1016/j.psc.2016.10.010

Heck, N. C., Flentje, A., Cochran, B. N. (2013). Intake interviewing with lesbian, gay, bisexual, and transgender clients: Starting from a place of affirmation. *Journal of Contemporary Psychotherapy, 43,* 23–32. doi:10.1007/s10879–012–9220-x

Hembree, W. C. (2011). Guidelines for pubertal suspension and gender reassignment for transgender adolescents. *Child and Adolescent Psychiatric Clinics, 20*(4), 725–732.

Hendricks, M. L., & Testa, R. J. (2012). A conceptual framework for clinical work with transgender and gender nonconforming clients: An adaptation of the minority stress model. *Professional Psychology: Research and Practice, 43,* 460–467.

Hepp, U., Kraemer, B., Schnyder, U., Miller, N., & Delsignore, A. (2005). Psychiatric comorbidity in gender identity disorder. *Journal of Psychosomatic Research, 58*(3), 259–261.

Herman, J. L. (2013). Gendered restrooms and minority stress: The public regulation of gender and its impact on transgender people's lives. *Journal of Public Management & Social Policy, 19,* 65–80.

ICATH. (n.d.). Informed consent for access to trans health care. Retrieved from https://www.icath.info/

Israel, T. (2006). Marginalized communities in the United States: Oppression, social justice, and the role of counseling psychologists. In R. L. Toporek, L. H. Gerstein, N. A. Fouad, G. Roysircar, & T. Israel (Eds.), *Handbook for social justice in counseling psychology: Leadership, vision, and action* (pp. 149–154). Thousand Oaks, CA: Sage Publications, Inc. doi:10.4135/9781412976220.n11

James, S. E., Herman, J. L., Rankin, S., Keisling, M., Mottet, L., & Anafi, M. (2016). The report of the 2015 U.S. Transgender Survey. Washington, DC: National Center for Transgender Equality. Retrieved from http://www.ustranssurvey.org/

Jorgensen, C. (2000). *Christine Jorgensen: A personal autobiography.* Berkeley, CA: Cleis Press.

Keo-Meier, C. L., Ducheny, K., & Hendricks, M. L. (2018). Identity and support letter. In M. R. Kauth & J. C. Shipherd (Eds.), *Adult transgender care: An interdisciplinary approach for training mental health professionals* (pp. 175–184). New York, NY: Routledge.

Keo-Meier, C. L., & Fitzgerald, K. M. (2017). Affirmative psychological testing and neurocognitive assessment with transgender adults. *Psychiatric Clinics, 40*(1), 51–64.

Kessler, S. J., & McKenna, W. (1978). *Gender: An ethnomethodological approach.* New York, NY: John Wiley & Sons.

Kins, E., Hoebeke, P., Heylens, G., Rubens, R., & DeCuypere, G. (2008). The female-to-male transsexual and his female partner versus the traditional couple: A comparison. *Journal of Sex and Marital Therapy, 34,* 429–438. doi.org/10.1080/00926230802156236

Knudson, G., De Cuypere, G., & Bockting, W. (2010). Process toward consensus on recommendations for revision of the DSM diagnoses of gender identity disorders by the World Professional Association for Transgender Health. *International Journal of Transgenderism, 12*(2), 54–59.

Kosciw, J. G., Greytak, E. A., Giga, N. M., Villenas, C., & Danischewski, D. J. (2016). The 2015 National School Climate Survey: The experiences of lesbian, gay, bisexual, transgender, and queer youth in our nation's schools. New York, NY: GLSEN. Retrieved from https://www.glsen.org/article/2015-national-school-climate-survey

Krieger, I. (2017). *Counseling transgender and non-binary youth: The essential guide.* London, UK: Jessica Kingsley Publishers.

Kuiper, A. J., & Cohen-Kettenis, P. T. (1998). Gender role reversal among postoperative transsexuals. *International Journal of Transgenderism, 2*(3), 1–16.

Lambda Legal. (2016a). Creating equal access to quality health care for transgender patients: Transgender-affirming health policies. Retrieved from https://www.lambdalegal.org/sites/default/files/publications/downloads/hospital-policies-2016_5–26–16.pdf

Lambda Legal. (2016b). *Transgender rights toolkit: A legal guide for trans people and their advocates.* Retrieved from https://www.lambdalegal.org/sites/default/files/publications/downloads/2016_trans_toolkit_final.pdf

Lambda Legal. (n.d.). Glossary of LGBTQ terms. Retrieved from https://www.lambdalegal.org/know-your-rights/article/youth-glossary-lgbtq-terms

Lating, J. M., Barnett, J. E., & Horowitz, M. (2009). Increasing advocacy awareness within professional psychology training programs. *Training and Education in Psychology, 3,* 106–110. doi:10.1037/a0013662

Levitt, H. M., & Ippolito, M. R. (2014). Being transgender: The experience of transgender identity development. *Journal of Homosexuality, 61,* 1727–1758. doi:10.1080/00918369.2014.951262

Linehan, M. (2014). *DBT® skills training manual.* New York, NY: Guilford Press.

Lurie, S. B. (2014). Exploring the impacts of disclosure for the transgender and gender non-conforming therapists. *Theses, Dissertations, and Projects.* Paper 822.

Masten. A. S. (2015). *Ordinary magic: Resilience in development.* New York, NY: Guilford Press.

McDonough, K. (2014). *Laverne Cox flawlessly shuts down Katie Couric's invasive questions about transgender people.* Retrieved from https://www.salon.com/2014/01/07/laverne_cox_artfully_shuts_down_katie_courics_invasive_questions_about_transgender_people/

McIntosh, P. (1991). White privilege: Unpacking the invisible knapsack. Retrieved from http://www.intergroupresources.com/rc/knapsack.pdf

Meyerowitz, J. J. (2009). *How sex changed: A history of transsexuality in the United States.* Cambridge, MA: Harvard University Press.

Mikalson, P., Pardo, S., & Green, J. (2012). *First, do no harm: Reducing disparities for lesbian, gay, bisexual, transgender, queer and questioning populations in California.* The California LGBTQ reducing mental health disparities population report. Office of Health Equity, California Department of Public Health.

Miller, T. (2018). *Echoing calls for co-conspirators: Death to the ally.* Retrieved from http://www.artforourselves.org/wtf-is-going-on/echoing-calls-for-co-conspirators-death-to-the-ally

Muehlenkamp, J. J. (2005). Self-injurious behavior as a separate clinical syndrome. *American Journal of Orthopsychiatry, 75*(2), 324.

Nadal, K. L., Skolnik, A., & Wong, Y. (2012). Interpersonal and systemic microaggressions toward transgender people: Implications for counseling. *Journal of LGBT Issues in Counseling, 6,* 55–82. doi:10.1080/15538605.2012.648583

National Center for Transgender Equality. (2018). ID documents center. Retrieved from https://www.transequality.org/documents

National Senior Citizens Law Center. (2011). LGBT older adults in long-term care facilities: Stories from the field. Washington, DC: Author, National Gay and Lesbian Task Force, Services and Advocacy for GLBT Elders, Lambda Legal, National Center for Lesbian Rights, & National Center for Transgender Equality. Retrieved from http://www.justiceinaging.org.customers.tigertech.net/wp-content/uploads/2015/06/Stories-from-the-Field.pdf

Nestle, J., Howell, C., & Wilchins, R. (Eds.). (2002). *Genderqueer: Voices from beyond the sexual binary.* Los Angeles, CA: Alyson Books.

Nichols, J. M. (2016). *Miss Major is a trans elder and Stonewall icon…And she's changing the world.* Retrieved from https://www.huffingtonpost.com/entry/miss-major-transgender-elder_us_579273 51e4b01180b52ef264

Nuttbrock, L., Hwahng, S., Bockting, W., Rosenblum, A., Mason, M., Macri, M., & Becker, J. (2010). Psychiatric impact of gender-related abuse across the life course of male-to-female transgender persons. *Journal of Sex Research, 47*(1), 12–23. doi:10.1080/00224490903062258

Olson, K. R., Durwood, L., DeMeules, M., & McLaughlin, K. A. (2016) Mental health of transgender children who are supported in their identities. *Pediatrics, 137*(3), 1–10. doi:10.1542/peds.2015-3223.

Ophelian, A. (2009). *Diagnosing difference* (film). San Francisco, CA: Floating Ophelia Productions.

Patient Protection and Affordable Care Act, 42 U.S.C. § 18001 (2010).

PFLAG. (n.d.). National glossary of terms. Retrieved from https://www.pflag.org/glossary

Porter, K. E., Brennan-Ing, M., Chang, S. C., dickey, l. m., Singh, A. A., Bower, K. L., & Witten, T. M. (2016). Providing competent and affirmative care for transgender and gender nonconforming older adults. *Clinical Gerontologist, 39*, 366–388. doi:10.1080/07317115.2016.1203383

Proctor, B. D., Semega, J. L., & Kollar, M. A. (2016). Income and poverty in the United States: 2015. (p. 13). Washington, DC: U.S. Census Bureau. Retrieved from https://www.census.gov/content/dam/Census/library/publications/2016/demo/p60–256.pdf

Ratts, M., Singh, A. A., Nassar-McMillan, S., Butler, S. K., & McCullough, R. (2016). Multicultural and social justice competencies: Guidelines for the counseling profession. *Journal of Multicultural Counseling and Development, 44*(1), 28–48.

Reisner S. L., Biello, K. B., White Hughto, J. M., Kuhns, L., Mayer, K. H., Garofalo, R., Mimiaga, M. J. (2016). Psychiatric diagnoses and comorbidities in a diverse, multicity cohort of young transgender women: Baseline findings from project lifeskills. *JAMA Pediatrics, 170*(5), 481–486. doi:10.1001/jamapediatrics.2016.0067

Reisner, S. L., White Hughto, J. M., Gamarel, K. E., Keuroghlian, A. S., Mizock, L., & Pachankis, J. E. (2016). Discriminatory experiences associated with posttraumatic stress disorder symptoms among transgender adults. *Journal of Counseling Psychology, 63*(5), 509.

Richmond, K., Burnes, T. R., Singh, A. A., Ferrara, M. (2017). Assessment and treatment of trauma with TGNC clients: A feminist approach. In A. A. Singh & l. m. dickey (Eds.), *Affirmative counseling and psychological practice with transgender and gender nonconforming clients* (pp. 191–212). Washington, DC: American Psychological Association.

Roberts, J., & Singh, A. A. (2014). Trans and gender non-conforming global leaders. In L. Erickson-Schroth (Ed.), *Trans bodies, trans selves.* New York, NY: Oxford Press.

Rotondi, N. K., Bauer, G. R., Travers, R., Travers, A., Scanlon, K., & Kaay, M. (2012). Depression in male-to-female transgender Ontarians: Results from the Trans PULSE Project. *Canadian Journal of Community Mental Health, 30*(2), 113–133.

Rowe, C., Santos, G. M., McFarland, W., & Wilson, E. C. (2015). Prevalence and correlates of substance use among trans* female youth ages 16–24 years in the San Francisco Bay Area. *Drug & Alcohol Dependence, 147*, 160–166.

Ryan, C., Russell, S. T., Huebner, D., Diaz, R., & Sanchez, J. (2010). Family acceptance in adolescence and the health of LGBT young adults. *Journal of Child and Adolescent Psychiatric Nursing, 23*(4), 205–213.

Shabanzadeh, D. M., & Sørensen, L. T. (2015). Alcohol consumption increases post-operative infection but not mortality: A systematic review and meta-analysis. *Surgical Infections, 16*(6), 657–668.

Shapiro, F. (2001). *Eye movement desensitization and reprocessing: Basic principles, protocols, and procedures* (2nd ed.). New York, NY: Guilford Press.

Shipherd, J. C., Maguen, S., Skidmore, W. C., & Abramovitz, S. M. (2011). Potentially traumatic events in a transgender sample: Frequency and associated symptoms. *Traumatology, 17*(2), 56–67.

Shumer, D. E., Reisner, S. L., Edwards-Leeper, L., & Tishelman, A. (2016). Evaluation of Asperger syndrome in youth presenting to a gender dysphoria clinic. *LGBT Health, 3*(5), 387–390.

Singh, A. A., & Burnes, T. R. (2010). Shifting the counselor role from gatekeeping to advocacy: Ten strategies for using the competencies for counseling with transgender clients for individual and social change. *Journal of LGBT Issues in Counseling, 4*(3–4), 241–255.

Singh, A. A., & dickey, l. m. (2017). Introduction to trans-affirming counseling and psychological practice. In Singh, A. A. & dickey, l. m. (Eds.), *Affirmative counseling and psychological practice with transgender and gender nonconforming clients*. Washington, DC: American Psychological Association.

Singh, A. A., Hays, D. G., & Watson, L. (2011). Strategies in the face of adversity: Resilience strategies of transgender individuals. *Journal of Counseling and Development, 89*, 20–27. doi:10.1002/j .1556–6678.2011.tb00057.x

Singh, A. A., & McKleroy, V. S. (2011). "Just getting out of bed is a revolutionary act": The resilience of transgender people of color who have survived traumatic life events. *Traumatology, 20*(10), 1–11. doi:10.1177/1534765610369261

Singh, A. A., Meng, S., & Hansen, A. (2013). "It's already hard enough being a student": Developing affirming college environments for trans youth. *The Journal of LGBT Youth, 10*(3), 208–223. doi: 10.1080/19361653.2013.800770

Smith, L. C., & Shin, R. Q. (2012). Moving counseling forward on LGBT issues: Speaking queerly on discourses and microaggressions. *The Counseling Psychologist, 40*(3), 385–408. doi:10.1177 /0011000011403165

Spade, D. (2000). Resisting medicine, re/modeling gender. *Berkeley Women's Law Journal, 18*, 15–37.

Spade, D. (2011). Some very basic tips for making higher education more accessible to trans students and rethinking how we talk about gendered bodies. *Radical Teacher, 92*(1), 57–62.

Stone, S. (1991). The empire strikes back: A posttranssexual manifesto. In J. Epstein & K. Straub (Eds.), *Body guards: The cultural politics of gender ambiguity* (pp. 121–142). New York, NY: Routledge.

Stryker, S. (2008). *Transgender history*. Berkeley, CA: Seal Press.

Stryker, S., & Aizura, A. (Eds.). (2013). *The transgender studies reader 2*. New York, NY: Routledge.

Stryker, S., & Whittle, S. (2006). *The transgender studies reader*. New York, NY: Taylor & Francis.

Substance Abuse and Mental Health Services Administration. (2014). SAMHSA's concept of trauma and guidance for a trauma-informed approach. Retrieved September 16, 2016, from http://www .store.samhsa.gov/shin/content/SMA14–4884/SMA14–4884.pdf

Substance Abuse and Mental Health Services Administration. (2015). *Ending conversion therapy: Supporting and affirming LGBTQ youth*. HHS Publication No. (SMA) 15–4928. Rockville, MD: Substance Abuse and Mental Health Services Administration.

Sue, D. W., Arredondo, P., & McDavis, R. J. (1992). Multicultural counseling competencies and standards: A call to the profession. *Journal of Counseling & Development, 70*(4), 477–483.

Tate, C. C., Ledbetter, J. N., & Youssef, C. P. (2013). A two-question method for assessing gender categories in the social and medical sciences. *Journal of Sex Research, 50*(8), 767–776.

Testa, R. J., Habarth, J., Peta, J., Balsam, K., & Bockting, W. (2015). Development of the Gender Minority Stress and Resilience Measure. *Psychology of Sexual Orientation and Gender Diversity, 2*(1), 65–77.

Testa, R. J., Rider, G. N., Haug, N. A., & Balsam, K. F. (2017). Gender confirming medical interventions and eating disorder symptoms among transgender individuals. *Health Psychology, 36*(10), 927.

Toporek, R. L., Gerstein, L. H., Fouad, N. A., Roysircar, G., & Israel, T. (2006). *Handbook for social justice in counseling psychology: Leadership, vision, and action.* Thousand Oaks, CA: Sage Publications, Inc.

Transgender Law Center. (2014). CA governor signs respect after death act. Retrieved from https://www.transgenderlawcenter.org/archives/11140

Transgender Law Center. (2016). *Know your rights: Transgender people at work.* Retrieved from http://www.transgenderlawcenter.org/wp-content/uploads/2012/05/01.28.2016-KYR-Trans-People-at-Work.pdf

Transgender Law Center. (n.d.). *Values.* Retrieved from http://www.transgenderlawcenter.org/about/mission

Travers, R., Bauer, G., Pyne, J., Bradlet, K., Gale, L., & Papadimitriou, M. (2012). *Impacts of strong parental support for trans youth: A report prepared for Children's Aid Society of Toronto and Delise Youth Services.* Retrieved from http://www.transpulseproject.ca/wp-content/uploads/2012/10/Impacts-of-Strong-Parental-Support-for-Trans-Youth-vFINAL.pdf

Vipond, E. (2015). Resisting transnormativity: Challenging the medicalization and regulation of trans bodies. *Theory in Action, 8*(2), 21–44. doi:10.3798/tia.1937–0237.15008

White, T., & Ettner, R. (2007). Adaptation and adjustment in children of transsexual parents. *European Child and Adolescent Psychiatry, 16*, 215–221. doi:10.1007/s00787–006–0591-y

White Hughto, J. M., Reisner, S. L., & Pachankis, J. E. (2015). Transgender stigma and health: A critical review of stigma determinants, mechanisms, and interventions. *Social Science & Medicine, 147*, 222–231. doi:10.1016/j.socscimed.2015.11.010

Williams, D. J., Prior, E., & Wegner, J. (2013). Resolving social problems associated with sexuality: Can a "sex-positive" approach help? *Social work, 58*(3), 273–276. doi:10.1093/sw/swt024

Winters, K. (2013). Australian "60 Minutes" report misrepresents trans youth medical care. GID Reform Advocates. Retrieved from https://gidreform.wordpress.com/2017/09/14/australian-60-minutes-report-misrepresents-trans-youth-medical-care/

Wiseman, J. (1996). *SM 101: A realistic introduction.* San Francisco, CA: Greenery Press.

Workers, N. A. (2008). *NASW code of ethics (Guide to the everyday professional conduct of social workers).* Washington, DC: NASW.

World Health Organization. (2016). *The ICD-10 classification of mental and behavioural disorders: Clinical descriptions and diagnostic guidelines* (5th edition). Geneva: World Health Organization.

Xavier, J., Bradford, J., Hendricks, M., Safford, L., McKee, R., Martin, E., & Honnold, J. A. (2012). Transgender health care access of Virginia: A qualitative study. *International Journal of Transgenderism, 14*(1), 3–17. doi:10.1080/15532739.2013.689513

**Sand C. Chang, PhD**, is a Chinese American nonbinary psychologist and trainer. They are the clinical practice consultant for Kaiser Permanente Northern California Transgender Services. They also have a private practice in Oakland, CA, specializing in trauma/EMDR, addictions, and eating disorders. Sand served on the task force that authored the 2015 APA Guidelines for Psychological Practice with Transgender and Gender Nonconforming Clients, and is past chair of the American Psychological Association (APA) Committee on Sexual Orientation and Gender Diversity (CSOGD). Outside of their professional work, Sand is a dancer, avid foodie, and pug enthusiast.

**Anneliese A. Singh, PhD, LPC**, is a professor and associate dean of diversity, equity, and inclusion in the college of education at the University of Georgia. Singh is cofounder of the Georgia Safe Schools Coalition to work on reducing heterosexism, transprejudice, racism, and other oppressions in Georgia schools. She is also cofounder of the Trans Resilience Project, where she translated her findings from fifteen years of research on trans people's resilience to oppression into practice and advocacy efforts. She is author of *The Queer and Transgender Resilience Workbook*. She's delivered widely viewed TEDx Talks, and recorded a podcast for APA on her research with transgender youth and resilience.

**lore m. dickey, PhD**, is a behavioral health consultant at North Country HealthCare in Bullhead City, AZ. He has a long history of LGBTQ advocacy and social justice work, and has presented throughout the world on trans-affirmative practice with gender-diverse people. His research and clinical work focus on addressing the needs of gender-diverse individuals. After working for several years in academia, lore recently took on a job working in an integrated behavioral health care setting. lore is the founder of My Bandana Project, which is a suicide prevention intervention for transgender people.

Foreword writer **Mira Krishnan, PhD, ABPP**, is a board-certified neuropsychologist and consultant. She is clinical assistant professor of psychiatry at Michigan State University, and cochair of the Committee for Transgender People and Gender Diversity, of Division 44 of the APA. In 2015, she was recognized as one of the Trans 100, an annual recognition of influential transgender Americans.

# Index

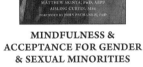

Register your **new harbinger** titles for additional benefits!

When you register your **new harbinger** title—purchased in any format, from any source—you get access to benefits like the following:

- Downloadable accessories like printable worksheets and extra content

- Instructional videos and audio files

- Information about updates, corrections, and new editions

Not every title has accessories, but we're adding new material all the time.

Access free accessories in 3 easy steps:

1. Sign in at NewHarbinger.com (or **register** to create an account).

2. Click on **register a book**. Search for your title and click the **register** button when it appears.

3. Click on the **book cover or title** to go to its details page. Click on **accessories** to view and access files.

That's all there is to it!

If you need help, visit:

NewHarbinger.com/accessories

new harbinger
CELEBRATING
**40** YEARS